Image Grammar

USING GRAMMATICAL STRUCTURES
TO TEACH WRITING

Harry R. Noden

Boynton/Cook
HEINEMANN
Portsmouth, NH

*To my wife Jan,
who through a lifetime, has given me precious love,
beautiful art, and two wonderful children.*

*To Eric, Kirk, Eileen, Mom and Dad,
who all helped shape the heart behind the words in this book.*

Heinemann
A division of Reed Elsevier Inc.
361 Hanover Street
Portsmouth, NH 03801–3912
www.heinemann.com

Offices and agents throughout the world

The author and publisher wish to thank those who have generously given permission to reprint borrowed material. Acknowledgments for borrowed material appear on page 214.

Library of Congress Cataloging-in-Publication Data
Noden, Harry R.
    Image grammar : using grammatical structures to teach writing /
Harry R. Noden.
      p.   cm.
    Includes bibliographical references.
    ISBN 0–86709–466–4
    1. Creative writing (Secondary education). 2. English language—Grammar
Study and teaching (Secondary). I. Title.
LB1631.N62 1999
808'.071'2—dc21
                                            99-26698
                                          CIP

Editor: Lisa Luedeke
Production: Vicki Kasabian
Cover painting: Jan Noden
Cover design: Jenny Jensen Greenleaf
Photographs of images on CD: Jerry Jividen
Manufacturing: Louise Richardson

Printed in the United States of America on acid-free paper
03   RRD   7 8 9 10

CONTENTS

Preface   vii

1   THE WRITER AS ARTIST: BASIC BRUSH STROKES   1

Concepts
Writing as Seeing / Painting with Five Basic Brush Strokes / Painting with
Participles / Painting with Absolutes / Painting with Appositives / Painting
with Adjectives Shifted Out of Order / Painting with Action Verbs /
Combining Strokes

Strategies
Create an Artist's Image Palette / Explore Images from Films of Best-Selling
Novels / Examine the Art of Sue Grafton / Stimulate Images with Derived
Poetry / Tour a Writer's Gallery / Copyedit "Gessi the Great" / Paint Models
from the *Nando Times*

2   THE ARTIST'S EYE: SEEING SPECIFIC DETAILS   25

Concepts
Getting Specific with Nouns and Verbs / Adding Details with Specific Verbs /
Adding Details with Adjectives and Prepositional Phrases / Specific Images
for Humor / Adding Details with Metaphors and Similes / Constructing
Specific Images in Dialogue / Constructing Specific Images in Poetry /
Expanding the Artist's Eye / Using Image/Word Relationships with Students

Strategies
Paint the Personality Behind the Clothes / Create a Shooting Script on
Location / Search for Details in Abstract Slides / Focus on Word-Image
Senses / Go on a Humor Hunt / Examine the Contents of the Mystery Purse

/ Breathe Life into Dead Character Descriptors / Paint a Setting with a List /
Replicate Olson's Experiment / Locate Humorous Images on the Internet /
Tour the Net Museums

3   THE ARTIST'S RHYTHMS:
    THE MUSIC OF PARALLEL STRUCTURES   49

    Concepts
    Listening for the Beat / Beating Rhythms of Literal Repetition / Beating
    Rhythms of Grammatical Repetition / Using Parallel Structure for Clarity /
    Extending Grammatical Rhythms to Paragraphs / Executing a Drum Roll
    with Periodic Sentences / Listening to the Music of Political Rhetoric

    Strategies
    Add Grammatical Music to a Sketch / Try a Rhythmic Experiment in Horror
    / Travel into the Twilight Zone / Revise Your Rhythm / Analyze the Music in
    "We Are Connectors" / Imitate the Rhythms of Parallel Structure / Explore
    Musical Rhythms to Write Poetry / Combine Brush Strokes and Parallel
    Structures

4   FROM IMITATION TO CREATION:
    LEARNING FROM THE MASTERS   69

    Concepts
    Imitating Without Plagiarizing / Providing Guidelines for Imitation /
    Experimenting with Variations of Imitation / Moving from Imitation to
    Creation / Creating with an Artist's Structural Palette / Moving Toward
    Creation with Method Writing / Creating with Scripted Fantasy

    Strategies
    Keep a Writer's Sketchbook / Paint from a Family Photo / Try Hamill's
    Imitation Approach / Imitate Poetic Sentences / Do Your Own Edgar Allan
    Humpty / Search for a Personal Voice / Read a Scripted Fantasy / Use a
    Second Structural Palette for Opinions

5   THE ARTIST'S SPECIAL EFFECTS:
    THE GRAMMAR-MEANING CONNECTION   94

    Concepts
    Creating Special Effects with Punctuation / Creating Special Effects with
    Sentence Structure / Creating Special Effects with a Greek Influence /

Creating Special Effects with Mood Filtering / Creating Special Effects with Tantalizing Titles

Strategies

Play with Fragments and Run-ons / Return to Erasmus / Listen to the Beat of Punctuation / Go Live on Channel Five / Search for Titles in the Amazon

6   TOWARD A GRAMMAR OF PASSAGES:
LINKING IMAGES BEYOND THE SENTENCE   109

Concepts

Exploring a Grammar of Passages / Tracking a Grammar of Passages in Exposition / Painting Passages Using Christensen's Approach / Introducing Logical Shapes with Periodic Passages / Introducing Logical Shapes with a Photo Shoot / Using Stadia to Explain Nontopic Sentence Sequences / Using Jon Franklin's Image Cluster Approach / Connecting Images with Transitions

Strategies

Paint Passages from Experiences of Touch / Construct Titles as Thesis Statements / Draw Conclusions from an Ad Campaign / Evaluate Henry's Paper on the Seasons / Solve the Gruesome Charles Benchley Murder / Perform a Magic Trick / Surf with Shaughnessy's Idea

7   STORY GRAMMAR AND SCENES: SHAPES FOR FICTION   141

Concepts

Understanding How Reading Teachers Define Story Grammar / Understanding How English Teachers Define Story Grammar / Painting Plot Patterns / Teaching the Art of Scene Writing / Providing Guidelines for Scene Writing / Painting Characters in Scenes / Moving from Scenes to Stories / Opening Stories with a Scene

Strategies

Paint a Character from Eight Perspectives / Build Visualized Scenes with Urban Myths / Discuss Comic Book Plot Paintings / Write Scenes from Short Story Films / Use Music to Paint Scenes / Build a Bulletin Board Photo Collection / Write a Setting for an Exotic Scene

8   NONFICTION FORM # 5:
    A CLOSE EXAMINATION OF A FEATURE ARTICLE FORM   162

Concepts
Writing Introductory Leads / Writing the Body of an Article / Writing
Conclusions / Putting It All Together / Avoiding the Rigidity Trap

Strategies
Stuff a Sack of Shapely Ideas / Run a Magazine Search Competition /
Experiment with Forms / Mix Forms with a Multigenre Research Paper /
Experiment with Images for Intros

9   SYSTEMATIC REVISION:
    FORM, STYLE, CONTENT, AND CONVENTIONS   182

Concepts
Recognizing Revision Roadblocks / Using Short Checklists for Systematic
Revision / Creating a Short Revision Checklist for Style / Creating a
Revision Checklist for Conventions / Creating a Short Revision Checklist
for Form / Creating a Short Revision Checklist for Content / Combining
Checklists

Strategies
Administer the Grammar Income Test / Punctuate That That Is Is That /
Editing the *County Line Newsletter* / Decoding Abstract Statements /
Evaluate "Lost" by Ben Dover / Review Writings on the Web

A Concluding Note   202

References   203

About the *Image Grammar* CD   214

PREFACE

Discussing grammar in the teachers' lounge is a little like stepping in between two opposing 350-pound NFL linemen just after the ball is snapped. Although the discussions are not quite that explosive, they seem to generate a similar competitive hostility. When grammar is the topic, teachers take a stand.

In one camp are the traditionalists who insist that students must be drilled in traditional grammar. If an *English Journal* survey is correct, 61 percent of secondary English teachers fall in this category (Warner 1993). In the other camp are the remaining 39 percent, equally adamant in their views. These teachers argue that teaching traditional grammar is linguistically unscientific.

For thirty years I've listened to teachers in these opposing camps debate. Back in the seventies I can recall two individuals in our English department who typified these opposite poles. (For the sake of anonymity, I'll call them Delaney and McLarken.) Each tried to lure department rookies like me to their way of thinking.

DeLaney, a relatively young teacher with twelve years of experience, championed the "research-based" view. "Any enlightened English teacher," he would say, "has to recognize the validity of the research. Would you go to a doctor who ignored medical research?" For Delaney the findings of research communicated an authority not unlike the word of God. His bible was the classic study by Richard Braddock, Richard Lloyd Jones, and Lowell Schoer (1963), which concluded that teaching grammar failed to improve student writing. "Teaching traditional grammar," Delaney would say, "takes valuable time away from writing and reading."

On the other side of the grammatical planet was Mrs. McLarken, a thirty-three-year veteran and proponent of an "experience-based" view. She felt research was a lot of "hokey." "Those college professors don't have a clue what public teaching is all about," she would say. "Besides, their studies just give an excuse for some teachers to avoid the hard work of teaching grammar." She liked to point out that she had produced many fine student writers with her traditional approach and delighted in arguing that writers like Poe, Steinbeck, and Hemingway were all raised on traditional grammar. "What worked for Steinbeck," she would argue, "will work for your students."

Personally, I felt both were fine teachers, each truly concerned for doing what was best for their kids, each teaching from a well-informed background and a foundation of experience. But since neither seemed more persuasive than the other, I tried both approaches.

At first, I taught traditional grammar because I knew this best. I drilled kids with worksheets and designed a flowchart to track students individually at their own pace through each aspect of mechanics and usage. At one point about 50 percent of my teaching time was devoted to traditional grammar. But in spite of my efforts, one glaring fact seemed obvious: there was no carryover from grammar instruction to writing.

So, I switched to a linguistic approach. This proved even more disastrous. Not only was there no carryover from transformational grammar to writing, but linguistic concepts seemed more difficult for students to grasp.

Recognizing this, scholars shifted their emphasis away from linguistics and began advocating the integration of writing and grammar. This seemed like an excellent idea, but most available textbooks just repackaged old approaches, failing to provide a new program that effectively accomplished this. I felt a little like a casualty in a scholarly war, left on the battlefield without a weapon to combat the hordes of grammar-deficient students.

Around this time whole language began to emerge and offered some exciting ideas for integrating reading, writing, and speaking. What made this movement so appealing to me was that its primary advocates were not scholars, but teachers sharing what worked well in their classrooms. However, on the question of grammar whole language offered little direction. While some strategies looked promising, to implement them required the kind of individualization only possible in an elementary classroom of twenty to thirty students. With 125 to 150 students, many of the one-on-one grammar strategies of whole language were almost impossible to use effectively.

With these scholarly roads leading nowhere, I began the journey that led to "image grammar." For almost thirty years I've traveled on this journey with more than four thousand students. From these encounters, I've developed and tested the ideas you are about to read.

I'd like to share with you some of the trails along this journey, but before we begin, let me caution you. First, this is not a journey into the nuances of conventions. If you come in search of clarifications for *lie* and *lay*, you'll be disappointed. *Image Grammar* explores only those concepts that help students "feel" what Joan Didion calls "the infinite power" of grammar, a power derived from images.

Second, image grammar grew from questions like How does Jack London make you feel you are not just reading, but living in the days of the Yukon gold rush? How does Erma Bombeck create images that trigger eruptions of laughter? It developed from the study of the writer as an artist and of grammatical structures as the artist's tools for creating images.

This view is not an analogy, but a new view of the relationship between grammatical images and writing, a view often expressed by professional authors. Pulitzer Prize–winning author Jon Franklin, for example, describes writing as an image journey with a single image as the molecule in the writing universe. Bradbury credits his childhood love of comic books with nurturing his skill as a science fiction writer. And Hemingway comments that the paintings of Cézanne helped him to develop his written descriptions of landscapes. These are not isolated instances, but a common theme among many writers.

In addition, working with image grammar has changed my concept of the limits of grammar. Traditionally, the study of grammar has dealt only with words, phrases, and clauses. However, when I began to see grammar as the process of creating art, it seemed unnatural—even impossible—not to view grammar as a continuous spectrum in a whole work. As I explored this view with my students, the connection seemed to bring grammar into a meaningful relationship with stories, novels, screenplays, poems, reports, songs—the ultimate products of the writer's art.

So, in the chapters of this book, you will find explanations and exercises on the relationship of image grammar to paragraphs, passages, and complete works. I tried to show how grammatical structures contribute to the whole and how the whole reflects back on smaller structures. In effect, I attempted to explore Mina Shaughnessy's notion that teachers need a grammar of passages.

Finally, this journey helped me to understand the need to teach grammar in an artist's studio. This means allowing for studio time when students can practice their art, writing with models—real, photographed, filmed, written, or staged. It means discussing the art of the masters, posting their passages, and sharing insights from reading in small group discussions and individual conferences. It means experimenting with multiple genres and maintaining portfolios.

The companion CD helps facilitate such a studio approach. (You will need a browser, such as Netscape or Internet Explorer, to access these files.) There are two sections: one for students and one for teachers. The student portion is designed to be uploaded as a website that can be accessed either from a school lab or from home. It contains images and links to image-rich sites for student writing.

The teacher's resource section contains a collection of teaching strategies and quoted examples from the book that can be printed out to be used as handouts, or for lesson ideas. This section is for teachers only and shouldn't be uploaded for use with students in class.

The strategies and quoted examples can be printed directly from your browser, making them ready to use as handouts or for use on an overhead projector. You can save material as text and add or delete sections with your word processor.

The image collection can be used in a variety of ways. You can show the images to an entire class if your computer is connected to a television. You can create overheads by printing copies on transparency film with a color printer. You can have students work with these images in small groups, around a single computer, or you can post the student website on the Internet from which students can access images from home.

The companion CD should help you to integrate the grammar and writing lessons in the book more effectively and more enjoyably with your students.

1
The Writer as Artist
Basic Brush Strokes

The writer is an artist, painting images of life with specific and identifiable brush strokes, images as realistic as Wyeth and as abstract as Picasso. In the act of creation, the writer, like the artist, relies on fundamental elements. As watercolorist Frank Webb (1983) explains, "Pictures are not made of flowers, guitars, people, surf or turf, but with irreducible elements of art: shapes, tones, directions, sizes, lines, textures, and color" (19). Similarly, writing is not constructed merely from experiences, information, characters or plots, but from fundamental artistic elements of grammar. Observe, for example, how James Michener paints a scene in his historical novel *The Bridges at Toko-Ri*:

> Now the great carrier struck a sea trough and slid away, her deck lurching, but relentlessly the bull horn cried, "Move jets into position for launching," and the catapult crew, fighting for footing on the sliding deck, sprang swiftly into action, inching two heavy Banshees onto the catapults, taking painful care not to allow the jets to get rolling, lest they plunge overboard with some sudden shifting of the deck. (1953, 5)

Or examine how Carl Sagan paints images of galaxies in his nonfiction work *Cosmos*:

> From an intergalactic vantage point we would see, strewn like sea froth on the waves of space, innumerable faint, wispy tendrils of light. These are the galaxies. Some are solitary wanderers; most inhabit communal clusters, huddling together, drifting endlessly in the great cosmic dark. Before us is the Cosmos on the grandest scale we know. We are in the realm of the nebulae, eight billion light years from Earth, halfway to the edge of the known universe. (1980, 5)

Hidden beneath these passages, often unnoticed and unappreciated, lies a grammar of style, a combination of artistic techniques as worthy of respect and awe as any museum canvas. To paint images like these requires an understanding of image grammar—a rhetoric of writing techniques that provides writers with artistic grammatical options.

Writing as Seeing

Developing a grammar of style begins with the writer learning to literally and metaphorically "see." When an author lacks a visual eye, his or her writing has no heart and soul: images lie lifeless like cadavers in a morgue. For example, compare the following two images, the first written by a high school student, the second by well-known novelist Brian Jacques:

> It was winter. Everything was frozen and white with snow. Snow had fallen from the sky for days. The weather was horrible.

> Mossflower lay deep in the grip of midwinter beneath a sky of leaden gray that showed tinges of scarlet and orange on the horizon. A cold mantle of snow draped the landscape, covering the flatlands to the west. Snow was everywhere, filling the ditches, drifting high against the hedgerows, making paths invisible, smoothing the contours of earth in its white embrace. (5)

Jacques writes with an artist's eye, using details and color to tease the reader's visual appetite; the high school student writes like a house painter, ignoring details and using color to simply cover the surface. One can see why Jacques' one word of advice to writers is paint: "Paint. That's the magic word. Paint pictures with words. That's the greatest advice I can give anybody. Paint the pictures with words. The pictures will appear in the imagination so the person reading it can say, 'I can see that'" (O'Neill 1995, 37).

The qualities of a writer's images—the details, colors, shapes, movement—derive from visual perception. An ineffective writer sees broad impressions that evoke vague labels; a powerful writer visualizes specific details that create a literary virtual reality. Some linguists (Whorf 1964) and most general semanticists (Weinberg 1959; Hayakawa 1941) argue that our language shapes our perceptions and our perceptions shape our reality. To any teacher who has observed students struggling with writing, this seems obvious. As Leavitt and Sohn (1964) explain, "The way you select words and organize them into whole compositions depends on the way you see human experience. If you literally do not see anything, you will of course have nothing to say" (7). But what does it mean to *see*?

Professional authors define two categories of *seeing*: *showing* and *telling*. Novelist Robert Newton Peck (1980) explains this concept in his *Secrets of Successful Fiction*:

> Readers want a picture—something to see, not just a paragraph to read. A picture made out of words. That's what makes a pro out of an amateur. An amateur writer tells a story. A pro shows the story, creates a picture to look at instead of just words to read. A good author writes with a camera, not with a pen.
>
> The amateur writes: "Bill was nervous."
>
> The pro writes: "Bill sat in a dentist's waiting room, peeling the skin at the edge of his thumb, until the raw, red flesh began to show. Biting the torn cuticle, he ripped it away, and sucked at the warm sweetness of his own blood." (4)

For student writers, learning to *show* is central in their journey toward powerful prose. Showing engages the reader's mind as a catalyst for visualization. Telling lulls the reader to sleep. If a student writes, "Mary was tired," the reader arrives at a mental dead end, left with no imaginative opportunities for envisioning. Compare this to a description such as "Mary shuffled into the kitchen, yawning and blinking. Collapsing into a chair, she closed her eyes, crossed her arms for a pillow, and slowly tucked her head onto the fold." The second description paints detailed images and compels the reader to participate by re-creating the action on an imaginary mental screen. No one has to *tell* the reader that Mary is tired: the reader watches the images unfold and makes conclusions much as she or he would if the experience were real.

Asked to describe an image of an old man, for example, a student or an amateur writer might *tell* with details such as "This is the face of an old man" or "The weird, old man is reaching for something." By contrast, a professional writer *shows* this image with details as Stephen King does in this painting of an old Gypsy in *Thinner*:

> And before Halleck can jerk away, the old Gypsy reaches out and caresses his cheek with one twisted finger. His lips spread open like a wound, showing a few tombstone stumps poking out of his gums. They are black and green. His tongue squirms between them and then slides out to lick his grinning, bitter lips. (1)

Or as Mark Halprin uses to portray an old man in *A Soldier of the Great War*:

> Limping along paths of crushed stone and tapping his cane as he took each step, he raced across intricacies of sunlight and shadow spread

before him on the dark garden floor like golden lace. Alessandro Giuliani was tall and unbent, and his buoyant white hair fell and floated about his head like the white water in the curl of a wave. (1)

A well-described fiction or nonfiction work creates the mental equivalent of a film, leading readers through a visual journey of endless images with close-ups, action scenes, and angle shots. Creating art that shows requires more than visual awareness: it requires a knowledge of technique, the ability to select words like colors on a palette and apply sentence structures like brush strokes to a verbal canvas. For the student writer this means developing an image grammar repertoire.

Painting with Five Basic Brush Strokes

Just as the painter combines a wide repertoire of brush stroke techniques to create an image, the writer chooses from a repertoire of sentence structures. Although professionals use an array of complex structures, students can begin to learn the art of image grammar by employing five basic brush strokes: (1) the participle, (2) the absolute, (3) the appositive, (4) adjectives shifted out of order, and (5) action verbs. To help students paint easily, teachers should simplify definitions, relying on modeling and expanding definitions as students increase their fluency.

Painting with Participles

To simplify the concept of the participle for students, teachers can define it as an *ing* verb tagged on the beginning or end of a sentence. (Variations using *ed* forms can be introduced later.) For example, picture in your mind's eye, a nest of snakes curling around some prey. One writer/artist might describe this with, "The diamond-scaled snakes attacked their prey." This image captures a little of what might be happening, but watch the effect when the writer adds a few participles (*ing* verbs) to the beginning of the sentence: **"Hissing, slithering, and coiling,** the diamond-scaled snakes attacked their prey."

The participles evoke action. Suddenly, we can see the snakes coiling and slithering. The sound of their hissing makes us feel that we are part of the experience.

Students can also add participial phrases, a participle along with any modifiers that complete the image. Visualize how this works when two participial phrases are added to our original sentence: **"Hissing their forked red tongues** and **coiling their cold bodies,** the diamond-scaled snakes attacked their prey." Both methods—adding several participles or adding one or two participial phrases—paint more detailed pictures. Using single participles creates rapid movement, while expanded phrases add details at a slower, but equally intense pace.

One of the clearest ways to define brush strokes for students is by showing models and having them imitate. Here are a few examples that helped clarify how professionals use participles and participial phrases.

Ernest Hemingway, for example, uses participial phrases to create tension and action in this excerpt from *Old Man and the Sea*:

> **Shifting the weight of the line to his left shoulder and kneeling carefully,** he washed his hand in the ocean and held it there, **submerged,** for more than a minute, **watching the blood trail away and the steady movement of the water against his hand as the boat moved.** (56-57)

In this passage Hemingway used the *ed* participle *submerged* for similar effect. When first working with brush strokes, students often confuse the *ed* form with the predicate of the sentence. So, it is best to begin with an *ing* definition and introduce the *ed* once students have control of the *ing* brush stroke.

The following student examples were written after several examples were created by the teacher using slide images. Only the minimal definition given above was presented. Notice how the student writers use participles and participial phrases to enhance the action and add visual detail.

> **Flying through the air on the wings of a dream,** the Olympic long jumper thrust the weight of his whole body forward. (Cathleen Conry)

> Melody froze, **dripping with sweat, hoping with all her might that they wouldn't hear the noise.** A beam of light swung out into the darkness, **searching.** (Becky Swab)

> The clown, **appearing bright and cheerful,** smiled and did his act with unusual certainty for someone who had just killed a man. (Christi Flick)

> The rhino, **caught in the tangled rope,** looked for freedom. (Erika Schreckengost) (Note that Erika generated this *ed* form before it was presented in class by imitating *ing* models.)

An equally powerful brush stoke that also adds to the action of an image is the *absolute*. An absolute is a two-word combination—a noun and an *ing* or *ed* verb added onto a sentence. Instead of saying "The cat climbed the tree," you can add two absolutes to give it detail: "**Claws digging, feet kick-**

ing, the cat climbed the tree." Either way the cat gets up the tree, but in the second instance, he climbs with flair, and the dog chasing him is amazed.

Painting with Absolutes

To help students understand absolutes, try this approach. Have them close their eyes and picture a mountain climber moving along a steep cliff. Pause for a moment and ask students to visualize this one sentence description: "The mountain climber edged along the cliff."

Next, explain that you are going to add a brush stroke, defined simply as a noun combined with an *ing* participle. (Again, *ed* participles can come later.) Then, with their eyes still closed, tell them to watch what happens as you add two absolutes. Read the sentence: "The mountain climber edged along the cliff, **hands shaking, feet trembling.**" Or in the reverse order: "**Hands shaking, feet trembling,** the mountain climber edged along the cliff." Although adding three absolutes overloads the picture and diminishes the effect, one or two creates a far more dynamic image than the original.

As with participles, explain to students that absolute phrases are also effective. For example, with the previous example, the climber might have been described with an absolute phrase, such as "**Feet trembling on the snow-covered rocks,** the mountain climber edged along the cliff."

Gary Hoffman in *Writeful* suggests another way of teaching absolutes— by asking students to imagine that the comma controls a telescopic lens that zooms in on images. Using the basic sentence "The rhapis palm sat in a large, white container" he demonstrates the zoom technique:

> The writer can zoom up on any part of the picture that is already framed by the original sentence. In this example, that means zooming up on either the container or the palm.
>
> For instance, assume the branches of the palm are the detail of interest. Without any word of transition, only a twist of a zoom lens represented by a comma, the sentence can now read: "The rhapis palm sat in a large, white container, **the branches stretching into the air...**" The writer can place a comma after "air" and zoom up something framed in this part of the sentence. This time the zoom can only be on the branches or air because the "camera" has focused on them, cutting the general description of the palm and container out of the picture.
>
> Suppose there is nothing of interest about the air, but the branches have interesting joints or nodes. Zooming in on those, the sentence would now read: "The rhapis palm sat in a large, white container, the **branches stretching into the air, fibrous joints knuckling the otherwise smooth surface.**" (20)

The zoom analogy works nicely for teaching students not only to use absolutes, but also participles, appositives, adjectives out of order, and a variety of other grammatical brush strokes. The zoom also helps to convey the proper use of commas to connect phrases to a simple sentence. Below are some sample absolute images created by professional and student writers. Using commas to zoom in on details, these writers telescoped images both at the beginning and end of their primary sentences. Showing examples such as these to students before they write can help them learn absolutes by imitating.

Notice how Anne Rice in this passage from *The Mummy* uses absolutes to zoom in for a close-up photo, capturing the specific images of the mummy's arm:

> The mummy was moving. The mummy's right arm was outstretched, **the torn wrappings hanging from it,** as the being stepped out of its gilded box! The scream froze in her throat. The thing was coming towards her—towards Henry, who stood with his back to it—moving with a weak, shuffling gait, **that arm outstretched before it, the dust rising from the rotting linen that covered it, a great smell of dust and decay filling the room.** (72)

In the following one-sentence examples, students painted with absolutes and absolute phrases as they observed slides:

> **Mind racing, anxiety overtaking,** the diver peered once more at the specimen. (Erin Stralka)
>
> I glanced at my clock, **digits glowing florescent blue in the inky darkness of my room.** (Jenn Coppolo)
>
> **Jaws cracking, tongue curling,** the kitten yawned tiredly, awaking from her nap. (Tara Tesmer)

One of the most common brush strokes in the action sequences of fiction, the absolute infuses action into a word painting. Just as the artist requires a variety of painting techniques to vary effect, the writer too needs a repertoire of devices to shape impressions. A third technique, the appositive, provides another option, often used to amplify still images.

Painting with Appositives

For student word painters, teachers can define an appositive as a noun that adds a second image to a preceding noun. Like the absolute, the appositive expands details in the reader's imagination. For example, by adding a second image to the noun *raccoon* in the sentence "The raccoon enjoys eating turtle eggs," the writer/artist can enhance the first image with a new perspective. For example, the writer might paint the sentence "The raccoon, **a scavenger,** enjoys eating turtle eggs."

Scavenger follows *raccoon* in the sentence; it's set off with commas and enriches the image of the painting. To add more vivid details, writers frequently expand the appositive to an appositive phrase with added details such as "The raccoon, **a midnight scavenger who roams lake shorelines in search of food,** enjoys eating turtle eggs."

Observe how Cornelius Ryan uses appositives in *June 6, 1944: The Longest Day.* He could have written: "A phalanx of ships and planes bore down on Hitler's Europe," but instead, Ryan expanded the image with appositives and then extended the picture with further specific examples:

> Plowing through the choppy gray waters, a phalanx of ships bore down on Hitler's Europe: **fast new attack transports, slow rust-scarred freighters, small ocean liners, channel steamers, hospital ships, weather-beaten tankers, and swarms of fussing tugs.** Barrage balloons flew above the ships. Squadrons of fighter planes weaved below the clouds. And surrounding this cavalcade of ships packed with men, guns, tanks, and motor vehicles, and supplies came a formidable array of 702 warships. (243)

With the same intent as Cornelius Ryan, eighth-grade students used appositives and appositive phrases to add a second noun image in each of the following sketches from photographs:

> The volcano, **a ravenous God of fire,** spewed forth lava and ash across the mountain. (Ben Quagliata)

> The old Navajo woman, **a weak and withered lady,** stared blankly. (Jon Vadnal)

> The waterfall, **a tilted pitcher,** poured the fresh, pure spray into the creek. The essence of natural beauty, tranquil and majestic, it seemed to enchant the forest with a mystical rush that echoed throughout the untouched virgin paradise. (Allie Archer)

> The fish, **a slimy mass of flesh,** felt the alligator's giant teeth sink into his scales as he struggled to get away. (Lindsey Kannen)

Working with fiction in the examples above, student-artists used appositives to expand the sensory details. In nonfiction authors more often use an appositive image to add clarity in phrases such as "Michael Jordan, the famous basketball player." All brush strokes work equally well for fiction, nonfiction, or poetry, but each genre creates a different emphasis.

Painting with Adjectives Shifted Out of Order

Adjectives out of order, used more often by authors of fiction, amplify the details of an image. We have all seen students overload their descriptions with too many adjectives in sentences like "The large, red-eyed, angry bull moose charged the intruder." Professional authors rarely commit this error. When they want to stack an image with three adjectives, they avoid a three-in-a-row string by using a technique called adjectives out of order. Leaving one adjective in its original place, the authors shift two others after the noun. With the sentence about the angry moose, a professional might transform it into "The large bull moose, **red-eyed and angry,** charged the intruder." The effect creates a spotlight and intensifies the image, giving it a profound rhythm instead of the elementary cadence of the original.

Sir Arthur Conan Doyle in *The Hound of the Baskervilles* uses this technique to shift three adjectives to the end of a sentence to describe a mysterious sound: "And then, suddenly, in the very dead of the night, there came a sound to my ears, **clear, resonant, and unmistakable**" (72). Had he placed the adjectives in their normal position, the description would have seemed childish. Listen to the loss of power when the sentence is written as "And then, suddenly, in the very dead of the night, there came a clear, resonant, unmistakable sound to my ears."

Similarly, in *The Alienist*, Caleb Carr describes arriving at the Insane Pavilion at Bellevue in New York City: "The Pavilion was a simple city, **long and rectangular**" (27). Again, shifting the adjectives out of their normal order creates a focus. Robert Newton Peck uses the same technique in this sentence from *A Day No Pigs Would Die*: "I could smell Mama, **crisp and starched,** plumping my pillow, and the cool muslin pillowcase touched both my ears as the back of my head sank into all those feathers" (12).

Students can learn to use this technique effectively as the following examples illustrate:

> The woman, **old and wrinkled,** smiled upon her newborn great-grandson with pride. (Stephanie Schwallie)

> The boxer, **twisted and tormented,** felt no compassion for his contender. (Chris Hloros)

> The cheetah, **tired and hungry,** stared at the gazelle, which would soon become his dinner. (Zach Vesoulis)

Painting with Action Verbs

Painting with action verbs gives writers another effective image tool. By eliminating passive voice and reducing *being* verbs, writers can energize action images. Verbs of passive voice communicate no action. The image is like a still photograph with the subject of the action frozen with the prepositions *by* or *with*. Typically, passive voice verbs require the help of a *being* verb. For example, these sentences are passive:

> The runaway horse **was ridden** into town by an old, white-whiskered rancher.

> The grocery store **was robbed** by two armed men.

Notice how the word *by* signals the noun performing the action. Passive voice can weaken images by freezing the action often inherent in a sentence. Compare the following revisions of the previous passive sentences and notice how active voice energizes the images:

> The old, white-whiskered rancher **rode** the runaway horse into town.

> Two armed men **robbed** the grocery store.

Even when not used as part of a passive voice, *being* verbs slow the action and tend to link complements that *tell*. Students can improve the power of their sentences by replacing as many being verbs as possible, often by creating an appositive. For example, examine these two sentences: "The Nerk Knocker is a strange mechanical contraption. It brews coffee while beating a drum solo." Both could be combined into a single, more powerful statement such as, "The Nerk Knocker, a strange mechanical contraption, brews coffee while beating a drum solo."

Action verbs replace still photos with motion pictures. With a little imagination, a writer can even bring an inanimate object to life by adding an action verb:

> *Being Verb:* The gravel road **was** on the left side of the barn.

> *Action Verb:* The gravel road **curled** around the left side of the barn.

By simply replacing *being* verbs, writers sharpen visual images. For example, when Shawn and Jerry first wrote the opening paragraph of their children's book *Goose Moon*, they used several *being* verbs. In their revision they removed these verbs, mobilizing the action of the children and the geese. Visualize the difference in the motion picture of your imagination as you compare these two drafts:

FIRST DRAFT

Rockwell was a beautiful lake. Canada geese could be heard across the water bugling like tuneless trumpets. Near the shore, two children were hidden behind a massive maple tree. Watching quietly, they hoped to see the first gosling begin to hatch. Tiny giggles escaped their whispers of excitement.

FINAL DRAFT

Rockwell Lake echoed with the sounds of Canada geese. Their honking bugled across the water like tuneless trumpets. Two children hid behind a massive maple tree. They silently watched, hoping to see the first gosling hatch. Tiny giggles escaped their whispers of excitement. (1)

Writers can strengthen sentences in which *being* verbs link vague noun complements. For example, in a sentence such as "The meal was wonderful," the being verb spotlights *wonderful*, a word that tells instead of shows, which characterizes instead of describes. Because of this quality, Burroway (1987) argues that most being verbs are "effectively passive," functioning like passive voice.

Students can locate being verbs and verbs of passive voice by using the find command on a word processor or simply by doing a visual search. With a little time spent eliminating these verbs, they can bring their images to life. However, when students cannot easily replace a being verb, it may belong in the sentence. Some being verbs function to define and others can convey a mood of passivity when a passage requires it for effect.

Combining Strokes

Once students have developed control of the five basic brush strokes, they begin to combine them spontaneously in longer works. Eighth grader Adam Porter, for example, blended several techniques in this scene from his horror story, inspired by the close-up image of a tarantula:

Then it crawled in. A spider, **a repulsive, hairy creature, no bigger than a tarantula,** crawled into the room. It crawled across the floor up onto his nightstand and stopped, as if it were staring at him. He reached for a nearby copy of *Sports Illustrated*, rolled it up, and swatted the spider with all his might.

He looked over only to see a hideous mass of eyes and legs. He had killed it. Just then, another one crawled in, **following the same path as the first.** He killed that one too. Then another one came, and another and another. There were hundreds of them! **Hands trembling, sweat dripping from his face,** he flung the magazine left and right, **trying to kill the spiders,** but there were too many. He dropped the magazine.

Helpless now, his eyes darted around the room. He could no longer see the individual spiders. He could just see a thick, black blanket of movement. He started squirming as he felt their fang-like teeth sink into his pale flesh like millions of tiny needles **piercing his body.**

In the same way and by using a photograph from *National Geographic,* Cary Cybulski spontaneously employed a variety of techniques in her description of an old man hugging a cello:

> The old man, **feeble and stiff,** tenderly embraced his beloved cello. A single tear slid down his wrinkled face. His arthritic hands shook as the bow quivered back and forth. He wore an out-of-style jacket, **an old fashioned plaid.** His shaggy eyebrows glistened with sweat, and his sideburns grew overgrown and wild. His cello, **a piece of art,** was old and had clearly been used. Decades of polishing made the wood shiny.
>
> In a scratchy, weak voice, the old man cursed his hands for being so stiff and sore. He suddenly gasped as a spasm of pain swept through his arm. **Exhausted,** he gently laid his cello in the soft velvet case and lowered himself onto his bed.
>
> As he lay there, memories of his childhood started to stir in his mind. He remembered coming home after school and practicing the cello for hours. He remembered playing solos in his high school orchestra, and then later in life playing with world known orchestras. **Smiling gently,** he brought his cello, **his life-long friend and partner,** close to him and fell asleep.

As students begin to play with these painting techniques, interesting image experiments emerge. One eighth-grade student, Michele Leighty, intrigued with the rhythm of absolutes, created the following poem:

> THE SNAKE
>
> Eyes darting,
> lips parting,
> the snake flicked its tongue.
>
> Body slithering,
> scales quivering,
> its rattle beat like a drum.
>
> Cold blood boiling,
> body coiling,
> the snake attacked its prey.
>
> Feet scurrying,
> paws hurrying,
> the mouse could not get away.

STRATEGIES

Having students recognize the beauty of an author's art differs from having them create their own art. From a practical "What do I do on Monday?" perspective, the question for teachers is How do I get my students to emulate outstanding writers by using techniques such as brush strokes?

The answer to this lies in the total literacy environment of the classroom: learning strategies, environmental opportunities for students to immerse themselves in print, options for collaboration, choices for learning modes, and so forth. This environment emerges from a combination of teaching-learning strategies including minilessons, discussion activities, small group inquiry, independent reading, independent writing, individual investigations, and conferences with peers and the teacher. (For more details see Noden and Vacca [1994].) What follows are several lesson strategies designed for this type of interactive environment, strategies that will help students apply image grammar.

Strategy 1: Create an Artist's Image Palette

To get a sense of the variety of images authors use, students can construct an "Artist's Image Palette," a collection of words and phrases used by professional authors to create powerful mental images. Give students the option of working in pairs or independently and ask them to search for powerful images written by favorite authors. Next, have them group these phrases in one of the several categories suggested in the handout that follows. Distribute An Artist's Image Palette to guide students. (This palette is also found on the companion CD, which includes other strategies, useful Internet sites, and images for in-class writing.)

AN ARTIST'S IMAGE PALETTE

Assignment (Part 1): Using a book by any author you have read this year or last, construct a palette of images used by that writer. Your images can range from one-word selections to four or five word phrases. After you have collected at least fifty images (half of which may be single words), classify them in one of the following categories or in categories of your own design:

Mood: reflective, humorous, fearful, stressful, relaxed, anxious, nervous, loving, angry, etc.

Activity: conflict descriptions (interactions with others, nature, animals, and so on), setting descriptions (city scenes, country scenes, wilderness scenes, interior scenes), character descriptions (facial features, dress, speech, actions).

Traditional parts of speech: noun images (people, places, buildings, objects, animals), verb images (actions, movements), adjective images (characteristics such as color, shape, size, sensory details).

Brush strokes: appositives, absolutes, participles, adjectives out of order, action verbs.

You may choose to work with a partner, but each of you must contribute 50 images for a combined list of 100.

Assignment (Part 2): Write a short descriptive paragraph mixing between 10 and 20 words from your artist's palette with 30 to 60 of your own. If you are working with a partner, each of you must create your own paragraph, but you may both use your combined list.

It is important for teachers to keep a balance between writing exercises and plagiarism. Chapter 4 provides guidelines for this purpose and further clarifies the rational behind these strategies.

Below are excerpts from one such assignment, written by teacher Tina Hughes for an inservice workshop. Tina's complete palette included a list of 150 images. Featured here is just a sampling to illustrate how the artist's palette works.

SAMPLE ARTIST'S IMAGE PALETTE
Images from *A Wrinkle in Time* by Madeline L'Engle

Movement
scudded frantically
feet padding softly
   as a kitten
fluttered up from her chair
sitting like statues
gushed from her eyes
rhythmic and flowing
   as a dance

Character Descriptions
strong, gentle fingers
glasses perched on his nose
gleam of avid curiosity
eyelids sagged
hair stringing about her face
nose a round soft blob

Moods
prickles of apprehension
flushed with rage
sullen fury
merry fire
savagely
perturbed

Parts of Speech
puny little brains
delighted smile
sweet autumnal smell
tingling faintly
jangling
grimly

Blending her own words with touches of images from *A Wrinkle in Time*, Tina created an original description, a paragraph of which is excerpted here. Words taken from the Artist's Palette are italicized.

> The teacher felt *prickles of apprehension* as she awaited the start of another year-long adventure. A heavy, *sweet, autumnal smell* floated through the opened windows as one final survey of the room revealed a state of readiness. The polished luster of the heavily waxed floor braced itself for the onslaught of the stampeding throngs of eager students. *Reverberating* through the halls, the *jangling* bell jolted the teacher from her moment of meditation.

Collecting written images builds the student's repertoire of techniques, allowing the student to play with word paintings of the masters and more clearly see how authors use brush strokes.

Strategy 2: Explore Images from Films of Best-Selling Novels

Hollywood producers adapt best-selling novels into films not only because the novel appeals to a large audience, but also because the images of the book provide a powerful visual guide for the director. The details of character, setting, and action scenes in the novel create an imaginary storyboard that simplifies the photographic decisions of the director. By taking excerpts from popular novels made into films and juxtaposing them against the representative scenes in the film versions, teachers can help students visualize the relationship between words and images.

This activity requires some prior research. First, you will need to locate copies of one or more of the films represented below from your local library or video store. Next, you will need to find the section of the film described in the text below.

With each film/text combination, show the film while projecting the author's description with an overhead. By viewing the projected text while simultaneously observing VCR cuts of the same film scene, students can work collaboratively in small groups to identify the brush stokes used to create both the film and novel images. The combination of written brush strokes and popular film cuts reinforces the concept of the writer as artist, making image grammar more significant for students, many of whom have been exposed primarily to multimedia imagery.

You can vary this assignment several ways. Students can work in collaborative teams or individually to identify techniques. Or to build a personal film-passage collection, you can give extra credit for each excerpt/video combination students bring to class. If the entire class is reading a novel made into a film, consider showing the film in parts and discussing how both the writer and director painted key incidents.

Sample Novel and Film Passages

RAIDERS OF THE LOST ARK BY ROBERT CAMPBELL

He stared at the bag, then at the idol in his hand, and then he was aware of a strange, distant noise, **a rumbling like that of a great machine set in motion, a sound of things waking from a long sleep, roaring and tearing and creaking through the spaces of the Temple.** . . . For a split second nothing happened. And then there was a faint whirring noise, **a creaking sound,** and the walls of the chamber seemed to break open as giant metal spikes, like the jaws of some impossible shark, slammed together in the center of the chamber. (7)

IN GOD WE TRUST ALL OTHERS PAY CASH (FILM ENTITLED THE CHRISTMAS STORY) BY JEAN SHEPHERD

He swept up the plastic trophy, **his symbol of superiority,** and rushed out through the dining room and into the living room. **Placing the lamp squarely in the middle of the library table,** he aligned it exactly at the center of the front window. We trailed behind him, **applauding and yipping.** He was unrolling the cord, down on all fours.

"Where's the damn plug?"

"Behind the sofa."

My mother answered quietly, in a vaguely detached tone.

"Quick! Go out in the kitchen and get me an extension!"

Our entire world was strung together with "extensions." Outlets in our house were rare and coveted, **each one buried under a bakelite mound of three-way, seven-way, and ten-way plugs and screw sockets, the entire mess caught in a twisted, snarling Gordian knot of frayed and cracked lamp cords, radio cords, and God knows what.** Occasionally in some houses a critical point was reached, and one of these electric bombs went off, **sometimes burning down whole blocks of homes, or more often blowing out the main fuse, plunging half the town into darkness.** (92-93)

JURASSIC PARK BY MICHAEL CRICHTON

Nedry opened the car door, **glancing back at the dinosaur to make sure it wasn't going to attack,** and felt a sudden, excruciating pain in his eyes, **stabbing like spikes into the back of his skull,** and he squeezed his eyes shut and gasped with the intensity of it and threw up his hands to cover his eyes and felt the slippery foam **trickling down both sides of his nose.** Spit. The dinosaur had spit in his eyes.

Even as he realized it, the pain overwhelmed him, and he dropped to his knees, **disoriented, wheezing. He collapsed onto his side, his cheek pressed to the wet ground, his breath coming in thin whistles through the constant, ever-screaming pain that caused flashing spots of light to appear behind his tightly shut eyelids.** (96)

CALL OF THE WILD BY JACK LONDON

For the most part, however, Buck's love was expressed in adoration. While he went wild with happiness when Thornton touched him or spoke to him, he did not seek these tokens. Unlike Skeet, who was wont to shove her nose under Thornton's hand and nudge and nudge till petted, or Nig, who would stalk up and rest his great head on Thornton's knee, Buck was content to adore at a distance. He would lie by the hour, **eager, alert,** at Thornton's feet, **looking up into his face, dwelling upon it, studying it, following with keenest interest each fleeting expression, every movement or change or feature.** Or, as chance might have it, he would lie farther away, to the side or rear, **watching the outlines of the man and the occasional movement of his body.** And often, such was the communion in which they lived, the strength of Buck's gaze would draw John Thornton's head around, and he would return the gaze, without speech, **his heart shining out of his eyes as Buck's heart shone out.** (64–65)

Nonfiction documentaries also provide excellent examples of some of these same techniques. Transcriptions of PBS documentaries offer a rich resource for analyzing brush strokes. The following excerpts from the film *The Hellstrom Chronicle* demonstrate how nonfiction models work equally well for analysis and discussion.

THE HELLSTROM CHRONICLE BY DAVID SELTZER

Their greatest enemy is the sun, **its scorching rays drying their protective walls to the consistency of dust. The mound ripped open,** they stand defenseless against attack. **Moving with sudden frenzy,** the soldiers assess the damage. With frightening efficiency the mound suddenly comes alive, **a troop of workers proceeding with incredible speed to heal their wound before the predators arrive. Exuding paste from special glands,** they fight to rebuild their shield. But in their work is desperation, for the drying rays of the sun begin to suck the life from them too.

Once students understand the concept of brush strokes, teachers can use a variety of models for collaboration, revision, and individual investigation.

Strategy 3: Examine the Art of Sue Grafton

In group discussions teachers can get accurate insights into how students perceive the art of literature. Once students have a working knowledge of sentence brush strokes, they more easily recognize the writer's art when responding to questions such as "What images did you especially enjoy in this piece?" or "Were there any words or phrases that struck you as especially powerful or interesting?"

With the aid of the following passage from *H Is for Homicide* by mystery novelist Sue Grafton, team students into small groups to locate as many brush stroke techniques as possible:

Bibiana got to her feet, groping blindly for her handbag. Too late. The couple converged on us. The blond woman placed a firm hand on my shoulder, effectively nailing me to the chair. The guy pressed a Browning forty-five against Bibiana's spine. I saw Jimmy reach for his thirty-eight, but the guy shook his head.

"I got the option to smoke her if there is any problem whatsoever. It's your choice."

Bibiana picked up her jacket and her handbag. Jimmy and I watched helplessly as the three of them moved toward the back door. The minute they were out of sight, he bolted for the front, attracting startled looks from all the patrons he bumped in passing. The front door banged open, and he was gone. I threw some money on the table and headed after him. By the time I hit the front street, he was already pounding toward the corner, elbows pumping, gun drawn. I ran after him, plowing straight through a puddle on the walk. . . .

I reached the intersection moments after Jimmy did. A Ford sedan shot out of the alley three doors down. Jimmy, as if moving in slow motion, took a stance and fired. The back window shattered. He fired again. The right rear tire blew and the Ford took a sudden fishtailing detour into a van parked at the curb. The Ford's front bumper clattered to the pavement and glass fragments showered down with a delicate tinkling. The front doors of the Ford seem to open simultaneously. The blond woman emerged from the passenger side; the big guy, from the drivers side, taking cover behind the yawning car door as he turned and took aim. I hit the pavement and flattened myself in the shelter of a line of trash cans. The ensuing shots sounded like kernels of popcorn in a lidded sauce pan. I heard three more shots fired in succession, one of them plowing in the pavement near my head. I feared for Jimmy and felt a sixth sense of dread for Bibiana, too. Someone was running. At least somebody was alive. I just wasn't sure who. I heard the footsteps fade. Then silence.

I pulled myself up onto my hands and knees and scrambled toward a parked car, peering over the hood. Jimmy was standing across the street. There was no sign of the blond. Bibiana, apparently unhurt, clung to the Ford's rear fender and wept hysterically. I approached her with care, wondering where the guy in the plaid sport coat had gone. I could hear panting, a labored moan that suggested both anguish and extreme effort. On the far side of the Ford, I caught sight of him, dragging himself along the sidewalk, blood streaming down the left side of his face from a head wound. He seemed completely focused on the journey, determined to escape, moving with the same haphazard of a crawling baby, limbs occasionally working at cross purposes. He laid his head down, resting for a moment before he inched forward again. A crowd had collected like the spectators at the finish of a marathon. No one cheered. A woman moved toward the injured man and dropped down beside him, reaching out tentatively. At her touch, a deep howl seemed to rise from him, guttural and pain filled. There is no sound so terrible as a man's sorrow for his own death. (39–40)

An awareness of brush strokes links reading to writing and gives students tools for reflection. This type of exercise helps students look beyond the content of a work to the artistry that created that content. (Note: An answer sheet with all the brush stokes identified can be found on the companion CD.)

Strategy 4: Stimulate Images with Derived Poetry

Shelly Tucker, author of *Writing Poetry*, suggests a variation of the artist's palette for poetry. She provides her students with a scrambled list of words from a poem by a well-known author. Students are then instructed to use these words as starting points for their own poems, letting the images suggest new combinations and themes.

Try Tucker's technique with a poem of your choice appropriate to the interests and age level of your students. For example, you might choose a poem like "Hector the Collector" by Shel Silverstein for middle school students or "Wolves" by John Haines for high school students.

Below is a list of the words used in these poems. Ask students to borrow words from one of the lists to generate an image starter for their own poem. Point out that only 25 to 30 percent of the words in their poem should be taken from the poet's palette. These should be used as springboards to original ideas and images.

WORDS FROM "HECTOR THE COLLECTOR" BY SHEL SILVERSTEIN

and	electric	models	shoelaces
all	for	my	shoot
airplane	fingers	more	stopped-up
bags	float	nails	small
bells	fit	not	string
bricks	gattlin guns	no	tires
broken	glistening	out	trains
bottles	gold	old	that
bits	handles	of	toot
boats	horns	people	twists
bent-up	Hecktor	paper	that
butter	heads	pieces	treasure
come	half	puzzles	trunk
called	his	picture	three-legged
came	it	patched-up	tracks
cracks	ice-cream	rings	these
collector	junk	rusty	things
collected	knives	ring	than
chipped	keys	soul	to
copper	locks	socks	the
chairs	looked	silly	vases
cups	loved	sightless	with
dried-up	leaky	share	would
dolls	leaves	sticks	wire
			worn-out
			with
			wouldn't

Middle school student Colin Culkin borrowed words from the list above, added them to his own images and created this poem.

THE ATTIC

My attic would appear to you
Old mangled things, replaced by new
Leaky cups and worn-out trains
Little bikes without chains

But to me it's so much more
Locked-up memories, many more in store

Cracked model planes, some soaring to heights
Mutilated disco balls, accompanied by lights

Rusty bells, patched-up vases
Much-loved treasures bringing back more-loved faces
Through thick and thin my attic stays
Never to be forgotten throughout my days

WORDS FROM "WOLVES" BY JOHN HAINES

an	find	my	so
afar	from	nigh	sleep
are	for	night	their
as	good	over	that
a	howling	only	they
and	heard	of	their
between	human	polished	through
by	he	rang	the
but	in	snow	tongues
brave	islands	sail	tomorrow
blown	licking	solitude	them
blinking	I	sound	voices
coming	ice	snowbound	wolves
continual	icy	sailors	water
drifting	know	stars	wind
death's	last	sing	with
eyelashes	moon	seamen	will
from	moonlit	should	yawning
frozen	much	sun	

As an in-class demo with words from "Wolves," the sample poem below was created by the author of this book. Notice that only about 25 percent of the images (those in italics) are borrowed from the original and these are scrambled in a new context. Using derived poetry works best as a catalyst with found images generating new images.

REDBIRD IN THE SNOW
by Harry Noden

ice wings fail to flutter
broken bird
cries un*heard*

lost in *snowbound solitude*
victim of the *wolf wind*
whipping, whirling
snapping, snarling
in *death's* dance of *frozen* embrace

Strategy 5: Tour a Writer's Gallery

Enlarge and post the following writing samples around the classroom. Divide the class into five or six small discussion groups to visit the pieces. Next, have each group discuss the artistic techniques they observed. Included are a few examples of sentence fragments for effect and the use of specific details for comic effect—techniques discussed in other chapters, but included here to arouse curiosity.

At daybreak Billy Buck emerged from the bunkhouse and stood for a moment on the porch looking up at the sky. He was a broad, bandy-legged little man with a walrus mustache, with square hands, puffed and muscled on the palms. His eyes were a contemplative, watery gray and the hair which protruded from under his Stetson hat was spiky and weathered. (John Steinbeck, *The Red Pony* [1973, 105])

An old lady sat at the kitchen hearthside—a big old lady, thin as a siding, but wide in the shoulders and so tall her head stuck up above the tidy of the rocker she was sitting in. The old lady was smoking a pipe and she kept her makings in the Dutch oven, which was built in one side of the fireplace. Every so often she'd knock her pipe out on the side of the fireplace, open up the iron door of the Dutch oven, get out her tobacco, bang the door shut, fill her pipe, open the door, bang it shut. Clack, clack, bang . . . bang. (Jessamyn West, *The Friendly Persuasion* [(1945) 1971, 110])

A baseball weighted your hand just so, and fit it. Its red stitches, its good leather and hardness like skin over bone, seemed to call forth a skill both easy and precise. On the catch—the grounder, the fly, the line drive—you could snag a baseball in your mitt, where it stayed, snap, like a mouse locked in its trap, not like some pumpkin of a softball you merely halted, with a terrible sound like a splat. You could curl your fingers around a baseball, and throw it in a straight line. When you hit it with a bat, it cracked—and your heart cracked, too, at the sound. It took a grass stain nicely, stayed round and smelled good and lived lashed in your mitt all winter, hibernating. (Annie Dillard, *An American Childhood* [1987, 100])

At the *Miami Herald* we ordinarily don't provide extensive coverage of New York City unless a major news development occurs up there, such as Sean Penn coming out of a restaurant. But lately we have become very concerned about the "Big Apple," because of a story about Miami that ran a few weeks ago in the Sunday magazine of the *New York Times*. Maybe you remember this story: The cover featured an upbeat photograph of suspected Miami drug dealers being handcuffed face-down in the barren dirt next to a garbage-strewn sidewalk outside a squalid shack that probably contains roaches the size of Volvo sedans. The headline asked: CAN MIAMI SAVE ITSELF?

For those readers too stupid to figure out the answer, there was this helpful hint: A City Beset by Drugs and Violence

The overall impression created by the cover was: Sure Miami can save itself! And some day trained sheep will pilot the Concorde. (Dave Barry, "Can New York Save Itself?" [1994, 327])

Long before the first rays of the sun proclaimed yet another brilliant day on the Monterey Peninsula, Ted lay awake thinking about the weeks ahead. The courtroom. The defendant's table where he would sit, feeling the eyes of the spectators on him, trying to get a sense of the impact of the testimony on the jurors. The verdict: Guilty of Murder in the Second Degree. Why Second Degree? he had asked his first lawyer. "Because in New York State, First Degree is reserved for killing a peace officer. For what it's worth, it amounts to about the same, as far as sentencing goes." Life, he told himself. A life in prison. (Mary Higgins Clark, *Weep No More My Lady* [1991, 167])

Strategy 6: Copyedit "Gessi the Great"

Have students imagine that they are copy editors for a popular magazine. The editor-in-chief has asked them to revise the paragraph below, cutting any unnecessary text and adding brush strokes.

The famous escape artist was hanging upside down above a parking lot in a straight jacket. He was suspended from a crane. His name was "Gessi the Great." He twisted and twirled in the wind as a crowd watched silently. The crowd was large with about fifty onlookers. Finally, Gessi wiggled out of the jacket and tossed it aside. He was lowered to the ground by the crane operator and greeted by cheers.

This should give students a feel for revising with brush strokes and generate paragraphs that resemble this:

Hanging upside down above the parking lot, suspended from a crane, "Gessi the Great," the famous escape artist, twisted and twirled in the wind. Below, a crowd of about fifty onlookers watched silently. Finally, Gessi wiggled out of the jacket and tossed it aside. The crowd erupted in cheers as the crane operator lowered him to the ground.

As a follow-up have students do a similar revision on a piece of their own writing.

Strategy 7: Paint Models from the Nando Times

Click on the *Nando Times* photo page at <http://www.nando.net/photopage/>. Each day the *Nando Times* displays sixteen key images from news events around the world. These images are always dramatic and high quality, providing an excellent resource for student writing.

Divide the class into five small groups and develop five learning stations—one area for reading, one for writing, one for discussion, one for listening, and one for writing on the Internet. Whether you have access in your room (or library) to only one computer or access to a block of four or five, you can assign a group of four to six students to explore one site, in this case, the photo page of *Nando Times*.

As they examine the photos, have students select an image they find fascinating and write a brief paragraph describing it, using the brush strokes described in this chapter. Explain that the small thumbnail images on the photo page can be enlarged by clicking on them. Also mention that the categories listed below the thumbnails lead to an archive of additional images.

You will find additional photographic resources for this strategy and others on the companion CD that accompanies this book.

2
The Artist's Eye
Seeing Specific Details

CONCEPTS

In the novels of writers such as Ursula Le Guin, J. R. R. Tolkien, Sue Grafton, and Harriet Beecher Stowe, characters never go "into the woods and build a fire," they walk "into the deep resin-scented darkness and gather dead sticks and cones to make a fire." A slave girl fearful her child will be sold into slavery doesn't just "leave the plantation with her child in her arms." Instead "the frosty ground creaks beneath her feet, and she trembles at the sound; every quaking leaf and fluttering shadow sends the blood backward to her heart, and quickens her footsteps." Why the difference? Professional writers paint with specific details. They use a camera eye with a telephoto lens to zoom in close on powerful images.

For example, picture in your mind the details in this sentence: "The child ran out of the shelter toward the beach, went into the water, and swam." Now watch how author Jean M. Auel transforms this vague, distant image by zooming in close on specific details:

> The naked child ran out of the hide-covered lean-to toward the rocky beach at the bend in the river. . . . She splashed into the river and felt rocks and sand shift under her feet as the shore fell off sharply. She dived into the cold water and came up sputtering, then reached out with sure strokes for the steep opposite bank. (1980, 1)

Auel creates a motion picture—and we are right there, hearing the splashing water, feeling the shifting sand between our toes, gasping for air. Specific detail makes the difference.

Veteran writing teachers have long advocated using specific details. Lucile Vaughn Payne in her book *The Lively Art of Writing* urges students to "transmit information to readers exactly as a filmmaker transmits it—through specific details that readers can see. Verbs can give you action shots. Specific details can supply the stills" (1982, 30). Writer and teacher Donald Murray notes that checking for specific details is the first thing he does when revising. "The more specific the language," Murray explains, "the more the reader believes and trusts the writer" (1995, 188).

So how does a teacher help students to apply this well-known maxim, especially to those students who write images of stick figures and smiley faces with no flesh or personality? One approach is to help them explore the qualities of individual words—words that explode detailed images like fireworks instead of puffing sketchy images like fog.

Words that shroud specific images give a reader's imagination very little to visualize. If a student describes Maxine as "nervous," he is firing an image blank, shooting with a fogged camera lens. The reader's imagination travels through a mental desert, barren, devoid of colorful details. However, if instead the writer describes Maxine "glancing at the midnight moon shadows from one side of the dark alleyway to the other, biting her nails as rivulets of perspiration soak her eyebrows," then the reader's mind turns on an internal video projector and participates in the experience. "In came a dog" is an image blank. "In came Charlie, the pit bull, frothing at the mouth" evokes a visual, sensory experience. "She loved her daughter" is an image blank. "She kissed three-year-old Carrie softly on the cheek and tucked in the covers as Carrie slept" is specific. Specific details, like brush strokes, show instead of tell.

Getting Specific with Nouns and Verbs

Teaching students to add specific details begins with helping them to see image qualities in two of the simplest grammatical structures: nouns and verbs. By the time students reach middle school and high school, they often view these structures as cliché, with an "I know what nouns and verbs are" attitude. Yet ironically, professionals with years of writing experience find these simple structures to be the overlooked engines that power good writing. As Robert Newton Peck notes, "Writing is not a butterfly collection of adverbs and adjectives. Good fiction is a head-on crash of nouns and verbs" (10).

When students discover this truth, their writing is transformed into vivid photography. Their use of specific nouns and verbs breathes life into cold corpse images. For example, notice the improvement in the use of specifics in the following two passages by eighth grader Lindsay Davis. The first was written early in the school year:

> Matthew had barely stepped into his house before Amos, his father's personal servant, had told him that his father wished to see him in the study right away. Matthew wouldn't have believed then, that anything his father could say would alter his mood. His heart sank as he saw the look on his father's face. He immediately realized he was going to receive a lecture.

The second sample, written two months later after Lindsay experimented with brush strokes and specific details, shows evidence of far more powerful images, even though the topic of this passage differs considerably:

> The clear, blue waves gently lapped against the large wooden ship. Waving in the wind, the black flag with skull and crossbones attached to the mast announced the coming of the grand ship. Captain James, a dangerous and cunning man, climbed on deck, his pegged leg clomping as he walked. The parrot Smee, annoying and loud, perched on his shoulder.

In the first passage Lindsay uses very few specific nouns and verbs. We learn, for example, that Matthew's father appears ready to give a lecture, but no nouns or verbs capture that vivid scene. In the second passage, we see noun phrases like "clear, blue waves" and a "black flag with skull and crossbones." We hear the waves as they "lap against the boat," watch Captain James "climb," and notice the parrot Smee "perched." The difference is dramatic.

In addition to making primary nouns specific, writers can add a second noun—an appositive—for greater detail. The appositive, described in Chapter 1, adds a second photograph. In *Seeing Through Language*, Ronald Carter and Walter Nash (1990) point out that writers of tabloid journalism rely on this device: "A dustman is not a dustman unless he can be called a 47-year-old refuse collector and father of two" (101).

In both fiction and nonfiction, appositives add authenticity. With fiction the use of appositives helps to re-create the illusion of reality, while with nonfiction appositives imply an underlying foundation of research. Notice how David Halberstam (1991) brings authenticity with an appositive phrase to his description of Henry Kissinger:

> This, then, was a fascinating scene unfolding in front of me: Kissinger, *Nobel Laureate, a symbolic figure of the old America, with its marvelous weapons systems, its dominant role among the superpowers,* standing in

front of these less celebrated public servants, who had to cope with brutal budgets, expanding social needs, deteriorating infrastructures, and public service institutions that often seem overwhelmed by the pressures they faced. America, I thought, meet America. (13)

Halberstam embellishes the image of Kissinger by adding the appositive "Nobel Laureate" and the second appositive phrase, "a symbolic figure of the old America, with its marvelous weapons systems, its dominant role among the superpowers." These added noun phrases create trust in the reader by implying Halberstam has a depth of knowledge.

Another method of adding noun images is a technique Weathers (1980) defined as "The List." In *An Alternate Style*, he explained: "Presenting a list of items is comparable to presenting a 'still life' of objects without indication of foreground or background, without any indication of relative importance, without any suggestion of cause-effect, this-before-that, rank, or the like" (20). Weathers gives an example from F. Scott Fitzgerald's story "The Crack-Up":

> Seen in a Junk Yard. Dogs, chickens with few claws, brass fittings, T's elbow, rust everywhere, bales of metal 1800 lbs., plumbing fixtures, bathtubs, sinks, water pumps, wheels, Fordson tractor, acetylene lamps for tractors, sewing machine, bell on dinghy, box of bolts (No. 1), van, stove, auto stuff (No. 2), army trucks, cast iron body, hot dog stand, dinky engines, sprockets like watch parts, hinge all taken apart on building side, motorcycle radiators, George on the high army truck. (1956, 20)

Authors often use the list to draw readers into images of setting as Norman Mailer does with this description of a street scene in ancient Egypt during the age of Pharaohs:

> Donkeys passed by with loads of straw—he looked at them from the ground, one eye open. Large-horned oxen, driven back from the market, crowded through the plaza, and walked around him. Fishermen passed with baskets of fish, and a baker with loaves, the pastry, meat, fruit, shoes, corn, sandals, onions, and wheat, the beads and perfume and oil, the honey and sleeping mats, bronze razors, pick-axes, baskets of corn and a brace of ducks, a vendor with leather bottles for wine passed him on their way to the market or back from it. (1983, 153)

Examining noun lists similar to these in literature increases student awareness for the quantity of specific details that surround us if we just take time to observe. An excellent companion piece for teaching the power of nouns is Tim O'Brien's short story "The Things They Carried." O'Brien weaves a portrait of several American soldiers in Vietnam by describing the things they carry—everything from love letters from a girl friend to an amputated thumb taken from an enemy.

Adding Details with Specific Verbs

In a reader's imagination, nouns flash slide shows of still images, but verbs project motion pictures. To keep the action moving, authors avoid verbs such as *looked, moved,* or *went,* and instead paint actions with lines like, "Gant snapped his eyes . . ." (Thomas 1977, 283); "My fingers whispered over his cheek" (Hesse 1994, 180); and "Wiglaf dodged, danced, flitted out of range" (Nye 1968, 91).

Professional writers choose verbs to drive their images, but casual readers can easily miss this. We don't notice the contribution that verbs make to moving images until we encounter writing in which the verbs leave us at a standstill. For example, read how Mark Twain harnesses the power of verbs:

> They presently emerged into the clump of sumac bushes, looked warily out, found the coast clear, and were soon lunching and smoking in the skiff. As the sun dipped toward the horizon, they pushed out and got under way. Tom skimmed up the shore through the long twilight, chatting cheerily with Huck, and landed shortly after dark. (1964, 549)

Twain's passage creates a lively image in the reader's imagination. Now, watch what happens to the images with the verbs neutered.

> They presently came out of the bushes. The coast was clear, so they got in the skiff. They had lunch and smoked. As the sun went down, they went out on the water. Tom moved along the shore. He talked and then came back to shore shortly after dark.

Verbs contribute images in a subtle but powerful way, so teachers need to help students understand the value of this ignored painting element. Some students might argue, however, that they just cannot think of good verbs. For them a device developed by poet Natalie Goldberg (1986) can help.

Goldberg suggests folding a sheet of paper in half and making two separate lists. On the left fold the student creates ten nouns. Then, on the right fold, without referring to the list on the left, the student creates a list of ten verbs that describe actions by people in some selected occupation. Next, the student unfolds the two lists and combines the nouns and verbs to see what happens. Goldberg demonstrated the technique with these sample lists. The verbs relate to the occupation of cook:

LEFT FOLD	RIGHT FOLD
lilacs	sauté
horse	chop
mustache	mince
cat	slice
fiddle	cut
muscles	heat
dinosaur	broil
seed	taste
plug	boil
video	bake
	fry
	marinate
	whip
	stir
	scoop (88)

Playing with combinations, she created these interesting verb images:

Dinosaurs marinate in the earth.
The fiddles boiled the air with their music.
The lilacs sliced the sky into purple. (88)

This brainstorming technique seems to work especially well with reluctant student writers, energizing passages that they felt were limp in the first draft.

Adding Details with Adjectives and Prepositional Phrases

In his *Journal of a Novel*, Steinbeck comments "I want to go through it [the novel *East of Eden*] before it is typed and take out even the few adjectives I have let slip in" (1969, 6). Hemingway in *A Moveable Feast* says Ezra Pound "taught me to distrust adjectives" (1964, 134). Why this invective against adjectives?

Certain types of adjectives paint scenes with image blanks. This not only happens with some predicate adjectives (as described in Chapter 1), but also with imageless adjectives that label. Adjectives like beautiful, as in "the beautiful mountains," are formless, creating an opinion instead of a picture. The English language abounds with such adjectives. Hess (1987) catalogued 179 of the more common examples used as "character descriptors." Here are a few from her list:

ambitious	fearful	nervous	responsible
annoying	friendly	observant	sarcastic
anxious	gullible	patient	sentimental
brave	happy	perceptive	shy
caring	immature	petty	sociable
cranky	insincere	playful	strong-willed
dependable	lazy	reliable	trusting
egotistical	naïve	religious	vain

As you read each word on this list, close your eyes and try to visualize an image. You will find that these adjectives project sterile labels, leaving nothing to engage the visual imagination. Words like *caring, gullible, reliable, vain* serve a purpose for generalizing, but should be used sparingly and followed or preceded by specific images.

A second problem with using adjectives is that too many can conflict, minimizing the significance of each as in the following student passage:

> Betty entered the room. A red ribbon contrasted her coal black hair, and she wore a pale blue dress with a violet flower design. Her new black patent leather shoes reflected her unusual red socks. Betty was chewing gum and carrying a small brown purse that did not match her outfit.

This is the type of unwanted writing teachers sometimes receive after asking students to add more description. The adjectives in this paragraph are poorly chosen: they lack purpose and seem to be jammed into the paragraph just to add details. This situation is analogous to a seven-year-old with her first camera, randomly shooting hundreds of photographs of anything in range. To be effective writers must exercise choice. Daniel Mendlowitz and Duane Wakeham (1993) in their book *A Guide to Drawing* emphasize this concept for all artists:

> Whistler decried "the purposeless copying" of every detail. Matisse cautioned, "What does not add to a [drawing] detracts from it." Selection and discrimination are an important part of expressive drawing; every line, shape, form, value, color requires judgment and thought—before the pencil is put to paper, during the process of drawing, and after the work is finished. (316)

Hemingway and Steinbeck recognized these problems with adjectives and obviously knew which adjectives to prune and which to nurture. Steinbeck's novels—even *East of Eden*, which he tightly edited—are rich with adjectives. Hemingway's *Death in the Afternoon* uses 770 adjectives in one eight-thousand-word sample (Miles 1967, 162). But his adjectives contribute to the art of his images.

Does not mean students should try to use only adjectives that suggest images? No. In *Cat Watching*, Desmond Morris (1986) begins a paragraph with the sentence, "Unlike humans, felines have very expressive ears" (52). The adjective *expressive* at first draws a blank. Yet, as the passage unfolds, Morris explains five ways cats use their ears to express emotion. The adjective works because it establishes a controlling idea for the passage that follows.

Similarly, a writer can use a vague adjective to set up supporting details within a sentence: "The dilapidated car pulled in the driveway, fenders rattling, the engine sending bellows of white smoke as the car came to a stop." The adjective *dilapidated* sets up the generalization, and the details about the fenders and engine provide support.

Teachers can help students understand the nature of adjectives by discussing samples collected in their Artist's Palettes and by working with passages that use an adjective as the controlling idea.

Prepositional phrases offer another avenue for painting specific details. Prepositions link additional noun images. These noun images, in turn, bring adjectives. The combination provides more details, color, sound, and so on. Observe how Stephen Crane ([1895] 1992) packs prepositional phrases in this sentence to paint an image of an insane soldier:

> And with his soiled and disordered dress, his red and inflamed feathers surmounted by the dingy ray with its spot of blood, his wildly swinging rifle and banging accouterments, he looked to be an insane soldier. (140)

Specific Images for Humor

Whether working with nouns, verbs, adjectives or prepositional phrases, one way to lure students into understanding specific images is through humor. Gene Perret—comedy writer for Bill Cosby, Bob Hope, and Carol Burnett—explains that "Most jokes are pictures. That is to say, with words we create an image in the listener's mind. The distortion or the ridiculousness of that image generates the humor" (1982, 61). Compare each of the following passages, the first written without any comic images, the second loaded with specific images for comic effect:

> Today's science topic is THE UNIVERSE. The universe has fascinated mankind for many, many years, dating back to when astronauts set out

to explore the boundless voids of space. Virtually every planet they found was inhabited, and finally the brave crew returned to earth.

Today's science topic is THE UNIVERSE. The universe has fascinated mankind for many, many years, dating back to the very earliest episodes of "Star Trek" when the brave crew of the starship Enterprise set out, wearing pajamas to explore the boundless voids of space, which turned out to be as densely populated as Queens, New York. Virtually every planet they found was inhabited, usually by evil beings with cheap costumes and Russian accents, so finally the brave crew of the Enterprise returned to Earth to gain weight and make movies. (Barry 1994, 472)

I'm from Long Island. My parents moved to Florida this past year. They didn't want to move to Florida, but they're in their sixties.

I'm from Long Island. My parents moved to Florida this past year. They didn't want to move to Florida, but they're in their sixties, and that's the law. There are leisure police that come and get you when you turn sixty. They have golf carts with sirens, "Okay, Pop, get the clubs right in the back. Drop the snow shovel right there, drop it." (Seinfeld 1993, 55)

One of the most astounding cases of clairvoyance is that of the noted Greek psychic, Archille Londos. Londos realized he had "unusual powers" by the age of ten. After a neighbor's husband had been missing for three weeks, Londos told them where to look. Londos could concentrate on a person's face and force the image to come out on a roll of ordinary Kodak film.

One of the most astounding cases of clairvoyance is that of the noted Greek psychic, Archille Londos. Londos realized he had "unusual powers" by the age of ten, when he could lie in bed and, by concentrating, make his father's false teeth jump out of his mouth. After a neighbor's husband had been missing for three weeks, Londos told them to look in the stove, where the man was found knitting. Londos could concentrate on a person's face and force the image to come out on a roll of ordinary Kodak film, although he could never seem to get anybody to smile. (Allen 1972, 12)

Writers can also create comic images by moving from a general notion to a specific image. Usually, humorists accomplish this with clauses and phrases, where a generalization introduces the setup and the specific image provides the punch line.

When Dave Barry describes reporting news in New York, he begins with a setup: "At the *Miami Herald* we ordinarily don't provide extensive coverage of New York City unless a major news development occurs up there," and then adds the specific image punch line: "such as Sean Pean coming out of a restaurant" (1994, 327). Erma Bombeck, describing her efforts to toss away useless items around the house, begins the first part of her sentence with the generalization: "In an attempt to clean out all the old things we never use any more." She then completes the sentence with the specific punch line "I realized that I had inadvertently set my husband at the curb on top of a rusted bicycle" (1985, 52).

Adding Details with Metaphors and Similes

Contrasting images not only work for comic effect, but also can enhance serious written art when developed as metaphors and similes. An excellent resource for class is the book *As One Mad with Wine and Other Similes* by Elyse and Mike Sommer (1991). It contains eight thousand similes by two thousand authors, from Shakespeare to Bob Dylan. Below are a few samples.

> A pure white mist crept over the water like breath upon a mirror. — A. J. Cronin (272)

> His eyes skewed round to meet yours and then cannoned off again like a pool-ball. —Sean Virgo (254)

> The smile of a man with a terminal headache. —T. Coraghessan Boyle (380)

> Her white silk robe flowed over her like a milk shower. —Harold Adams (95)

> A desolate, cratered face, sooty with care like an abandoned mining town. —Joseph Heller (154)

> Love is like a wind stirring the grass beneath trees on a black night. —Sherwood Anderson (258)

> . . . felt like a deer stepping out before the rifle of a hunter. —Piers Anthony (162)

> Eerie as a man carving his own epitaph. —William McIlvanney (389)

Metaphors and similes generate an image webbing pattern in the reader's mind, where added power comes from one image linking to another and to another. For example, reading McIlvanney's simile "Eerie as a man carving his own epitaph," an individual might envision a midnight graveyard with images of tombstones, bones, and dark shadows. Another reader might associate images of ghosts walking through solid doors and howling into the night. Similes and metaphors, more than other structures, lead readers on a uniquely personal journey down their own imaginative trail.

Constructing Specific Images in Dialogue

When students write dialogue, teachers can help them learn to use specific detail as part of the conversation. Authors frequently mix images with quotes. Examine how Gary Paulsen in this excerpt from *The Island*, evokes images through dialogue, images loaded with specific details:

> "What's the matter?"
>
> "Nothing. The guy came and fixed the plumbing. Short guy with a bald head and chewing snoose all the time, hair out his shoulders . . ."
>
> "And a dog that goobers in your ear. That's Emil Aucht."
>
> "Yeah. That's the one. I got too close to his truck and the dog got me. He came and fixed the plumbing."
>
> "So what's the matter?"
>
> "It's your mother—she's in the kitchen."
>
> Wil went across the room and into the kitchen, where his mother was leaning over the sink, scrubbing with a sponge, her eyes closed while the hot water poured. She looked up when Wil walked in. "You could have told me . . ."
>
> "Told you what?"
>
> "Told me we'd have to boil the whole house after he left." Her face was gray. "I mean he walked over and spit in the sink. Just walked over and let go with this big . . ." She couldn't finish. (1988, 25)

Dialogue can build conflict, pique curiosity, shape character, or enhance the writing in a hundred ways when crafted with specific images.

Constructing Specific Images in Poetry

Every type of writing can be improved with specific detail. However, poetry, because of its compact nature, seems to demand images. Yet some students write poetry as summary statements arranged in a poetic shape. The following anonymous piece is a good example:

> LOST FRIEND
>
> I felt so bad
> When my friend moved away
> We were so close
> And shared so much
> We had many great memories
> I'll miss her

Although the student who wrote this felt strongly about her loss, she failed to paint enough specific details to re-create the experience for the reader. By contrast, eighth grader Melody White paints a poem on the loss of her grandfather with dynamic details and as a result the reader can share her memories:

ONE LAST WISH

If I were given one last wish,
It would be for you grandpa.
I'd wish that you were still here,

For one last Mickey Mouse pancake,
One last push on the tire swing,
One last read aloud of "The Night Before Christmas."

If my wish came true, I could have
You cheering me on at my soccer games,
Applauding loudly at my ballet recitals,
Holding my hand tight when we walk to church,
And showing me how to hammer without hitting my thumb.

But most importantly I'd want,
If my wish came true,
A final hug,
A warm embrace,
A kiss on my cheek,
And one last smile to see on your face.

Expanding the Artist's Eye

Specific details may uniquely appeal to our new-millennium students. Sol Stein, author and teacher, comments: "Twentieth-century readers, transformed by film and television, are used to seeing stories. The reading experience for twentieth-century readers is increasingly visual. The story is happening in front of their eyes" (1995, 122–23). This relatively recent shift to visual learning may parallel a shift in the writing styles of authors. Alan Spiegel (1976) in *Fiction and the Camera Eye* argues that the invention of the camera, the emergence of film and television, and the development of the computer has influenced writers to be more visual that their premedia predecessors. So, it is possible that, separated by one generation, students relate to images more intensely than teachers.

Recognizing the appeal of media to students, teachers can use art and film as tools for enhancing details. Janet Olson (1992) does this by having her students draw scenes from their own writing to help kids understand visual detail. In *Envisioning Writing* she describes a four step procedure in which she asks students to (1) write a description, (2) draw and color an image of the description, (3) discuss the drawing with a friend or teacher, and then (4) revise the original written description after comparing it to the drawing.

With one example, taken from the work of a sixth grader, Olson illustrates the results of this approach. Below are two paragraphs, one written before the student creates an image and one after.

BIG GUY

James weighs 240 pounds and use to be the champ. He beat Mohammed Ali for the crown. He's 38 know and he has drugs and pot. He's been in jail for 5 years and that ended his career. He's had a tough time finding a job. His face is scared. He wares a ripped T shirt with knee pants. He's trying to make a come back in the boxing world. He's black.

And "Big Guy" after the student created the artwork:

The lonely man stood in a ring holding tight to the ropes. His head was bald. His chest was hairy and sweaty. His legs looked like they were planted to the ground like stumps. His muscles were relaxed in the dark ring. His mouth looked mean and tough the way it was formed. He was solid looking. His boxing gloves had blood stains on them. His still body structure glowed in the darkness. He braced himself against the ropes. His white pants had red strips. The hair on his chin prickled out like thorns. (54)

Creating a sketch of the writing and discussing the details in the sketch helped the student to visualize details.

Well-known artwork can also be used to teach students to use specific details. To demonstrate how visual details suggest specific details of character, Judithe Douglas Speidel (1977) had her students write descriptions of famous portraits from the Renaissance and Baroque periods, asking students to include details that suggested character traits.

As part of this lesson, Speidel shared with students written characterizations by Charles Dickens, Willa Cather, Sir Arthur Conan Doyle, and Norman Mailer. Then, as a follow-up exercise, she gave students a list of the contents of a woman's purse and asked them to discuss inferences about the appearance, age, social position, personality, and activities of its owner.

Using control group studies to assess the growth of students who were taught with this lesson, Speidel found (1) that students who worked with this lesson doubled their specificity scores from a pretest to a posttest, (2) that higher teacher grades correlated with greater specificity, and (3) that students of below-average ability (based on SAT scores) improved more than students of higher ability (69–70).

More recently, Janice M. Gallagher, a teacher in Cleveland, has used this approach with her gifted students. Gallagher has her students choose an artwork from several reproductions posted around the room. Then, she and her students discuss their impressions of the work—suggested meanings, subtle details, choice of color, and facial expressions if the work is a portrait. And finally, they write about the work, interpreting it in the genre of their choice. Some students spin off short stories; others compose essays; still others create poems. Gallagher found that her approach generated richer specific detail in the writings of her students.

An excellent resource for locating artwork for this type of lesson is the Paris Web Museum Internet site (http://mistral.culture.fr/louvre/). The Paris Web Museum showcases works from the Louvre and displays one of the most extensive repositories of famous online art. In a lesson that replicated Gallagher's approach, Chris Hloros wrote these observations about Picasso's self-portrait, *Facing Death*.

> The feeling I think Picasso was trying to represent in this was that of sadness and depression. There are many clues. First off, the colors used in the painting are not bright. They are very dull and dreary, creating a mood of sadness and mystery. The blue gives you the feeling that this man is very unhappy with his life, and the green is a sickly color, making me think that this man is not in the best of health—maybe even in the last stages of his life about to die. The red in the eyes makes them seem bloodshot. This may be from insomnia, possibly because of a horrific nightmare. His hair is also red, perhaps symbolizing blood or death on his mind. These colors truly add feeling to this painting.
>
> One thing that was very apparent to me was the shape of teardrops used throughout the face. Picasso used a particularly large one that seemed to be in the center of the picture. This hints to unhappiness, possibly even a trauma that may have caused many tears to flow. Also, the nose is in the form of a teardrop, and the eyes are almost teardrop shaped, creating a feeling of great sadness and depression.

With advanced students in an AP English class, teachers might want to extend this writing-art relationship by examining the book *Painting Literature* by Constance Pedoto (1993). Pedoto discusses specific painting techniques like the *sfumato* technique of the early Renaissance painters and demonstrates how passages from literature appear to use the same device with words. Pedoto explains this parallel referring to the work of Kafka:

The sfumato technique used by earlier Renaissance painters, most notably by Leonardo da Vinci, has the tendency to sculpt painted forms, by using the soft gradation of tones and colors, which blurs the outlines of the painting's subject matter, and to create a sort of hazy or misty quality in the work, which engulfs its protagonists. This same misty veil in Franz Kafka's *The Castle* clouds K.'s vision of "the castle" and blurs his relationship with others, with himself and his purpose in the Castle community, and with Time. (128–129)

With middle school students, teachers can find resources for relating art and writing in a less complex book, *Activities for Creating Pictures and Poetry* by Janis Bunchman and Stephanie Bissell Briggs (1994). Bunchman and Briggs show students how poets and painters work with similar images. For example, Rudyard Kipling's poem "Tiger! Tiger!" is presented with Henri Rousseau's painting *Tropical Storm with a Tiger*. After viewing both, students are engaged in several activities such as

Pretend that you are in one of Rousseau's tropical environments. What animals do you see? Are there lions, elephants, and beautiful tropical birds around? Describe what they look like. What color is the wildlife? Tell us what they are doing. Do you see a tiger hunting, a gorilla playing or a lion at rest? (59)

Writers and artists have always collaborated on works where an artist illustrated a writer's text, but in a few instances a writer has created text to enhance an artist's images. Author Harlan Ellison and artist Jacek Yerka collaborated this way in the book *Mind Fields*. The coauthors took turns setting the scene for each other. First Ellison created a story, and Yerka illustrated it. Then Yerka created a painting, and Ellison wrote about it. Similarly, in *A Poet and His Camera* Gorden Parks presents poems that he wrote about his photographs and shows photographs that he took to illustrate his poems.

Using Image/Word Relationships with Students

Examining models such as these can be a visual warm-up for getting students to think of words as images and images as words. Once students understand this relationship, teachers can encourage them to think visually as they write, even when there are no paintings or photographs to use as a reference. For example, with the following passage, eighth grader Keir Marticke was asked to read this text carefully, visualizing the specific images that were left out:

Smoke, flames and noise woke me at 3:00 A.M. Looking out the window I saw that the old coat factory down Van Allen Street was on fire. The flames were very high. The heat was intense. I knew the situation was serious when fire fighters began to evacuate our block. Their talk about the factory's big fuel tank scared us all. My family and neighbors had to go to the Osborne School for shelter. We waited nervously all night. We were happy in the morning when we learned the fire was finally under control. (Blau 1995)

After reading the passage, Keir was asked to revise it adding words and phrases that would better picture the scene. She was encouraged to "look" in her imagination for specific images and "listen" for specific sounds. Here is her revision incorporating the images she imagined:

I awoke to the early morning wail of sirens as fire engines screamed down the chaotic street. Peering out my window, I discovered a thick screen of dry smoke, as though someone had rung a gray wool blanket over my window. My eyes searched through the cloud, and I discerned the Van Allen Coat Factory, enveloped in a raging blaze. The flames extended their contorted tongues, hungrily licking the skyline. Searing heat spread through the area like warm butter over bread.

"It's out of control!" I heard a fireman scream in despair. "Everybody out!"

I trembled at his helpless words. My family and neighbors were hustled to the Osborne School for shelter. We waited nervously all night. Finally, as the early morning sun broke the horizon, we received word that the fire was under control.

To replicate this with your students, see strategy four in the next section. You will also find other strategies you can use to help students to think visually for specific details.

STRATEGIES

Strategy 1: Paint the Personality Behind the Clothes

In the corner of the room hang two sets of clothes: one for a man and one for a woman. Ask the class to imagine what type of individuals wore these clothes. Have them picture their personalities, occupations, and social lives.

Did they know each other? Were they friends, enemies, or just acquaintances? After brainstorming aloud or silently, have students write a description or a story about one or both imaginary individuals. (If you don't have some interesting clothes around the house, consider purchasing a few items at a Goodwill store or borrowing a few things from the local theatre costume collection.)

Strategy 2: Create a Shooting Script on Location

Divide the class into teams of four or five. Explain that they are going to create a "shooting script"—short decriptions of scenes that could be used by a photograph to film a documentary. Instruct each team to go on location to a place in the school they feel might be interesting—the cafeteria, the gym, a science lab, a band room, a sporting event—and to write a series of short descriptions of scenes they feel would work well in a film featuring school life.

Before students write, have teams share their thoughts on possibilities for close-up shots, shots from interesting perspectives and of interesting details that might captivate the viewer's attention. Also, ask teams to discuss what images would best convey the impression they want to communicate.

After teams develop their "shooting scripts," ask members to review each others work and select a few highlights to share with the class. As a bonus assignment, you may want to invite those teams who have exceptional scripts to film their scenes with commentary.

Strategy 3: Search for Details in Abstract Slides

Find the images entitled Abstract Series on the accompanying CD. With each slide ask students to describe what they see in as much detail as possible. These slides are common objects photographed in such a way that they are difficult to identify. While students are writing, ask them not to announce what they believe the abstract slides represent. Students can share their perceptions later.

After everyone has finished writing, compare descriptions and discuss the use of specific details. Generally, in this strategy, the more difficult the image is to identify, the more specific the descriptions of details become. If you repeat this exercise, a good source for abstract images is from *Games* magazine. For years in each issue they featured a page of abstract images for readers to identify.

Strategy 4: Focus on Word-Image Senses

Specific details emerge as the writer/artist sees, hears, smells, tastes, and touches an imaginary or real world. This lesson is designed to move students imaginatively from word to visual images and back. First read the following first-draft paragraph to the class:

> Running almost ten feet ahead of her competition, Jenny raced toward the finish line. As she crossed in victory, the crowd went wild. Jenny was exhausted, and her coach held her up as she congratulated her on the victory. The loudspeaker announced a new school record as friends raced onto the track to share in the excitement.

Next, ask students to close their eyes and visualize the event just described. Tell them to listen to the sounds—of the crowd, the runners, the loudspeaker, the wind. Ask them to listen for comments that might be used as quotes, adding to the drama of the race.

Next have them use a zoom lens to look closely at specific details. Ask them "What images can you see when you zoom in on the runners, looking at their faces, arms, legs, in close-up detail? What images emerge from the crowd as the camera zooms in on individuals: the coaches, the timer, parents, friends?"

Next have them smell the odors and aromas that surround the track meet. Ask them to smell the sweat, the grass, the food from the concession stand, the blacktop, Gator Aid.

Then have students concentrate on the senses of taste and touch: the track, the wind, hugs, water, sweat. Finally distribute the following sensory guidelines and ask students to rewrite the original paragraph, adding their own detailed images.

GUIDELINES FOR PICTURING SPECIFIC DETAILS

Sounds: the crowd, the runners, the loudspeaker, the wind, dialogue
Zoom Images: close-up shots of runners (their faces, arms, legs), the crowd, the coaches, the timer, parents, friends
Odors/Aromas: sweat, grass, food, suntan lotion, blacktop, Gator Aid
Tastes: sweat, water, dryness, food
Touch: feet on the pavement, fists clenching, headband, muscles, arms, legs, stomach, embraces

Another variation on this idea is to play sound effects (from a tape or a CD) and have students in the class follow the same procedure, identifying images evoked by the sounds. Here is one example of this assignment using the sound effects of a rain storm:

SENSES OF A STORM
by Kate Cooke

Fog appearing, puddles splashing, the storm carried on. Everything suffered from the wetness because of the newly fallen rain. The sky turned charcoal as rain fell hurriedly out of the metallic clouds. The lighting, a yellow flash, brightened the backyard as if it were daytime. Large globs of rainwater slipped off the corners of the sopping patio furniture.

Tapping above my head, drops of water struck the roof, interrupted only by the piercing thunder booming as loud as a dinosaur's roar. I opened the window, and everything was much louder. The leaves on the trees rustled from the strong winds.

Out of the window I stuck my arm. Cold drops soaked through my sleeve, gripping against my arm, causing me to shiver. The wind, breezy and cold, blew against my face. In the darkness and cold, the storm and I were one.

Strategy 5: Go on a Humor Hunt

Drop by your local library and pick up several comedy CDs or tapes. Some that are generally appropriate for in-class use include those of Bill Cosby, Erma Bombeck, Bob Newhart, Bob and Ray. Check out videotapes of comics doing monologues: Seinfield, Leno, and Comedy Club Skits. Play selected cuts in class and have students identify specific images that contribute to the humor.

You can also assign students to locate audio and video humor models as long as you allow time to preview them. Doing this as an extra credit project works best, creating fewer samples to preview for class use.

Strategy 6: Examine the Contents of the Mystery Purse

Using Speidel's suggestion, purchase six large inexpensive purses at a Goodwill store. In each purse place several unusual items that might generate discussion. You might include a want ad, an article from the newspaper on a recent crime, a map, a financial statement, a letter, a photograph, a paperback book, and so on.

Divide the class into six small groups, give each group a purse full of objects, and ask them to speculate about the owner. After they have had time to discuss the contents and reach some tentative conclusions, have each group select a spokesperson to share how the specific details of the items enclosed led them to conclusions about the purse's owner.

Strategy 7: Breathe Life into Dead Character Descriptors

Xerox and enlarge one copy of the list below for each of your classes. Cut a set of individual words for each class, folding each word to conceal it and placing the words in a large can. Ask students to draw one word out of the can and reflect on a time when she or he experienced this emotion.

To ensure that students find an emotion they can relate to, allow them to draw a second and a third time. Finally, have students write a short paper describing a situation in which they or someone they know (friend, relative, neighbor, or the students themselves) experienced this emotion. Be sure to have them zoom in on specific details that support the impression given by the word they drew. Here are some words from a much longer list by Karen Hess (1987) in her book *Enhancing Writing Through Imagery*.

WORDS THAT LABEL EMOTIONS

ambitious	fearful	nervous	responsible
annoying	friendly	observant	sarcastic
anxious	gullible	patient	sentimental
brave	happy	perceptive	shy
caring	immature	petty	sociable
cranky	insincere	playful	strong-willed
dependable	lazy	reliable	trusting
egotistical	naïve	religious	vain

Once students have selected an emotion and recalled an incident, you might want to get them started by reading either Russell Baker's character sketch of his Uncle Harold in Chapter 10 of *Growing Up* or Jay Leno's description of his father in the first chapter of *Leading with My Chin*. Both models capture humorous emotions and characterize with excellent specific examples.

Strategy 8: Paint a Setting with a List

Ask students to select a setting they perceive as crowded with people and objects. Using a list as F. Scott Fitzgerald and Norman Mailer did in the passages shown earlier, have students describe the setting. To motivate their thinking, you might suggest a few settings, such as a cafeteria, a dance, the lobby of a movie theatre, a well-attended sporting event, an art show, a concert hall, a dress shop, or a coffee shop/bookstore.

Strategy 9: Replicate Olson's Experiment

Try replicating the exercise Jane Olson conducted. After your students have written a piece, have them draw an image that represents the main focus of the writing. (If possible, have them use color.) Next, divide the class into groups to discuss the details in their drawings.

To ensure a productive discussion, you may want to use the following questions, adapted from an article by Robert Probst (1990) in which he formulated questions for discussion based on Rosenblatt's theories of reading and writing. Here the word *text* is replaced by *drawing*.

First Reaction: What is your first reaction or response to the drawing? Describe or explain it briefly.

Feelings: What feelings did the drawing awaken in you? What emotions did you feel as you looked at the drawing?

Perceptions: What did you see happening in the drawing? Paraphrase it—retell the major events briefly.

Visual Images: What related images did you picture as you looked at the drawing?

Associations: What memory does the drawing call to mind—of people, places, events, sights, smells, or even of something more ambiguous, perhaps feelings or attitudes?

Thoughts, Ideas: What idea or thought was suggested by the drawing? Explain it briefly.

Selection of Textual Elements: Upon what, in the drawing, did you focus most intently as you looked at it?

Judgments of Importance: What is the most important part of the drawing?

Patterns of Response: How did you respond to the drawing—emotionally or intellectually? Did you feel involved with the drawing, or distant from it?

Literary Associations: Does this drawing call to mind any other artwork or literary work (poem, play, film, or story)? If it does, what is the work and what is the connection you see between the two?

Finally, have the students revise their writing using ideas for images that arose from the discussion.

Strategy 10: Locate Humorous Images on the Internet

Have students search the Internet for a humorous photograph. Ask them to describe the photo using exaggerated specific details similar to the techniques used by Dave Barry, Jerry Seinfield, and Woody Allen. Two of the best sources for locating images of all types are the Yahoo Image Surfer and the AltaVista Photo finder. Ask students to surf these sources for comical images. Once they locate an image, have them download it to use temporarily in class when sharing writings.

The Yahoo Image Surfer can be found at <http://isurf.yahoo.com/>. The AltaVista Photo Finder can be found at <http://image.altavista.com/cgi-bin/avncgi>.

These search engines help you to travel the Internet for any image category that interests you. They organize image searches around categories such as arts, entertainment, science, people, and recreation. With the Yahoo Image Surfer and the AltaVista Photo Finder, you can locate images of everything from Hanson's latest concert to photos of mountain gorillas in the Virunga Mountain Range.

Strategy 11: Tour the Net Museums

Have students locate a piece of artwork that fascinates them. Ask them to write their impressions. Below you will find a list of several prominent museums along with descriptive quotes from their web pages:

Louvre Museum
http://mistral.culture.fr/louvre/louvrea.htm
Established in 1793 by the French Republic, the Louvre Museum, in the company of the Ashmoleum Museum (1683), the Dresden Museum (1744) and the Vatican Museum (1784) is one of the earliest European museums. The collections of the Louvre Museum represent works of art dating from the birth of the great civilizations of the Mediterranean area until the western civilization of the Early Middle Ages to the middle of the nineteenth century.

National Gallery of Art
http://www.nga.gov/
The National Gallery of Art houses one of the finest collections in the world illustrating major achievements in painting, sculpture, and graphic

arts from the Middle Ages to the present. Search the collection by specific artist, title, or a combination of criteria.

The Smithsonian
http://www.si.edu/newstart.htm
The Smithsonian is composed of sixteen museums and galleries and the National Zoo and numerous research facilities in the United States and abroad. Nine Smithsonian museums are located on the National Mall between the Washington Monument and the Capitol.

Metropolitan Museum of Art
http://www.metmuseum.org/
The Metropolitan Museum of Art is one of the largest and finest art museums in the world. Its collections include more than two million works of art—several hundred thousand of which are on view at any given time—spanning more than 5,000 years of world culture, from prehistory to the present.

Museum of Contemporary Art
http://mcachicago.org/exhibit/envision/index.html
Chicago's newest major museum and one of the nation's largest facilities devoted to the art of our time, the Museum of Contemporary Art (MCA) offers exhibitions of the most thought-provoking art created since 1945.

Los Angeles County Museum of Art
http://www.lacma.org/
Welcome to LACMA—The Los Angeles County Museum of Art! LACMA is the premier visual arts museum in the Western United States. Its holdings include more than 150,000 works spanning the history of art from ancient times to the present.

Museum of Modern Art, New York
http://208.215.131.139/
The world's largest and most inclusive collection of modern painting and sculpture comprises some 3,200 works dating from the late nineteenth century to the present. It provides a comprehensive overview of the major artists and movements since the 1890s, from Paul Cézanne's *The Bather* and Vincent van Gogh's *The Starry Night* to masterworks of today.

World Wide Web (WWW) Virtual Library Museums Pages
http://www.comlab.ox.ac.uk/archive/other/museums/index.html
If these museums do not appeal to your students' artistic interests, have

them visit the World Wide Web (WWW) Virtual Library Museums Pages. This is a directory of online museums and museum-related resources.

You can find more photographic resources on the CD that accompanies this book.

3
The Artist's Rhythms
The Music of Parallel Structures

Each week from 1959 to 1964 through 156 episodes, thousands of television viewers sat riveted to their sets, listening to the lure of these familiar words:

> There is a fifth dimension beyond that which is known to man. It is a dimension as vast as space and as timeless as infinity. It is the middle ground between light and shadow, between science and superstition, and it lies between the pit of man's fears, and the summit of his knowledge. This is the dimension of imagination. It is an area which we call . . . THE TWILIGHT ZONE. (Zicree 1989, 31)

Written by Rod Serling, these words mesmerized viewers with their enchanting rhythm. So compelling were they that almost forty years later, advertisers are still imitating Serling's sentence structure in advertisements for films like Universal's *12 Monkeys* and United Artists' *Lord of Illusion*:

> Between the past and the future, between sanity and madness, between dreams and reality, lies the mystery of the 12 Monkeys. (Universal Studios)

> Between what can be seen and what must be feared, between what lives and what never dies, between the light of truth and the darkness of evil, lies the future of terror. (United Artists)

The grammatical rhythms of writers like Serling sing and sometimes shout. They march. They skip. They float like the song of a sparrow on a midnight summer breeze. Writers beat rhythms of musical syntax as backgrounds to ideas of joy, love, and anger. In every genre from science fiction to journalism, they use the subtle cadences of structure to enhance a variety of moods.

Listening for the Beat

While authors create these rhythms with a myriad of word and sentence devices, they employ one technique repeatedly—parallel structure. Parallel structure refers to identical grammatical structures that add rhythm and balance to images. These structures give prose a musical quality that adds emphasis and sound to central images. Listen to the following excerpts and see if you can hear how the rhythms of the structures in bold amplify the images.

From Charles Kuralt's *A Life on the Road:*

> If you are in search of the authentic America, **seek out the little river** that runs under the bridge at Concord. **Pay your respects to the Suwannee, the Shenandoah, the Appomattox. Walk in the grass** beside the Little Bighorn and think about what happened there. **Spend an afternoon** waist-deep in the Henry's Fork with a fly rod in your hand, in the fall when the trumpeter swans fly low over the river. **Walk down to the banks** of the Missouri, which used to change its course so often that farmers along it complained they never knew whether their crop was going to be corn or catfish.
>
> America is a great story, and there is a river on every page of it. (1990, 166)

From Carl Sagan's *Cosmos:*

> The Cosmos is **all that is or ever was or ever will be.** Our feeblest contemplations of the Cosmos stir us—there is **a tingling in the spine, a catch in the voice, a faint sensation,** as if a distant memory of falling from a height. We know we are approaching the greatest of mysteries.
>
> The size and age of the Cosmos are beyond ordinary human understanding. Lost somewhere **between immensity and eternity** is our tiny planetary home. In a cosmic perspective, most human concerns seem insignificant, even petty. And yet our species is **young and curious and brave** and shows much promise. In the last few millennia we have made the most astonishing and unexpected discoveries about the Cosmos and our place within it, explorations that are exhilarating to wonder. They remind us **that humans have evolved to wonder, that understanding is a joy, that knowledge is a prerequisite to survival.** (1980, 4)

From the *Bible* (Ruth I.16):

> **Where thou goest, I will go; and where thou lodgest, I will lodge; thy people shall be my people, and thy God, my God.** (Scofield [1945] 1967, 317)

Through the ages authors have relied on the musical rhythms of prose. In the phrases and clauses from early editions of the Bible to the latest Dean

Koontz horror novel, one can hear the subtle drumbeats of parallel structure. To help students learn to use these patterns, teachers can present two broad categories of sound devices: (1) literal repetition, and (2) grammatical repetition. With a few brief definitions and numerous models, students can learn to emulate these lively rhythms.

Beating Rhythms of Literal Repetition

Using the parallel structure of literal repetition, writers repeat the exact same words to create an echo, a trancelike refrain. Although authors construct literal repetition for dramatic effect, everyone inadvertently repeats phrases and words when under emotional stress. For example, Leo Buscalia in his *Living, Loving, and Learning* published an anonymous letter written by one of his students to her boyfriend, a Vietnam soldier. The power of the letter emerges from perhaps unintentional literal repetition:

> Remember the day I borrowed your brand new car, and I dented it? I thought you'd kill me, **but you didn't.** And remember the time I dragged you to the beach, and you said it would rain, and it did? I thought you'd say, "I told you so," **but you didn't.** Do you remember the time I flirted with all the guys to make you jealous and you were? I thought you'd leave me, **but you didn't.** Do you remember the time I spilled strawberry pie all over your car rug? I thought you'd hit me, **but you didn't.** And remember the time I forgot to tell you that the dance was formal, and you showed up in jeans. I thought you'd drop me, **but you didn't.** Yes, there were lots of things you didn't do. But **you put up with me,** and **you loved me,** and **you protected me.** There were lots of things I wanted to make up to you when you returned from Vietnam. **But you didn't.** (1982, 75–76)

While this letter may illustrate accidental repetition, writers usually craft repetitions for specific effects. In "The Tell-Tale Heart," Edgar Allan Poe repeats a clause to create tension as a murderer describes the haunting beat of his dead victim's heart:

> I talked more quickly—more vehemently; **but the noise steadily increased.** I arose and argued about trifles, in a high key with gesticulations, **but the noise steadily increased.** Why would they not be gone? I paced the floor to and fro with heavy strides, as if excited to fury by the observation of the men—**but the noise steadily increased.** (1938, 306)

Students can learn to orchestrate similar beats in their own prose. Listen to a few examples of rhythmical excerpts from the writings of eighth graders as they experiment with literal repetition.

At the climax of a mystery story, Morgan McKinney writes,

> It was all so clear now. She knew who had killed Sylvia. It was **someone who** hated her, **someone who** had been a friend of hers, **someone who** never forgave her for how she had treated him, **someone** from high school, **someone who** knew her old nickname was Syl. It was Bruce Crystal!

At the conclusion of a nonfiction article, David Haile sums up the struggle for amateur athletes to become pros:

> Every day some kid makes a big name for himself in high school or college, but **only the best make it to** the NFL. **Only the best of the best make it to** the Hall of Fame. And running backs are a breed apart, lone warriors facing minefields of destruction, and in this dog-eat-dog league, **only the best** survive.

In a piece on victory, Kristen Parker writes,

> **They march off so victoriously, or so they say. They die so victoriously, or so they think.** But how **victorious** is it to bid good-bye to the sentiments they once knew.

Beating Rhythms of Grammatical Repetition

Grammatical repetition, the most common repetition used by writers, repeats identical grammatical structures, but with different words. Subtler than literal repetition, grammatical repetition beats a rhythm that can build into a crescendo as the following passage taken from Abraham Lincoln's Gettysburg Address:

> But, in a larger sense, **we can not dedicate—we can not consecrate—we can not hallow—**this ground. The brave men, **living and dead,** who struggled here, have consecrated it, far above our poor power to **add or detract.** The world **will little note, nor long remember, what we say here, but it can never forget what we did here.**

Authors create grammatical repetitions using structures such as parallel clauses, participial phrases, prepositional phrases, infinitives, and so on. Almost any grammatical element can be used as long as the sound pattern is consistent. For example in the well-known quote attributed to Julius Caesar, **"I came; I saw; I conquered,"** the sentence structure in each clause is identical and the syllables nearly identical, creating a musical effect that pounds a rhythm behind the writer's words. Or take the classic phrase from Lincoln's Gettysburg Address: "government **of the people, by the people, and for the**

people." Had Lincoln written "government of, by, and for the people" the emphatic combination of ideas and rhythm would have been lost.

Patterns of parallel structure can be constructed with every type of grammatical element. However, this concept can be simplified for students by demonstrating rhythms in three categories: (1) structures connected with conjunctions (coordinating and correlative), (2) structures created with repeated phrases (infinitive, participle, gerund, prepositional), and (3) clauses (dependent, independent, relative).

Using Conjunctions

When authors pound a drumbeat with coordinating conjunctions, they balance identical grammatical structures with the words *and, or, for, nor,* and *but.* For example, a writer might use a conjunction to balance two participle brush strokes and establish a gentle rhythm in a statement such as "The king's power was **shifting and shrinking.**" Or the author may attempt a more dramatic rhythm by balancing two participial phrases: "The king's power was **shifting in the countryside and shrinking in the villages.**" To create this rhythm, the author uses the word *and* to highlight the musical repetition.

Also, correlative conjunctions (both/and, neither/nor, not only/but also, either/or, not/but, and whether/or not) can create a drumbeat. Franklin Roosevelt used this technique in his 1944 tax bill veto message: "It is **not a tax bill, but a tax relief bill,** providing relief **not for the needy but for the greedy.**" David Halberstam described a Japanese tradition by saying that "Anyone in Japan who uses too much, whether it be food, or money, or personal freedom of speech, **is not merely perceived to be taking too much from the nation but is presumed to be taking it at the expense of others**" (1991, 83).

Both coordinating and correlative conjunctions provide a natural fulcrum for balancing structures.

Repeating Phrase and Clause Structures

Often, however, writers repeat grammatical structures without the help of conjunctions. For example, Loren Eiseley in *Unexpected Universe* creates rhythm with repeated infinitive phrases:

> Man, for all his daylight activities, is, at best, an evening creature. Our every addiction to the day and our compulsion, manifest through the ages, **to invent** and use illuminating devices, **to contest** with midnight, **to cast** off sleep as we would death, suggest that we know more of the shadows than we are willing to recognize. (1964, 195)

Other writers create rhythm with prepositional phrases as these students have done:

> **With the scorching prairie fires,** it came. **With the surging floods,** it came. **With the defensive Indians,** it came. **With every step,** death came to the wagon trains. (Kati Moseley)

> **Between what breathes absolute death and what breathes glorious life, between what laughs and what never cries, between the hope of joy and the fear of pain,** lies the emotion of the soul. (Christi Flick)

> **With the cutting of each branch, with the sawing of each tree, with the depletion of each forest,** the world continues to lose valuable wilderness. (Annie Diorio)

In a similar way, authors use repetitious clause structures. In James Herriot's description of the Bellerbys, he repeats a similar dependent clause after each verb:

> I had always marveled at the Bellerbys. They seemed to me to be survivors from another age and their world had a timeless quality. They were never in a hurry; they rose **when it was light,** went to bed **when they were tired,** ate **when they were hungry** and seldom looked at a clock (1972, 60).

The concluding phrase "seldom looked at the clock" adds finality to the beat because it breaks the pattern and concludes the sequence. Although Herriot enhanced his rhythm with the subordinate conjunction *when,* any type of grammatical structure—words, phrases, or entire sentences—can create a powerful beat. Once students realize this as they imitate, they learn to play with these patterns and devise original beats.

As with all play, students learn the rules of the game with continued experience. So all they need to begin hearing, seeing, and creating rhythms are simple explanations accompanied by models. Detailed definitions can come later. Here are a few examples of middle school students playing with rhythms:

> The terrible, dreaded order comes in the form of a telegram. There is **no choice, no hope, and no escape.** We meet in the town square, **terrified, frightened, and uncertain** of what's ahead. (Meredith MacMillan)

> I consider myself one of their true believers, **a hypnotic witness to the dreams they hold so dearly, a scientist of their curious nature, a witness to their spells, a witness to the crystal explosion of their gentle eyes,** overlapped with a shattering sense of truth and life. (Cassie Lynott)

The truth is **as deadly as a rattlesnake and careless as a two-year-old.**
(Kristine Naylor)

This was a fight between two beasts: **a lion who loves and a lion who
kills.** (Kirstin Anderson)

He was a man **who knew his enemies and friends, who could talk the
Pope out of Catholicism, who could lure any woman into his strong
grasp.** (Allie Archer)

Childhood is the joy. Adolescence is the craziest, but adulthood must
be the pits. (Nefertori Donerson)

Selecting structures for rhythmic effect is like selecting notes for a song:
the choices offer endless opportunity for creativity. As with other devices of
grammatical style, authors often employ these techniques as a tool for revision.

When an author feels a need for an added touch of detail or hears sour
rhythms in an oral reading, he or she reshapes the musical pattern. Note the
following example from the writing of E. B. White. In his first draft of an essay
on the first moon landing for the *New Yorker*, White described the moon in a
quick sketch, but in his final revision he added the beat of parallel structure
transforming his initial thoughts into a powerful etude of images:

FIRST DRAFT

The moon still influences the tides and the tides lap on every shore,
right around the globe. The moon still belongs to lovers, and lovers are
everywhere—not just in America. (Elledge 1984, 360)

FINAL (SIXTH) DRAFT

Like **every great river and every great sea,** the moon **belongs to none
and belongs to all.** It **still holds the key** to madness, **still controls the
tides** that lap on shores everywhere, **still guards the lovers** that kiss in
every land under no banner but the sky. (Elledge 1984, 366)

Using Parallel Structure for Clarity

Just as parallel structures can enhance images, the lack of parallel structure
can disrupt them. Choppy rhythms distort perceptions and interrupt the
consistent flow of ideas. In a sentence like "Melvin enjoyed rock music,
football, and to collect stamps" the uneven rhythm of "to collect stamps"
acts like an abrasive, static noise in the middle of a quiet song. To flow
smoothly, the sentence requires a steady rhythm: "Melvin enjoyed music,
sports, and stamp collecting." Or "Melvin enjoyed listening to music, play-

ing sports, and collecting stamps." The grammatical elements need to play a consistent melody.

This is true with all grammatical structures. Notice similar problems in the examples below, representing disjointed beats in verbs, adjectives, and adverbs.

VERBS

Choppy: Lulu pushed the hair from her eyes, wiped the sweat from her forehead, and the volleyball was served.

Rhythmic: Lulu pushed the hair from her eyes, wiped the sweat from her forehead, and served the volleyball.

ADJECTIVES

Choppy: Bubba was tall, muscle-bound, and often acted mean.

Rhythmic: Bubba was tall, muscle-bound, and mean.

ADVERBS

Choppy: The cat crawled through the weeds stealthily, cautiously, and he moved at a slow pace.

Rhythmic: The cat crawled through the weeds stealthily, cautiously, and slowly.

Extending Grammatical Rhythms to Paragraphs

Besides sentence structures, writers communicate music through the contrasting rhythms of entire paragraphs—the drumbeats of long crescendo sentences, mixed with short booms, blended with medium rolls. Gary Provost in *Make Your Words Work* illustrates this musical quality of sentence variety:

> This sentence has five words. This is five words too. Five word sentences are fine. But several together become monotonous. Listen to what is happening. The writing is getting boring. The sound of it drones. It's like a stuck record. The ear demands some variety. Now listen. I vary the sentence length and I create music. Music. The writing sings. It has a pleasant rhythm, a lilt, a harmony. I use short sentences. And I use sentences of medium length. And sometimes when I am certain the reader is rested I will engage him with a sentence of considerable length, a sentence that burns with energy and builds with all the impetus of a crescendo, the roll of the drums, the crash of the symbols, and sounds that say listen to this, it is important. (1990, 55)

Sometimes, authors play with the rhythms of sentences for other purposes. In *The Fight*, a book describing the heavyweight boxing championship between Mohammed Ali and George Foreman, Norman Mailer uses the rhythm of sentence structures to capture the exchange of punches:

> Foreman threw a wild left. Then a left, a right, a left, a left, and a right. Some to the head, some to the body, some got blocked, some missed, one collided with Ali's floating ribs, brutal punches, jarring and imprecise as a collision at slow speed in a truck. (1975, 181)

In another passage, later in the fight, Mailer captures a slightly different volley:

> Across that embattled short space Foreman threw punches in barrages of four and six and eight and nine, heavy maniacal slamming punches, heavy as the boom of oaken doors, bombs to the body, bolts to the head, punching until he could not breathe, backing off to breathe again and come in again, bomb again, blast again, drive and steam and slam the torso in front of him, wreck him in the arms, break through those arms, get to his ribs, dig him out, dig him out, put the dynamite in the earth, lift him, punch him, punch him up to heaven, take him out, stagger him—great earthmover he must have sobbed to himself, kill this mad and bouncing goat.
>
> And Ali, gloves to his head, elbows to his ribs, stood and swayed and was rattled and banged and shaken like a grasshopper at the top of a reed when the wind whips, and the ropes shook and swung like sheets in a storm, and Foreman would lunge with his right at Ali's chin and Ali go flying back out of reach by a half-inch, and half out of the ring, and back in to push at Foreman's elbow and hug his own ribs and sway, and sway just further, and lean back and come forward from the ropes and slide off a punch and fall back into the ropes with all the calm of a man swinging in the ringing. (195-196)

Paragraph rhythms can also harmonize with the visual images of text, adding another artistic dimension. Janet Burroway in *Writing Fiction* demonstrates this with two examples, the first of which illustrates a lifeless, slow rhythm:

> The first impression I had as I stopped in the doorway of the immense City Room was of extreme rush and bustle, with reporters moving rapidly back and forth in the long aisles in order to shove their copy at each other, or making frantic gestures as they shouted into their many telephones. (1987, 89)

In her second example, the rapid succession of repeated participles hits a rhythmic tempo that communicates images of activity:

> I stopped by the doorway. The City Room was immense, reporters rushing down the aisles, shoving copy at each other, bustling back again, flinging gestures, shouting into telephones. (89)

The quick cadence of this second example enhances and harmonizes with the bustling images of a news team rushing to meet a deadline.

Executing a Drum Roll with Periodic Sentences

Another musical element of prose is the periodic sentence, first identified by Aristotle who characterized it as a "compact" sentence. Periodic sentences communicate a final emphasis—a dramatic drumbeat at the end of the sentence. Feel, for example, the power of Peter Benchley's periodic sentence, which describes an attacking shark:

> Rising at him from the darkling blue—slowly, smoothly—came *the shark*. (1974, 287)

Benchley arranged the order of this sentence to create a surprising ending. "Loose" sentences, by contrast, are not written for emphasis and can be rearranged in a variety of ways without changing the meaning. If Benchley had written this in a loose style, the suspense would have been lost, as the following illustrates:

> The shark rose toward him slowly, smoothly from the darkling blue.

Authors frequently use the arrangement of words to shape the way readers build images. Such musical exclamation marks occur in about 20 percent of the sentence structures used by contemporary writers (Connors and Glenn 1992, 267).

To heighten the climax of a paragraph, authors sometimes delay the conclusion with intervening parallel structures. For example, notice how Red Smith, the Pulitzer Prize–winning sports columnist, used this combination in the opening of one of his articles:

> It could happen **only** in Brooklyn. Nowhere else in this broad, untidy universe, **not in Bedlam nor in Babel nor in the remotest psychopathic ward nor the sleaziest padded cell** could The Thing be.
>
> **Only** in the ancestral home of the Dodgers which knew the goofy glories of Babe Herman **could a man win a World Series game by striking out.** (1982, 154)

This same technique, known as the *periodic paragraph* in some contexts, is also a common device in fiction. To create suspense in his novel *The Horse Hunters*, Robert Newton Peck delays identifying the most important fact until the last three words of this passage:

The voice I was now hearing didn't belong to a loudspeaker or a rodeo. In fact, it was a new voice, one that I'd never before listened up. Then I heard a very sharp sound and it was close to my left ear.

Click!

Opening my eyes, I felt the steely hardness on my neck, right below my ear. Then I realized what the click was.

A gun hammer. (1988, 107)

Learning from models like these, students can create similar effects. Notice how these eighth graders combined parallel structures with a dramatic conclusion:

When Santa Claus does not come down the chimney anymore, **when** the boogie monster no longer lurks under your bed, **when** the tooth fairy turns out to be only your parents, **then** childhood dies. (Chris Hloros)

He was a guy **who had no** fear of death, **who had no** sense of worry, **who had no** regrets—a sky diver. (Lindsey Kannen)

When the crimson sun sinks below the horizon, **when** the mosquitoes turn the air into a cloud of stinging beasts, **when** the jaguars and pumas rule the jungle floor, **when** all the sane men are asleep, **then** out come the cannibals. (Zach Vesoulis)

Listening to the Music of Political Rhetoric

Some of the richest sources for classroom examples of parallel structure can be found in the speeches of politicians. Speech writers use rhythms to create the illusion of profundity, capturing the listener's ear as the following samples illustrate.

From John F. Kennedy's Inaugural Address:

Let every nation know, **whether it wishes us well or ill,** that we shall **pay any price, bear any burden, meet any hardship, support any friend, oppose any foe,** in order to assure the survival and success of liberty. This much we pledge—and more. (January 20, 1961)

From President Reagan's Comments on the *Challenger* Tragedy:

We pray that the special power of this season will make its way into your sad hearts and **remind you of some old joys. Remind you of the joy it was to know** these fine young men and women, **the joy it was to witness the things they said and the jokes they played, the kindness they did and how they laughed.** . . . **For love is never wasted, love is never lost; love lives on** and sees us through sorrow. (Noonan 1990, 261)

And from Martin Luther King Jr.'s famous "I Have a Dream" speech:

> **I have a dream that one day on the red hills of Georgia, sons of former slaves and former slave-owners** will be able to sit down together at the table of brotherhood.
>
> **I have a dream that one day the state of Mississippi, a state sweltering with the heat of injustice, sweltering with the heat of oppression,** will be transformed into an oasis of freedom and justice.
>
> **I have a dream** that my four little children will one day live in a nation where they will **not be judged by the color of their skin but by the content of their character. I have a dream** today! (King 1986, 194)

Playing recordings of classic speeches can help students recognize the power of parallel structures. The appeal to the ear of both the listener and the reader provides another avenue for learning. The sound of writing helps exaggerate the qualities of rhythm; many writers make a habit of reading works aloud. Authors such as Ray Bradbury often read drafts to small gatherings of friends. Oral reading not only emphasizes the flow of ideas, but also helps the writer recognize punctuation problems, syntax confusions, and glitches in clarity.

Reading aloud has long been advocated by secondary reading teachers as a way of helping writers focus on issues of clarity. James Moffett, for example, in designing his language arts program in the 1970s advocated teaching punctuation by having students correct an unpunctuated passage while listening to the passage on tape. Several of the classroom strategies that follow encourage teachers to train students to listen to the rhythms of grammar.

STRATEGIES

Strategy 1: Add Grammatical Music to a Sketch

Ask students to close their eyes and picture a remote mountain cabin. Have them re-create sensory details in their minds as you paint a picture beginning with the sentence: "The old cabin made me feel close to nature." Explain that instead of adding additional sentences to make this painting, you are going to expand the basic sentence by adding details created with a rhythm of repeated prepositions or subordinate conjunctions and relative pronouns. Demonstrate with the following: "The old cabin **with its rustic stone fireplace, with its handmade log furniture, with its view of Lake Papatachi,** made me feel close to nature." Point out how the repeated *with* phrases add detail and rhythm.

Give a second example using the subordinate conjunction *when*, adding the following clauses: **"When I awoke to the aroma of burnt fire logs, when I looked out the window and saw the morning fog roll across the lake, when I felt the slight chill of the mountain air,** the old cabin made me feel close to nature."

After you have modeled this technique, have each student imitate it, using an image taken either from the companion CD or from one of the suggested Internet image sites.

Invite students to describe a picture of their choice, but have them use either the list of prepositions or the list of subordinate conjunctions and relative pronouns that follow to create parallel structures. Encourage students to add sensory details that are not necessarily represented in the photograph—sounds, smells, or any related images.

PREPOSITIONS

about, above, according to, across, after, against, ahead of, along, alongside, along with, amid, around, as well as, at, before, below, beneath, beside, besides, between, beyond, by, but (except), concerning, despite, down, due to, during, except, for, from, in, in addition to, in between, in front of, inside, instead of, in spite of, into, like, minus, near, of, off, on, onto, opposite, out, outside, over, past, plus, prior to, since, through, throughout, till, to, together with, toward, under, underneath, up, upon, until, via, with, within, without.

SUBORDINATE CONJUNCTIONS AND RELATIVE PRONOUNS

after, although, as, as if, as though, before, because, even though, even if, how, if, since, so that, than, that, though, unless, until, what, whatever, when, whenever, where, wherever, who, whoever, whom, whomever, which, whichever, whether, while, why, whereas, whose.

Have students create two additional descriptions using images from magazines at home. (For students who might not have magazines available, ask the librarian for discards.) Students should cut out selected images from the magazines and attach them to their writing before turning in the assignment.

Strategy 2: Try a Rhythmic Experiment in Horror

Try this experiment created by Arch Obler, a radio announcer and horror writer of the late thirties and early forties. Obler once recorded this "Experiment in Horror," which utilizes the repetition of words and phrases to create a chilling effect. If you can locate a copy of Arch Obler's "Lights Out" recording, produced in 1970 by Capitol Records, you will find Obler's reading effective. If not, read the following excerpt taken from that recording:

> This is Arch Obler. In a horrific time, in a horrible world, I have been asked to try and horrify you—all in fun, of course. A challenge in horror so to speak. Now I know that you're not a person who is easily frightened. Monsters, ghosts, the dead. Who gets scared of that sort of thing anymore? You don't. Or do you? Do you ever think of the undead, the ghostly ones crowded under the gravestones, the restless dead, millions of them there under the ground?
>
> May we try something? Turn your lights out. Yes, all of them. Lights out. Everybody. Now then, sit down in a chair and turn your back to the loudspeaker. Yes, turn your back. Now sit quietly, very quietly. The room, very quiet. Now whatever I say, don't turn around. Remember that. Don't turn around. (Pause)
>
> Do you hear that? Now don't turn around. Something is coming up behind you. No, no, don't turn around. It's coming closer and closer and closer. It's something . . . Oh no. Dead. It's been dead so very long. No, don't turn around. Closer and closer. Decay. The odor of decay. Don't turn. It's putting out its hand toward your neck, skeleton hand reaching for your neck, touching your neck. [At this point a loud, piercing scream concludes the experiment, usually causing students to shiver and sometimes scream.]

Repeat Obler's instructions, but this time ask students to identify words or phrases that repeat, words such as "Now sit quietly, very quietly. The room, very quiet." (All of the repeated words and phrases in this passage are identified on the accompanying CD.)

This minilesson works well for middle school students, but for high school students you may want to introduce this concept by playing a recording of Edgar Allan Poe's "The Tell-Tale Heart," which illustrates the same techniques in greater number and complexity. Helping students to hear models of parallel structure is a first step toward helping students to write them.

Strategy 3: Travel into the Twilight Zone

Another experiment in sound can be created using any of the many introductions from Rod Serling's *Twilight Zone* series. To begin, either read the excerpt below or play a video cassette of the original introduction to *The Twilight Zone*. (The cassette may be available at a local library, but if not, you may purchase a copy from CBS/Fox Video 1211 Avenue of the Americas, New York, NY 10036.) Ask students to identify examples of repetition and parallel structures in Serling's introduction. Typically, students will identify those in italics:

> There is a fifth **dimension** beyond that which is known to man. It is a **dimension as vast as space and as timeless as infinity.** It is the middle ground **between light and shadow, between science and superstition,** and it lies **between the pit of man's fears, and the summit of his knowledge.** This is the **dimension** of imagination. It is an area which we call . . . THE TWILIGHT ZONE. (Zicree 1989, 31)

Next, read or play the passage from the conclusion of Rod Serling's screenplay, "The Monsters Are Due on Maple Street" (originally broadcast on March 4, 1960 and available on videotape from CBS/Fox Video), transcribed by Marc Scott Zicree in *The Twilight Zone Companion*:

> The tools of conquest do not necessarily come with **bombs and explosions and fallout.** There are weapons that are simply **thoughts, attitudes, prejudices**—to be found only in the minds of men. For the record, **prejudices can kill and suspicion can destroy,** and a thoughtless, frightened search for a scapegoat has a fallout all its own—**for the children, and the children yet unborn.** And the pity of it is that these things cannot be confined to the Twilight Zone. (Zicree 1989, 91)

Ask students to identify the rhythmic examples. (Examples are italicized.) Finally, divide the class into several groups of five or six students and distribute the following template of Rod Serling's classic introduction.

THE _____ ZONE

> There is a fifth dimension beyond that which is known to man. It is a dimension as _____ as _____ and as _____ as _____. It is the _____ _____ between _____ and _____, between _____ and _____, and it lies between the _____ of _____ _____, and the _____ of his/her _____. This is the dimension of _____. It is an area which we call . . . THE _____ ZONE.

Explain to the class that the task of each group is to create an imaginary zone, filling in the blanks to create a parody. They can select a subject from school (math class, history class, lunch, a dance, a sport) or from an outside interest (MTV, sports figures, actors/actresses, novelists, political personalities). Below a group of eight-grade students collaborated to demonstrate how this assignment might be written about math:

> There is a fifth dimension beyond that which is known to man. It is a dimension as acute as one degree and as obtuse as 179 degrees. It is the vast plane between simple addition and advanced calculus, between infinity and probability, and it lies between the teacher's daily cup of hot coffee and the student's daily pile of homework problems. This is the dimension of chalkboard scribbles. It is an area which we call the Math Zone.

Strategy 4: Revise Your Rhythm

Have students select a piece of writing that they want to energize. Ask students to look for sentences that can be expanded in one of the following six ways using parallel structures:

1. Use prepositional phrases, as in " History will show that he walked away *with . . . with . . . and with . . . .*" Or "She walked *down . . . through . . . and across . . . .*"
2. Use *who* clauses, as in "She was a woman *who . . . who . . . and who. . . .*" (Or an idea *that . . . , that . . . , and that. . . .*)
3. Use infinitive *to* phrases, as in "Students need to help their troubled friends *to . . . , to . . . , to . . . .*"
4. Use clauses, as in *"If we are to . . . , If we are to . . . , If we are to . . . ,* then we must act now." Or "This was a place where . . . , where . . . , and where . . . ."
5. _____ing, _____ing, _____ing, the . . . . (Or have students try this same structure with two complete phrases, such as "Diving through the branches, swerving around a tree trunk, the chickadee landed on the ranger's arm.")

Strategy 5: Analyze the Music in "We Are Connectors"

Intense emotion often produces powerful musical melodies. Anxious to make an appointment, a nervous friend might say to her spouse, "Al, we have to go. We have to go now! We have to go now or we're going to be late." Dramatic examples of repetition often arise from simple events where speakers feel deep emotions. Ask students to identify qualities of music in the following opening school address, which was written and delivered by Alliance, Ohio, high school mathematics teacher William Carli. This activity might be done with a small group or individually.

> Our students, like children of previous generations, have to be connected to the human experience. They have to be connected to the first people who used tools, planted crops, and rode horses. They have to be connected to Greek geometry, the Chinese abacus, and the African algebra. They have to be connected to the gentle wisdom of Confucius, the glorious genius of Mozart, and the expressive passion of Elizabeth Barrett Browning.
>
> They have to be connected to the excitement of sport and solemnity of ritual, to the joy of art and the sorrow of the blues, to the value of work and the emptiness of hatred, and to the complexity of science and the simplicity of love.
>
> We are the connectors. We are the high priests and priestesses of our generation. For some of our students, the school, our temple, is an oasis of order in an otherwise chaotic life. In it we dispense discipline without abuse, morality without superstition, and judgment without bias, by connecting them to concern, wisdom, and justice.
>
> We are the connectors. We connect our children not only to the other five billion currently early occupants, but to the millions who have lived before, some brave, some brilliant, some evil beyond words, some merely grandmas and grandpas, but all part of our human heritage.
>
> We are the connectors. Without us civilization ends. Without us, the computers will crash, the assembly lines will stop, the great stories will be forgotten, the flame will go out.
>
> We are the connectors. We are teachers. Welcome back.

Strategy 6: Imitate the Rhythms of Parallel Structure

This strategy, designed as a warm-up for imitation in Chapter 5, helps students feel the rhythm of sentences and paragraphs. Ask students, working in groups or individually, to fill in the parallel image blanks below. Following this experiment, discuss how meaning changes with rhythmic patterns.

1. Between what _____ _____
    _____ and what _____ _____
    _____, between what _____ and what never
    _____, between the _____ of
    _____ and the _____ of _____
    lies the _____ of _____.

2. Some days you _____ _____. Some days you
_____ _____. Some days
you_____ _____. Some days you

_____ _____ _____
_____. Some days are made for _____.

3. If there are no _____, if _____ really don't
exist, if _____ are only a myth, then how do you explain
the _____ ? How do you explain the_____ ?
And most of all, how do you explain the _____? Beyond
_____ lies the _____.

4. When _____, when
_____, and when
_____, only then will
_____.

5. This is a (man / woman) who _____, a (man
/ woman) who _____, and a
(man / woman) who _____.
This is _____.

6. This was a place where _____ _____
_____, where
_____ _____

_____, and where_____
_____.

Strategy 7: Explore Musical Rhythms to Write Poetry

Have your students use rhythms to create poetry. Playing with parallel structure can create surprises in the cadence of a poem. For example, listen to
the sound of grammatical repetitions in this poem by middle school student
Gary Anderson:

> IF I WERE A COW IN BOMBAY
>
> If I were a cow in Bombay,
> I'd laze. I'd loll. I'd loiter all day,
> wandering the streets wagging my tail,
> listening to all people tell me, "Hail, hail."

You know in India they worship a cow.
Whenever they see one, they take a bow,
Not to worry, not to care, not a fly in my hair.
No butchers, no hamburgers, no steaks anywhere.

Ah, if I were a cow born in Bombay,
I'd invite all my friends to come share my hay.
munching and crunching and swallowing seven times.
(Regurgitating is a very hard word to rhyme.)
We'd love our life in the streets of Bombay,
and feel sorry for the poor cows in the ole U.S.A.

All techniques discussed in this chapter can be applied to writing poetry and song lyrics as well as fiction and nonfiction. With works that have a strong rhythm, audiotapes and oral readings can dramatize these qualities. To introduce grammatical rhythms, try reading or playing recordings of poems that beat rhythms of parallel structures. You might try Tennyson's "Charge of the Light Brigade," Poe's "The Raven," or Prelutsky's "Werewolf" for starters.

Strategy 8: Combine Brush Strokes and Parallel Structures

From the Internet sites below or from accessing them off the CD, have students select an interesting image of a person. Ask students to describe this individual as though they were writing a scene from a short story. Remind them to incorporate specific details and the brush strokes that they learned earlier; however, at the conclusion of this description, have students use parallel structure to create a dramatic ending.

PORTRAITS AND SELF-PORTRAITS BY ARTISTS

National Portrait Gallery
http://www.npg.si.edu/

Portraits From the Web Museum, Paris
http://sunsite.unc.edu/wm/paint/auth/

Rembrant
http://sunsite.unc.edu/wm/paint/auth/rembrandt/

Renoir
http://sunsite.unc.edu/wm/paint/auth/renoir/portraits/

Van Gogh
http://sunsite.unc.edu/wm/paint/auth/gogh/self/

Cezanne
http://sunsite.unc.edu/wm/paint/auth/cezanne/portraits/

IMAGES OF THE HOMELESS

Vagrant Gaze (photos of and by homeless people)
http://www.perfekt.net/~vagrant/homeless.htm

Covington's Homeless
http://www.intac.com/~jdeck/Covdex2.html
Meet Characters like Bones and Backpack Bill, and Art and Patty, a
homeless couple who fell in love.

IMAGES OF ATHLETES

ESPN
http://ESPN.SportsZone.com/

CNN / Sports Illustrated
http://www.cnnsi.com/

CBS Sportsline
http://www.sportsline.com/

ABC Sports
http://www.abcsports.com/

4
From Imitation to Creation
Learning from the Masters

CONCEPTS

What do Robert Lewis Stevenson, Somerset Maugham, William Dean Howells, Vincent Van Gogh, and Pablo Picasso have in common? At one time in their careers, they all imitated the techniques of artists and authors they admired. Imitation for them was an important prerequisite to original creation, a workout in the writing (or painting) gym, as author Pete Hamill explains:

> I would see a paragraph describing a typhoon in Joseph Conrad, and I would change it in my journal to a snowstorm.
>
> The journal is sort of like going to the gymnasium. It's not the fight itself. It's preparing you for it. It's working on certain aspects of what you do. In writing, if you took a typhoon and turned it into a snowstorm, first of all, all the nouns change and then all the verbs change. (Callahan 1993, 46)

Imitating structure—whether it's the structure of sentences, the structure of paragraphs, or even the structure of entire works—has been used successfully by teachers for decades. Bonniejean Christensen's *The Christensen Method* (1979), a comprehensive writing program for high school students based on Francis Christensen's work, relies heavily on imitating sentence and paragraph structures. In *Art of Styling Sentences*, Waddell, Esch, and Walker (1972) argued that imitation dramatically improved the writing of their university students (vii). Similarly, research by Daiker, Kerek, and Morenberg (1990) at the University of Miami found that freshman composition students who imitated professional sentence structures "for a semester wrote papers that were graded higher than those written by students who had not" (4).

Imitating Without Plagiarizing

Used properly, imitation internalizes writing techniques that students can later apply in infinite ways. However, imitation is a dangerous cliff above the cavern of plagiarism. Students can plunge into unethical depths if the teacher doesn't emphasize the difference. By imitating, a writer attempts to internalize the structural design, not the specific content. The approach is analogous to an artist imitating types of lines (hatching, cross-hatching, contour, scribbled tones), which then she uses to create an original drawing. Imitation emulates the techniques that produced the art; plagiarism attempts to duplicate the entire art.

Even casual readers easily recognize this difference. For example in 1997, fans of romance novels began to notice plagiarized passages in the work of Janet Daily, passages that were obviously copied from novels written earlier by Nora Roberts. Daily eventually admitted to plagiarism after fans began posting comparative passages like these on the Internet:

FROM NORA ROBERTS' SWEET REVENGE

"Talk to me."

"It was just a dream, as you said."

"You're hurting." He touched her cheek. This time she didn't jerk away, only closed her eyes. "You talk, I'll listen."

"I don't need anyone."

"I'm not going away until you talk to me."

FROM JANET DAILEY'S NOTORIOUS

"Talk to me, Eden."

"It was only a dream, just as you said." She kept her gaze fixed on the water glass.

"It was more than that." His fingers brushed her cheek, pushing back a strand of hair. She closed her eyes at the contact.

"You need to talk about it. I'll listen."

"I don't need anyone," she insisted stiffly.

"I'm not leaving until you tell me about it" (CNN Interactive 1997)

FROM SWEET REVENGE

But it was only a whisper of a kiss, the brush, retreat, brush of mouth against mouth.

FROM NOTORIOUS

His mouth brushed her lips in a mere whisper of a kiss, lightly rubbed and retreated, again and again. (CNN Interactive 1997)

These examples are radically different from imitation. Daily copied sentence structures, content, and specific images with only slight variations.

Providing Guidelines for Imitation

In spite of incidents like this, the benefits of imitation far outweigh the risks of plagiarism. As novelist R. V. Cassill (1975) explains, "Those with enough equanimity to try a few imitations now and then will learn something about their craft that can hardly be learned so quickly in any other way" (38). However, using imitation requires some guidelines to help students avoid plagiarism and focus on technique.

Imitation might be presented to students as analogous to dressing a mannequin. Once you understand the structure, the shape, and the movement of each part of the body, you can dress the figure in infinitely original ways. With writing, the structure of sentences, paragraphs, and passages represent the mannequin. These structures are finite, but often unrecognized by students. The content, represented by the clothes, provides the opportunity for originality and creativity.

This perspective is the basic premise behind most guidelines for imitation. For example, Cassill offers five suggestions for imitating an author's structural techniques in fiction:

1. You have to imitate the number of sentences and their relative length and complexity, their grammatical structure.
2. You have to imitate detail that characterizes scene and actors.
3. You have to imitate the point of view.
4. You have to imitate the use of proper names and pronouns.
5. You have to imitate the emotional state of the characters that gives them their relationship to the scene. (38–39)

Frank D'Angelo (1985) in his *Process and Thought in Composition* also provides guidelines for imitating structure but not content. D'Angelo's list is less specific, but applies to both fiction and nonfiction and works well in combination with that of Cassill's:

1. Select a short passage from a writer's work that has excellencies of style and is relatively complete in itself.
2. Read the model carefully, preferably aloud at first to get the full impact, in order to get an overview of the dominant impression.
3. Analyze the model carefully, noting the sentence length, the sentence types, and the word choice.

4. Do either a close or loose imitation of the model by selecting a subject that differs from the model's but is suitable for treatment in the model's style. (355)

Experimenting with Variations of Imitation

With guidelines, students can learn to emulate rather than duplicate the art of professionals. However, not every type of imitation will necessarily help students. As Lindemann (1995) notes, imitation is only effective if students are shown "how" to re-create the technique being imitated (252). To simply copy a passage word for word as the ancient Greeks did doesn't appear to internalize techniques, but four types of imitation seem to help: the Franklin approach, the Hamill approach, the Pooh Perplex approach, and the Van Gogh approach.

The Franklin Approach

Ben Franklin attributed the development of his writing skills to time spent attempting to duplicate passages from the *Spectator*. Franklin would reread a selection that he especially enjoyed and take notes on its content. Then, a few days later, "Without looking at the book, [I] tried to complete the papers again, by expressing each hinted sentiment at length and as fully as it had been expressed before, in any suitable words that should come to hand" (Franklin, 20). By comparing his rewrite with the original, Franklin discovered how his writing differed from that of professionals.

Teachers can emulate Franklin's approach with a sample passage and a list of notes. By creating lists prior to imitation, teachers can avoid problems with students who list too many or too few details to learn from this approach. Here is an example of a classroom application of this technique using a passage from Arthur C. Clark's *July 20, 2019*. First, students were given Clarke's description of Arthur, a future-world computer butler that does everything from brewing coffee to buying stocks:

> Arthur woke Palmerston at 5:00 A.M. each day by warming his bedroom until he couldn't sleep any longer. Palmerston's body became so accustomed to the ritual, he first opened his eyes within three minutes after the mercury hit 79 degrees F. Encephalosensors in Palmerston's pillows told Arthur precisely when the first visual images reached Palmerston's brain. Seconds later, the house made Palmerston's coffee, blending caffeinated and decaffeinated in accordance with Palmerston's mood. When Palmerston was happy, he got mostly decaf. To determine his mood, Arthur monitored how long he stayed in the shower, how hot he

wanted the water, and whether he sang or whistled. . . . (Clarke 1986, 179–80)

After reading the passage, they were provided with these notes:

1. Arthur woke Palmerston at 5:00 A.M.
2. Warmed his room to arouse him
3. Palmerston always followed a pattern
4. Opened eyes within three minutes of 79 degrees F
5. "Encephalosensors" in pillow sense Palmerston's first visual images
6. Made Palmerston's coffee, blending to match Palmerston's mood
7. Happy: decaf
8. Arthur determined mood by length of shower, how hot Palmerston wanted his water, singing versus whistling in shower

The next day, students were given only a copy of the notes and asked to reconstruct the original passage. High school student Troy Raeder produced this rewrite:

> Arthur woke Palmerston at 5:00 A.M. by warming his room. Palmerston was used to this and opened his eyes within three minutes after the temperature reached 79 degrees F. Encephalosensors in Palmerston's pillow told Arthur exactly when Palmerston saw his first visual images. Arthur then made Palmerston's coffee, blending it to match his mood. Arthur determined Palmerston's mood by how he wanted his water, and whether he sang or whistled in the shower.

The value of Franklin's imitation approach comes from comparing the original to the rewrite. What makes the original more effective? What sentence structures, arrangements, and subtle devices did Clarke use that were overlooked in the imitation?

As a follow-up to Franklin's approach, teachers might locate several versions of a popular news story from different sources: two from current magazines, one from a local paper, one from an online news magazine, and perhaps one from an evening newscast. Using these as a basis for comparing style, teachers can generate interesting discussions about grammar and rhetoric.

Another variation of Franklin's approach is sentence combining, where teachers give students a list of unconnected sentences and ask them to create a smooth flowing passage. In this exercise, students are not shown the original until after they have created their own imitation. Here is a typical example in which students were given the following list from *Jurassic Park*:

1. It moved toward the rear.
2. It banged the passenger door shut.
3. It moved toward Grant.
4. He stood there.
5. Grant was dizzy with fear.
6. His heart pounded inside his chest.
7. He could smell the rotted flesh in the mouth.
8. The animal was close.
9. The flesh smelled like sweetish blood-smell.
10. The smell was the sickening stench of the carnivore.

Eighth grader Micki Keyser rewrote the passage this way:

It moved toward the rear, banging the passenger door shut. Grant just stood there, dizzy with fear, his heart heavily pounding inside his chest. The animal was close. He could smell the rotted stench of the carnivore.

The original paragraph by Michael Crichton read:

Then moving toward the rear, it banged the passenger door shut, and moved right toward Grant as he stood there. Grant was dizzy with fear, his heart pounding inside his chest. With the animal so close, he could smell the rotten flesh in the mouth, the sweetish blood-smell, the sickening stench of the carnivore. (1990, 189)

With sentence combining, the value also comes from follow-up discussions. Teachers and students can explore questions such as What makes one version more or less effective than another? Are two choices equally valid for different impressions? This follow-up discussion is essential. Without involving students in discussion, one would have to agree with critics like Moffett (1968), Williams (1979a), and Elbow (1985), who have argued that combining sentences fails to engage students in the thinking process essential to writing.

Focusing students on the rhetorical effects of sentence combining seems to help them internalize options as tools. A similar effect seems to occur with imitation, which may be more beneficial than sentence combining. A study by Williams, comparing sentence combining to sentence imitating, concluded that students learning from imitation retained techniques longer and used them more effectively (1979b, 24–40).

The Hamill Approach
As Pete Hamill explained in his quote at the opening of this chapter, he learned his craft by imitating. Hamill would imitate the structure of pas-

sages, but completely change the content. As a result, he uncovered image-creating techniques central to the writer's art. Students can acquire similar insights in the same way. Here are a few examples of high school students imitating with the Hamill approach.

From Gary Paulsen's *Brian's Winter*:

> At first he didn't recognize what was coming. He saw the moose stiffen and turn his head, his huge ears alert and forward, and then in a shadow he saw a flash of gray, just a touch, moving across to the rear of the moose. (1996, 121)

Brad Wicklund's imitation:

> At first he didn't realize what was happening. He saw the car rumble and flash its lights, its huge engine roaring and grinding, and then in the shadow he saw a flash of red, just a touch, moving across the hood of the car.

From Michael Shaara's *The Killer Angels*:

> Lee sat down against a rail fence. A band came by, playing an incoherent song, fifes and bugles. The sky was overcast with blowing white smoke, the smell of hot guns, of blasted earth, the sweet smell of splintery trees. Lee was in the way, in the road; men were gathering around him, calling to him. (1974, 106)

Mike Metzger's imitation:

> Jack leaned on the store window. Airplanes flew by, leaving a trail of smoke, gray and cloudy. The sun was setting and the smell of fear, and salty sweat overcame Jack. He wanted to run away, far away; men had surrounded him, interrogating him.

Hamill's approach invites students to look over the shoulder of a talented writer and watch how she or he paints each image, brush stroke by brush stroke. This type of imitation generates questions. When students find a new structure that supercharges writing, they ask about it. Consequently, teachers need to be aware of some of the most common structures that can arise in these discussions, so they can expand student insights into the craft, helping them build a repertoire of image-creating devices. A few advanced brush strokes that students often inquire about when using the Hamill approach are listed below, which are illustrated with examples from established writers.

1. Absolutes with an *ed* or *en* Participle:
   Milt turned around and looked at the big, clumsy man, **his shirt stuffed into his trousers and held there by a rope belt.** (L'Amour 1990, 5)

In the basement, he had found an old wheelchair, **covered with dust and cobwebs.** (Draper 1997, 19)

2. Subordinate Conjunctions

   The hawk hit only a few rods from **where I was standing in the clover.** Just the yonder side of a juniper bush **where the clover wasn't nearby at all,** and **where it once had been open meadowland for pasture.** (Peck 1984, 63)

3. Infinitive Strokes

   To be ignorant is **to be poor.** (Nightingale 1969, 100)

4. Verb Chain

   He **made** more friends, **had** more fun, **fooled** more people, **presided** over more sustained prosperity, **incurred** more debt, **controlled** more nuclear missiles, **encouraged** more individual freedom at home and abroad, and **escaped** responsibility for more scandals than any president in the history of the Republic. (Reston 1991, 431)

5. Relative Pronouns

   He went through the Bible book by book and sinner by sinner. He prayed in the name of Adam, **who had sinned and fallen short of grace;** of Moses, **who had lost the Promised Land;** of David, **who had looked with desire on another man's wife.** (L'Engle 1994, 16)

Pooh Perplex Approach

The Pooh Perplex approach is named after Frederick Crews' book, which spoofs literary analysis by analyzing *Winnie-the-Pooh.* Like the Hamill approach, this technique also imitates structure, but in addition, it creates a parody of a serious piece of writing. For example, note the underlying structure of the following two parodies by tenth-grade students, the first of the well-known introduction to *A Tale of Two Cities* by Dickens and the second a takeoff on the Gettysburg Address:

> It was the best of times, it was the worst of times, it was the age of wisdom, or was it? It was our teenage years, it was the season of darkness, but only if you got caught in the act of doing something wrong. It was the spring of hope, hope that your parents would let you go out tonight even though last weekend you came home 15 minutes past curfew. (Nikki Pietro)

> Seven years and seven months ago a baby girl was brought forth on this continent, conceived in a family, and dedicated to the promise that all children are created equal.
>
> Now this girl and her brother are engaged in a great battle, testing whether she can endure the pain of his brutal words. Today we meet in

the yard of this battle, the backyard, as a dedication and appreciation to the girl who endured so much—so many harsh words. It is very appropriate and right that we should do this. (Jenny Hastings)

For years writers across the country used this type of parody to poke fun at Hemingway's unique sentence structures. In a competition sponsored by Harry's Bar in California, the owners solicited "a really good page of bad Hemingway" and awarded the winner a trip to the original Harry's Bar in Florence, Italy. Listen to the Hemingway rhythm in these excerpts from the competition:

THE OLD MAN AND THE SEAL

He was an old man who fished alone when he fished by himself. For 358 days now he had been fishless. Maybe if I used bait, he thought. And a hook. The last fish he caught was still in his pants pocket, forgotten.

"Que stencho," the old man said. "No wonder I fish alone. But bad smell does not matter to a man, though this smell is very bad." (Mark Silber, *Best of Bad Hemingway* [1989, 30])

ACROSS THE MALL AND INTO THE WHITE HOUSE

The President looked at the woman he called Nancy. He knew in his heart that other men had also called her Nancy—it was her name. But he did not wish to think about that now.

They were seated at a table. The table was strong, like wood, but shiny, and not afraid of spilled condiments. Maybe a formica tree was killed for it, the President thought. He looked at it admiringly, for he knew that to kill a formica tree was not an easy thing and required much courage to do the job truly and well. Even with a chainsaw. (Daniel R. White, *Best of Bad Hemingway* [1989, 111])

The Van Gogh Approach
The Van Gogh approach, a spin-off of the Pooh Perplex approach, emphasizes structure in a writer's voice. Voice—an elusive concept for most students—can be defined as the rhythm and sound of an author's words. Voice is the distinctive grammatical style of a writer. As Coe (1981) points out, voice creates a persona of the author's personality (160). Most writers project a voice, easily recognized by their avid readers.

One way to introduce voice is by showing students contrasting artistic styles of artists such as Van Gogh, Picasso, Monet, and Chagall. The artistic patterns of these artists are so unique that their artwork is easily identified on a casual walk through a museum. Writers project similar identifying qualities in their written voice.

To draw the parallel with writers, teachers can show students written passages with similar dramatic contrasts in style. Columnist Russell Baker did this when he demonstrated how "Little Red Riding Hood" might have sounded had it been written in the voice of a corporate bureaucrat. The opening few paragraphs of his satirical piece make the point:

> Once upon a point in time, a small person named Little Red Riding Hood initiated plans for the preparation, delivery and transportation of foodstuffs to her grandmother, a senior citizen residing in a place of residence in a forest of indeterminate dimension.
>
> In the process of implementing this program, her incursion into the forest was in mid-transportation process when it attained interface with an alleged perpetrator. This individual, a wolf, made inquiry as to the whereabouts of Little Red Riding Hood's goal as well as inferring that he was desirous of ascertaining the contents of Little Red Riding Hood's foodstuffs basket. (Baker 1980, 47)

A number of years ago *Read* magazine published two contrasting versions of the classic Humpty Dumpty story. One was written with the voice of Edgar Allen Poe; the other, in a typical voice of a newspaper reporter:

THE FALL OF THE HOUSE OF DUMPTY

> As I made my way up the long dank pathway through the gnarled wood past the gray hedgerow, I saw the mansion of my friend Humpty Dumpty, the last scion of an old and honorable family. How long he had begged that I sojourn for a fortnight with him and his butler in his rockbound mansion by the sea! But I could not shake off a chill of dread and impending doom as I made my way past the garden and toward the mossy brick wall that was his favorite resting place. (*Read* 1973, 23)

NEWS REPORT FROM MOTHER GOOSE LAND

> Coroner Jack Horner tentatively concluded today that the death of Humpty Dumpty was accidental. Mr. Dumpty fell from a wall late yesterday on his estate and could not be restored despite frantic rescue attempts. After a complete investigation on the site of the fatality, Mr. Horner announced to a press conference that no foul play had been involved. (*Read* 1973, 23)

Experimenting with voice is one of the most difficult tasks for students but one that not only improves writing, but also influences the way students read. As students imitate, they search for their own voice. They make connections—noticing structure, details, effects, links, transitions. Like other experiments in imitation, explorations with voice generate questions in small group discussions, questions such as What makes Stephen King sound so different than Jean Auel? Why can I always recognize a piece written by

Dave Barry and know it isn't the writing of Bill Cosby or Steve Allen? Such questions help students and teachers to discover how grammatical choices characterize an author's craft.

Moving from Imitation to Creation

The purpose of all imitation is, of course, to enrich the grammatical options for original creation. Teachers can begin to accomplish this by having students imagine that they are painting branches on an image tree. With this approach, first suggested by Tufte (1971, 142), students picture a sentence to be a large fallen tree. For example, examine Figure 4–1 and picture the simple sentence as the trunk.

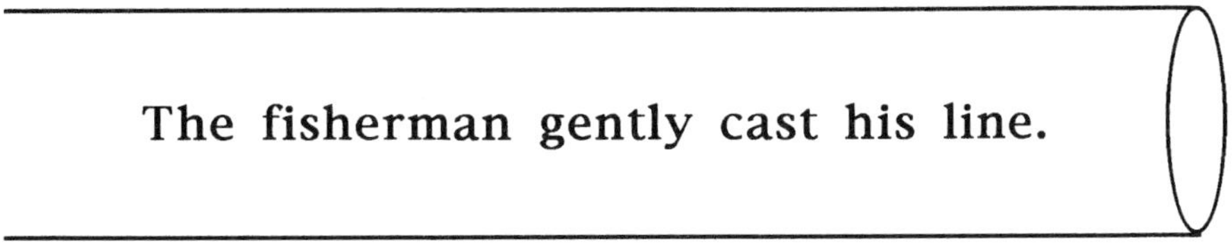

The fisherman gently cast his line.

FIGURE 4–1. Fallen tree trunk

If the tree has fallen to the left, students can add branches to the beginning of the sentence as in Figure 4–2.

If the tree has fallen to the right, students can add branches to the end of the sentence as in Figure 4–3.

If students wish to add branches in the middle, they can imagine the tree has fallen either way and add branches as in Figure 4–4.

The tree analogy can also show students how branches added in different places create different nuances of meaning. Figure 4–2 creates a power-

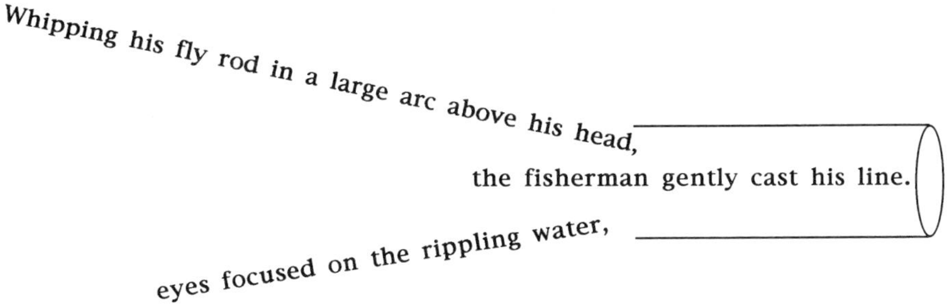

Whipping his fly rod in a large arc above his head,

the fisherman gently cast his line.

eyes focused on the rippling water,

FIGURE 4–2. Left branching tree

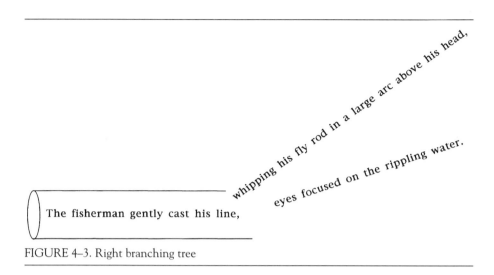

FIGURE 4–3. Right branching tree

ful image of the rod in an arc above the fisherman and emphasizes the fisherman's eyes. Figure 4–4 seems almost out of order and gives more emphasis to the identification of the fisherman rather than the action of his cast.

An alternative for viewing the three arrangements of branches on a fallen tree is to view sentences as variations of three forms: sentence openers, subject-verb splits, and sentence closers. This is the approach Don Killgallon (1997, 1998) uses in his workbook series on sentence composing. Killgallon provides exercises and examples appropriate for middle school, high school, and college students, using a minimum of terminology to help students more easily apply grammatical knowledge to writing.

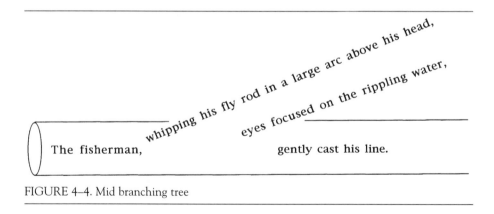

FIGURE 4–4. Mid branching tree

Creating with an Artist's Structural Palette

Another way to move students from imitation to creation is with an Artist's Structural Palette, a variation of the Artist's Image Palette described in Chapter 1. The Artist's Structural Palette provides structural dabs of paint for student writers, encouraging them to add a touch of participle here, an appositive there—to inject grammatical structures in the same way they injected words and short phrases from their image palettes. The difference is that the strucural palette provides only structures and not images.

Although teachers can customize structural palettes based on the individual structures students have learned through imitation, the best way to begin is by introducing a structural palette based on the five basic brush strokes, a palette similar to this:

1. Absolute (with *ed* or *ing* participles added)

    Junior stood on top of the bard, **arm outstretched, legs apart.** (Betsy Byars [1986, 1])

    Far into the night she awoke with a start and saw Jutta standing in the tree, **rain shrouding her like a second skin.** (Ursula Hegi [1994, 190])

2. Appositive

    There would be a glimpse of green—**the landscaped lawn around the Central Plaza; a bush on the riverbank.** (Lois Lowry [1993, 97])

3. Participle (*ing*/*ed* forms)

    It was tiring and awkward, **standing there trying to hold my weight against the walker and clutching the slippery sides of the small sink,** my eyes squinched shut. (Cynthia Voight [1986, 60])

    He could feel perspiration **trickling down his neck onto his shoulders, then down his arms.** He, too, lay on his stomach, **hidden by trees and grass and bushes.** (Virginia Hamilton [1968, 40])

4. Adjectives Shifted Out of Order

    At the edge of sand was a line of tangled bushes, some of them bearing flowers of red and blue. And beyond them, the stumps of buildings, looking like candles that had burned down almost to their ends, **melted and blackened.** (Ben Bova [1995, 72])

5. Action Verbs

    When the cold comes to New England, it **arrives** in sheets of sleet and ice. In December, the wind **wraps** itself around bare trees and twists in between husbands and wives asleep in their beds. It **shakes** the shingles from the roofs and **sifts** rough cracks in the plaster. (Alice Hoffman [1997, 246])

After reviewing the Artist's Structural Palette, teachers might ask students to write a short description of an image using examples of the palette structures. Here are a few examples of eighth-grade students mixing structures:

> **Wheels racing, fire spitting,** the sleek car burst through the roaring flames with an echoing explosion. The driver, **a young mastermind behind the vehicle,** triumphantly zoomed across the finish line. (Micki Keyser)

> The night was cold, and the wind was whipping the leaves, **dead and limp,** into my face. I lay on the cold wet grass and looked up into the dark velvet sky, lit with fiery candles, **glistening bright against black emptiness.** (Katie Chapell)

> An elderly man sits next to the creek. **Heart aching, eyes watering,** he thinks of his deceased wife. **Touching the water as if it were part of her,** he reflects. The water, **a calmer of people,** helps comfort the man. It sheds tears for him, as it streams along by his fingers. (Meredith Bucur)

> The husky, **an animal of radiant beauty,** peered across the knife's edge of Mt. Kahtadin. Its eyes, **keen and gray,** missed nothing. **Fur bristling, ears deciphering,** it waited. Then apparently satisfied, it turned and trotted away. (Keir Marticke)

Moving Toward Creation with Method Writing

"Method Writing," a technique developed by Colleen Mariah Rae in her book *Movies of the Mind* provides another catalyst for helping students move from imitation to creation. Borrowing from the Stanislavski approach to acting, the writer imagines a scene that conveys a strong emotion and paints images from the natural flow of emotions. As Rae explains, "It is absolutely impossible to have an emotion in your body without having a concomitant sensory image in your mind's eye—and vice versa" (1996, 25). To illustrate how images, emotions, and effective writing work in unison, Rae uses the following exercise with her students:

> Close your eyes. You are sitting outside a hot dog stand on a busy city street. A hot dog stand. Outside. Eating. And all of a sudden you hear

the sound of cars colliding, and in that instant, just as you're turning, you hear a woman shriek, "My baby!" . . .

What happens inside of you when you hear those words in your mind's eye? Try imagining it again, more vividly. Watch the way the feeling plays through you. Does your stomach knot? Do chills course over your body? It's not the words that make you feel; it's the fact that you are imaging—hearing the words in your mind's eye. (26)

The images in the passage, as well as the images in the imagination of the listening students, create an emotional response that seems real. Students who have control of basic brush strokes can draw from their repertoire of writing techniques, using their knowledge of grammatical structures to capture the emotions and images suggested by these scenes.

Author Joan Didion describes her approach to writing as a very similar process. For her, writing begins with constructing images, images real and imagined.

When I talk about pictures in my mind I am talking, quite specifically, about images that shimmer around the edges. . . . Look hard enough, and you can't miss the shimmer. It's there. You can't think too much about these pictures that shimmer. You just lie low and let them develop. You stay quiet. You don't talk to many people and you keep your nervous system from shorting out and you try to locate the cat in the shimmer, the grammar of the picture.

Just as I meant "shimmer" literally I mean "grammar." Literally. Grammar is a piano I play by ear, since I seem to have been out of school the year the rules were mentioned. All I know about grammar is its infinite power. To shift the structure of a sentence alters the meaning of that sentence, as definitely and inflexibly as the position of a camera alters the meaning of the object photographed. Many people know about camera angles now, but not so many know about sentences. (1984, 6–7)

For Joan Didion meaning and structure harmonize: the more intense the meaning, the more powerful the grammatical structures. Connie Weaver describes this as "grammar emerging from writing." Observing students, Weaver has found that "sophisticated grammatical structures may emerge when teachers focus on developing ideas for writing and on using descriptive language, without focusing on particular parts of speech or on particular grammatical constructions" (1997, 3). The approach of Didion and Weaver, similar to Rae's "method writing," is one way to nurture emerging grammar; another is scripted fantasy.

Creating with Scripted Fantasy

For decades psychologists have used *scripted fantasy* to help their patients re-create the real or imagined emotions of an experience. A scripted fantasy is a short passage describing an imaginary scene that is designed to evoke strong images in the mind of the listener. Psychologists such as Freud, Jung, Caslant, and Desoille found scripted fantasy useful in unlocking details of buried memories, and some psychologists have even used it to enhance classroom performance (Hall, Hall, and Leech 1990, 1–3).

More recently, however, scripted fantasy has been used as a tool for developing effective images in writing. Karen Hess in *Enhancing Writing Through Imagery* has developed a comprehensive collection of scripted fantasy lessons designed to use images as a springboard for fiction, nonfiction, poetry, and drama. For example, helping students create a mystery story, she walks them through images for setting, character, and plot. To create the setting, she has students open a phone book to the yellow pages and select an ad, observing and recording any key details. Then she reads the following script, pausing on the ellipses.

> You will be creating a scene and place from which to view the action of the story. Read over the information you've written down about the place of business. Close your eyes and see this place . . . read the sign with the name on it . . . notice what the sign is made of and where it is on the building . . . examine the building and take a guess at its age . . . look to the right, noticing what is located there . . . [longer pause] . . . and now to the left . . .[longer pause] . . . walk slowly to the door . . . listen to and feel the door as you open it . . . enter the building and notice what strikes you as you enter . . . [longer pause] . . . now, like a movie camera, pan in slow motion, taking in the entire scene . . . [longer pause] . . . take in every detail . . . face the door now from the inside . . . and leave the building . . . (1987, 138)

Continuing the script outside the building and creating details about the random name in the phone book, students construct images for a mystery. The scripted fantasy discourages students from crafting plot summaries, helping them to more clearly paint their mental images. This approach offers one more way to help students transfer the methods learned from imitation to the process of original creation.

STRATEGIES

Strategy 1: Keep a Writer's Sketchbook

Most artists keep a sketchbook, containing quick sketches for future reference, to capture moments of inspiration. Pass out the following guidelines and have your students develop a writer's sketchbook.

A WRITER'S SKETCHBOOK

Artists carry sketchbooks to capture images they find fascinating. We are going to do the same thing, but we will capture our images with words. Sometimes we will write from still images in class. Sometimes we will write from film images. Sometimes, if it can be arranged, we will describe guest speakers or scenes from field trips—all for the purpose of painting.

Like an artist, you will be asked to use your sketchbook to create your own artwork and also to study the writing of the masters. For this assignment you will need to locate a folder with two pockets—one pocket for paragraphs created by you, and one for copied or xeroxed paragraph sketches written by published authors.

Over the next four weeks, you will need to create ten original images of one or two paragraphs each and locate ten professional sketches of one or two paragraphs each. If you create or find a technique we have discussed in class and can identify it, you will earn bonus points. Your task is to experiment and explore. Let your camera eye tell you what images look powerful in what you read and what you write. Any work of fiction or nonfiction may be used.

Strategy 2: Paint from a Family Photo

From old family photos, have students choose a photograph of one of their parents or grandparents when they were about the same age as them. Ask students to spend 20 minutes looking for details in the photograph. Then have them write their impressions. The form of the writing may be descriptive, narrative, persuasive, or informative. It can be humorous or serious. The primary requirement is that they capture and embellish images from the photograph.

For students who are unable to locate a photograph of one of their parents or grandparents in their youth, offer two alternatives: (1) Have them locate a photograph of themselves in a situation that brings back memories with strong emotions—joy, fear, surprise, sadness, or (2) Have them find a magazine photo that reminds them of an experience they or one of their parents or grandparents once had.

After students have written about their experiences, ask them to revise using the Artist's Structural Palette, and then seek out volunteers to share their writings.

Jim Kagafas, a writing instructor at the University of Akron, has used a variation of this idea with his college freshmen for fifteen years. Kagafas introduces the assignment with "Looking for My Mother," an excerpt from Chapter 28 of Roland Barthes' novel *Camera Lucida*, and shows students a companion photograph of Barthes' mother (Scholes 1994, 44). In the essay, Barthes writes about the photograph and discusses what an image can capture and miss.

Reflecting on student responses to this assignment, Kagafas said, "I found the writing produced from this lesson to be richer with metaphor, sensory inventories, lyrical passages, and active verbs than other assignments. Surprisingly, too, the students made fewer punctuation errors." Although not statistically documented, Kagafas' observations lend some support to the notion that the quality of writing may correlate with the emotional involvement of the writer.

Strategy 3: Try Hamill's Imitation Approach

Have your students select two of the following models to imitate, using Pete Hamill's method. Remind them that they need to keep the sentence structure as close to the original as possible, but must change the content. For example, the rainstorm in the first model might be changed to a snowstorm.

> She sat in her room and watched heavy black clouds boil up over the lake, turning dusk to night. Rain began pounding the roof in buckets, and as the wind came up she could make out the trees bent over like it was easy. She could hear the crackling and crashing of branches torn from the mother trunk. Lightning bolted across the sky, turning the world white then black then white again. In that ghastly light she caught a glimpse of the water, a mass of furious waves. The clap of thunderous noise that followed the lightning seemed to come from their roof, making her jump from her window seat. (Slepian 1985, 113)

> The grown males went forward, their leader at the center. The females and young watched from behind, screaming defiance. The males displayed at each other, fangs barred, manes bushed, bellowing not their

ritual challenge calls, but older ones, a hoarse repetitive bark which till now they had not known they knew. (Dickinson 1992, 143)

They left then, stepping carefully through the darkness, eyes trained on the low light the candle flame shed. Pallas, bred in the overlight of Los Angeles in houses without basements, associated them with movie evil or trash or crawly things. She gripped Seneca's hand and breathed through her mouth. But the gestures were expressions of anticipated, not genuine alarm. In fact, as they climbed the stairs, images of a grand-mother rocking peacefully, her arms, a lap, a singing voice soothed her. The whole house felt permeated with a blessed maleness, like a protect-ed domain, free of hunters but exciting too. (Morrison 1998, 176–177)

Spade turned and with angry heedlessness tossed his glass at the table. The glass struck the wood, burst apart, and splashed its contents and glittering fragments over the table and floor. Spade, deaf and blind to the crash, wheeled to confront the fat man again.

   The fat man paid no more attention to the glass's fate than Spade did: lips pursed, eyebrows raised, head cocked a little to the left, he maintained his pink-faced blandness throughout Spade's angry speech, and he maintained it now. (Hammett 1930, 93)

Of course the ordinary soldiers didn't have much fun. For one thing there was the snow. It came down in a great blizzard about a week after the troops had started to build their encampment. Their huts were not finished and they were forced to work in bitter cold and storm. The cold was a problem. The huts were really just tiny log cabins with big stone fireplaces making the whole rear wall. In cold weather they had a lot of trouble getting the mortar to set. Because of this the chimneys leaked so badly that half the smoke blew back into the room. The snow made hew-ing wood difficult, too. Sam told us that they were having an awful time getting the huts finished. Even when they were done they weren't much to live in—twelve soldiers jammed into a 14 by 16 room, breathing more smoke than air and having to stumble over people whenever they wanted to move around. And the snow never stopped falling. By January it cov-ered the countryside three feet deep, so that the stone walls disappeared. You could drive a sled over the snow anywhere you wanted without pay-ing attention to where the roads were. (Collier and Collier 1974, 177)

They murdered him.
   As he turned to take the ball, a dam burst against the side of his head and a hand grenade shattered his stomach. Engulfed by nausea, he pitched toward the grass. His mouth encountered gravel, and he spat frantically, afraid that some of his teeth had been knocked out. Rising to his feet, he saw the field through drifting gauze but held on until everything settled into place, like a lens focusing, making the world sharp again, with edges. (Cormier 1974, 3)

If students are keeping an Artist's Sketchbook, give them the option of imitating one or two of the passages they collected. Research suggests that students can learn more emulating authors they admire (Kehl 1979, 137–138) If you are working with advanced high school students, an excellent resource is *Style and Statement* by Edward Corbett and Robert Conners (1999). Their approach is similar to Hamill and includes imitation models by Dryden, Defoe, Irving, Austen, as well as numerous contemporary writers.

Strategy 4: Imitate Poetic Sentences

Poets craft their words with thoughtful precision. Consequently, their use of language provides interesting models for image grammar. With this strategy, you must first find a short poem consisting of one to four sentences, a poem that contains some interesting image grammar techniques. Excellent examples can be found in any anthology, but a few recommended poems include Carl Sandburg's "Fog," Langston Hughes' "The Dream Keeper," Anne Sexton's "Welcome Morning," Robert Frost's "The Rabbit-Hunt," Alfred Lord Tennyson's "The Eagle," and John Haines' "Wolves."

Once you have located some models, have students create their own poem, imitating the sentence structure of an original. For models, show students the following two examples: one based on Sandburg's "Fog" and created by teacher Mike Fejes, the second written by one of Mike's students, Elizabeth Hunsberger, and based on the sentence structure of Hughes' "Dream Keeper."

LIGHTNING
Mike Fejes

The lightning sizzles in
on dragon wings.
It spears the night
stabbing building and house
with bony white legs and talons
then dissolves in the darkness.

WISH KEEPER
Elizabeth Hunsberger

Bring me all of your hopes
Believers
Bring me all of your
Trusting faith
That I may wrap it

In a blanket of sky
A new wish comes true
With every falling star

Strategy 5: Do Your Own Edgar Allan Humpty

Ask the elementary librarian in your school system to loan you thirty well-known children's books. After sharing the Red Riding Hood and Edgar Allen Poe parodies quoted earlier in this chapter, have students select a children's book such as *The Three Bears, Snow White,* or *Cinderella,* and rewrite a portion of it in a totally different voice. They might try writing it in the voice of an evening news broadcaster, a sports commentator, an author you are reading in class, or perhaps in the voice of a popular celebrity with an accent.

Strategy 6: Search for a Personal Voice

Ask students to write an opinion piece but with a very special twist. In this they must attempt to create a personal voice, writing that has a conversational tone. For starters, share this excerpt from an article written by eighth-grade soap opera fan Cathleen Conry:

WARNING! SOAP OPERAS AREN'T FOR EVERYONE

Arrest me already! Throw me in a cell! Darkness, starvation, misery—I can take it! But please, whatever you do, don't turn off the soaps! I know, I know; it all seems so dramatic, and trust me—I'd rather live with darkness, starvation, and misery than give up soap operas, but there are those who would beg to differ.

"Sharon, you know I only want what's best for you and Nick," Grace says with a sincere smile. Inside, the wheels are turning—she's got to think fast if she wants to move in on Nick, the rich and extremely good-looking young entrepreneur, who also happens to be her best friend's husband! And if that's not enough, Sharon, Grace's best friend, and Nick's wife is pregnant with Nick's child!

Sound a little unbelievable? It sure should! This is just a fraction of a typical day in Genewa City, the fictional town where the cast of "The Young and the Restless" live their dramatic lives. Sure, some of the story lines are stupid, unrealistic, and sometimes even (gasp!) boring, but it's all worth it once you taste those thrilling cliff-hangers, right? Those juicy love scenes that some viewers live for can be a bit extreme or just plain ridiculous at times. Then all this leaves us with a question: Why do so many people (mostly women and teenage girls) get hooked on soap operas?

You can hear Cathleen almost as though she were sharing her views over lunch with friends. Ask students to try capturing a similar tone.

Strategy 7: Read a Scripted Fantasy

Turn out the lights, ask students to close their eyes, and then read the following scripted fantasy:

> Close your eyes and picture a machine (any machine but a lawn mower)—a particular type of car, a can opener, garbage disposal, water sprinkler—any mechanical device powered by electricity, gas, or the wind. Now, look closely at each detail of the machine. . . . Watch how its parts move. . . . Listen to its sounds. . . . Smell any aromas or odors it emits. . . .
>
> Now, think of an animal that the object reminds you of. Visualize how the animal looks. . . . Picture its colors, sounds, smells. . . . Observe it as it moves. . . . Look at each muscle and watch its rhythm. . . . Notice its mood and the details that made you realize that mood. . . . Watch what it does and where it goes. . . . Look around your animal and notice where it is. Look above it, to the right, to the left, below. . . . OK. Open your eyes.

Explain to the class that they are going to use the images they just pictured to write a poem. Ask them to concentrate on the images one more time as you reread the script. Next, have them use the images they visualized as they follow this sequence:

1. Identify the machine with two or three words.
2. Describe it with a one-word metaphor and a participle.
3. Add an absolute phrase showing what it's doing.
4. Use a prepositional phrase to tell where the animal is located.
5. Add another participle describing its actions.
6. Use a prepositional phrase to conclude the poem.

After students have finished, ask volunteers to share their poems. Explain that this scripted fantasy was designed to help them use grammatical structures to create poetic images.

Some students may have difficulty following this procedure. If so, present the sample below (written by the author) before asking students to create their own. Mention that the rhyme in the sample wasn't necessary, but added for effect.

SAMPLE POEM

lawn mower,
a shark devouring its prey,
teeth slicing its way
through oceans of green,
attacking prey unseen
with mindless
devotion

Strategy 8: Use a Second Structural Palette for Opinions

This is a two-part strategy. The first part asks students to locate information. The second places requirements on their writing, which is based on the information they find.

Part 1
Ask students to visit any one of these listed Internet sites dealing with a controversial issue and collect information for an opinion paper supporting or opposing a position.

Euthanasia
The Voluntary Euthanasia Society of Scotland (Pro)
http://www.euthanasia.org/index.htm

International Anti-Euthanasia Task Force (Con)
http://www.iaetf.org/

Abortion
Ultimate Pro Life Resource List
http://www.prolife.org/ultimate/opinions.html

Pro-Choice Resources
http://adtech.net/acsa/choice.html

Gun Control
Ohio University site (Pro and Con)
http://www.tcom.ohiou.edu/OULanguage/project/guns.html

Vouchers
Cato Policy Analysis (Pro and Con)
http://www.cato.org/pubs/pas/pa-269.html

Heartland Institute (Pro)
http://www.heartland.org/education/whatis.htm

National Education Association (Con)
http://www.policy.com/issuewk/97/1013/101397f.html

Global Warming
Storm Smart (Pro and Con)
http://stormsmart.wics.com/expert/warming/explain.html

Scientific American (Pro and Con)
http://www.sciam.com/0597issue/0597karl.html

Sierra Club (Global Warming Is a Threat)
http://www.sierraclub.org/news/global-warming/

Heartland Institute (Global Warming Is *Not* a Threat)
http://www.heartland.org/studies/gwscience.htm

Ask students to review the information on the site, take a pro or con stand, and then write the first draft of a one-page opinion.

Part 2
Next, stretch your students' abilities by introducing a new structural palette based on parallel structures—the Artist's Structural Palette II. Review with students the examples of parallel structure in Chapter 3 and explain that their task will be to revise their opinion drafts by injecting at least two structures found on the following palette:

1. Literal Repetition

   Perhaps I am very ill, I thought. **Perhaps I am** imagining things. **Perhaps I am** a little delirious. (Roald Dahl [1994, 89])

2. Grammatical Repetition
   a. Repeated Clause Structures (subordinate/coordinate conjunctions, relative pronouns)

   Near the banks of the Muscatatuck **where once the woods had stretched, dark row on row,** and **where the fox grapes and wold mint still flourished,** Jess Birdwell, an Irish Quaker, built his white clapboard house. (Jessamyn West [1971, 3])

   b. Repeated Phrases (absolutes, appositives, participles, prepositions, noun and verb phrases)

Without the hatchet he had nothing—**no fire, no tools, no weapons.**
(Gary Paulsen [1987, 174])

Beyond the tennis courts and the big oval track, beyond the stand of pine trees that bordered the school campus, a charming lake emptied into a wild, white river. (Caroline Cooney [1990, 41])

With this palette teachers may want to distribute the list of prepositions, subordinate conjunctions, coordinate conjunctions, and relative pronouns on page 61 to help students create structural patterns. So students can see a few examples of these techniques used by other students, pass out these samples:

> When man starts to respect himself, when man and nature come together, and when all of mankind live in harmony, only then will there be peace. (Micki Keyser)

> In his mind he can create them. In his soul he can believe them. In his heart he can feel them. He is a writer, one who shows fact and fiction to the world. (Katie Chapell)

> Listen to the trees. Listen to the birds. Listen to the winds. Listen to nature. (Meredith Bucur)

> Beseeching were his eyes; fretting were his folds. Unwavering was his demeanor. But behind his sorrowful gaze lies a mind more complex than you perceive, more deadly than he'll ever know. (Keir Marticke)

Although there has been no research into using structural palettes with writing, the use of these formats for imitation seem to help students develop a subconscious repertoire of grammatical techniques for painting images.

5
The Artist's Special Effects
The Grammar–Meaning Connection

CONCEPTS

Try this experiment. Examine the punctuation in each of the following sentences and mark the sentence as either (C) correct or (I) incorrect.

_____ 1. That part was settled, their compact had been subscribed by the photographer, they trusted one another, affection had triumphed for once in a way.

_____ 2. Outside on the square it had stopped raining and the moon was trying to get through the clouds.

_____ 3. [Her] childlike resourcefulness—to get a job in publishing, to become a gifted potter!—bewilders the imagination.

_____ 4. If the merchandise has not been forfeited I shall be glad to substitute a certified check in the amount of $3.56 for the check I sent you on March third.

_____ 5. Then at midnight I ordered everyone out. A cold night. A bright moon. The rattle of drums.

_____ 6. Nothing had happened since, nothing could happen.

_____ 7. Then something bellowed tremendously above his head, he heard human voices, a bell jangled and the sound ceased and the mist vanished.

_____ 8. Frank Conroy loves his yo-yo tricks, Emily Dickinson her slant of light.

Be sure not to read on until you have carefully reviewed your answers.

If you marked all of these correct, you are either a horrible textbook grammarian or an incredibly insightful reader. Each sentence above was written—exactly as punctuated—by the following authors: 1. E. M. Forster, 2. Ernest Hemingway, 3. Joan Didion, 4. James Thurber, 5. Gore Vidal, 6. Katherine Anne Porter, 7. William Faulkner, and 8. Annie Dillard.

Were these rare oversights? Did these skilled authors simply make errors that went unnoticed? Not according to scholars like John Dawkins (1992, 1995) and Charles Meyer (1987) whose research has shown that prominent authors ignore the conventions of punctuation when those conventions conflict with desired nuances of meaning.

Authors often consciously craft grammatical structures and push conventions beyond textbook limits to create special effects of meaning. Sometimes authors create special effects by enhancing meaning with simple arrangements and choices of structures. At other times they add power to meaning by violating conventions.

Creating Special Effects with Punctuation

Although some grammar handbooks acknowledge occasional violations of punctuation rules by authors, most imply that this practice is rare. Dawkins (1995, 1992) disagrees. Using eighteen renowned authors in his study, Dawkins demonstrated that good writers use "incorrect" punctuation to create meanings that otherwise couldn't be expressed.

Many of these meanings are communicated through the length of pauses in text. Using a hierarchy similar to one developed by Meyer (1987), Dawkins charted the relationship between the length of a punctuation pause and the intended effect. As you review Dawkins' chart, notice how the meaning of the sample sentences changes slightly with each change in punctuation.

DAWKINS' PUNCTUATION HIERARCHY

Maximum Separation (the period, the question mark, and the exclamation mark)
Example: I looked up. And there she stood.

Medium Separation, Emphatic (the dash)
Example: I looked up—and there she stood.

Medium Separation, Anticipatory (the colon)
Example: I looked up: And there she stood.

Medium Separation (the semicolon)
Example: I looked up; and there she stood.

Minimum Separation (the comma)
Example: I looked up, and there she stood.

Zero Separation
Example: I looked up and there she stood.
(1992, 10–11)

Each choice of punctuation communicates a slightly different emphasis. Maximum separation is a dramatic stop that spotlights the sentence that follows. Medium separation connects ideas more closely. The colon, for example, conveys a sense of anticipation; the dash, a strong emphasis on whatever follows. Minimum separation with the comma invites readers to join related images with quick flashes. Finally, placing no punctuation where punctuation is expected runs one idea into the next like automobiles racing down an entry ramp, merging onto a crowded freeway.

Some teachers might question sharing these options with students for fear it would lead to confusion. However, Dawkins' ideas have several classroom advantages. First, they show students the relationship between meaning and punctuation, making both conventions and their violations more understandable. Second, the approach generates positive rather than punitive perceptions. Examining punctuation for its purpose and power, students view writing as an act of creation rather than a burden of correction.

For example, a teacher might introduce the use of a colon by saying, "In addition to its use in the business letter, a colon can be used to join two sentences together when the second explains or amplifies the first." This emphasizes the convention. However, look at the difference if the teacher introduces the colon with a comment such as "When joining two sentences, a colon communicates anticipation. This is one way authors use the colon to express meaning." The first approach provides a rule; the second approach emphasizes how the colon is a vehicle for communicating meaning.

Looking at rhetoric rather than rules takes away the negative feelings associated with error and invites students on an exciting journey of image play, experimentation, and special effects of meaning. This perspective encourages teachers to dwell less on rules and focus more on meaning, as Dawkins explains:

> To punctuate well one needs to know—not book grammar—only an independent clause and its attachments when one writes them (a knowledge that is essentially intuitive, psycholinguistics tells us). . . . Indeed, one claim for this theory is that anyone—writer or student— will punctuate more effectively and efficiently because of a concern for meaning rather than a concern for rules. (1991, 16)

Creating Special Effects with Sentence Structure

Special effects of meaning can also be generated with variations of sentence structure. Teachers can show students subtle shifts of meaning with three types of examples: (1) the selective use of fragments and run-ons, (2) the careful placement of clauses and phrases, and (3) the use of highly stylized sentence structures.

Fragments and Run-ons

Fragments and run-ons are legitimate and powerful structures used by professional writers. Like variations of punctuation, writers create meaning in fragments and run-ons with pauses. The meaning of fragments is enhanced with an abrupt unanticipated pause, and the meaning of run-ons builds from the endless flow of ideas without a pause. For example, notice how the pauses in the following fragments create a quick succession of fragmented images that conveys the feeling of flashing close-up camera shots:

> I am very beat. Lipstick. Hair combed. Bandage on my leg from raincoat lining. Typewriter in lap. Staring up at the spot where the little thin line of light is growing, like hope. (Anne Beaumont [1989, 179])

> What could he say? After the phone calls and beating. After the desecration of his locker. The silent treatment. Pushed downstairs. What they did to Goober, to Brother Eugene. What guys like Archie and Janza did to the school. What they would do to the world when they left Trinity. (Robert Cormier [1974, 225])

> Man of forty-one with a thirty-two-inch waist. Wearing white sharkskin tennis shorts and a white cotton knit shirt, his lucky favorite. Thirty-five-dollar Tretorn shoes, the best, the kind that cushioned the arch, softly snugged the heel and made his reflexes feel improved. The shoes would be ruined after this; they'd probably dry stiff. (Gerald A. Browne [1976, 3])

The pauses created by the fragments dramatize key images, giving them greater significance than they would have had if buried in the flow of a normal sentence. Conversely, the lack of anticipated pauses also alters meaning. Watch how Tom Wolfe uses run-ons to embellish meaning in this passage from the *Right Stuff*:

> To take off in an F-100 at dawn and cut in the afterburner and hurtle twenty-five thousand feet up into the sky so suddenly that you felt not like a bird but like a trajectory, yet with full control, full control of five tons of thrust, all of which flowed from your will and through your fingertips, with the huge engine right beneath you, so close that it was as

if you were riding it bareback, until you leveled out and went super-
sonic, an event registered on earth by a tremendous crackling boom
that shook windows, but up here only by the fact that you now felt
utterly free of the earth—to describe it, even to wife, child, near ones
and dear ones, seemed impossible. (1979, 30)

Wolfe creates a rhetorical effect, using run-ons to capture a feeling of
acceleration. For Wolfe as with most authors, meaning takes precedence over
rules. Teaching this notion to students can actually strengthen their understanding of conventions, rather than diluting it as some teachers might expect.
When teachers help students see conventions as an aid to meaning, struggling
students can better recognize when fragments and run-ons don't work, and
confident students can better understand why writers break the rules.

With those students who have control of conventions, teachers can
encourage experimentation with similar effects. In the following passage,
middle school student Caitlin McNally uses fragments to intensify images
of a gorilla in captivity:

> Gorilla. Stormy gray eyes. Anger. Staring at the far away lights.
> Wondering. When he will be alone? Far off noises taunting him.
> Repetition. His life has changed after coming to this new caged world.
> Waiting. When will he escape? This thought stays only to be torn. The
> truth comes forward. He is a prisoner.

Combining run-ons and fragments, eighth-grade student Emelia
Hiltner plays with the rhythms of fire in the following piece. Running clauses and phrases together, injecting fragments, Emelia captures the feeling of
a raging fire, flaming out of control:

> The fire roared, rushing from building to building, devouring every-
> thing in its path, destroying and wasting, hot and hungry, quick and
> powerful, like a starving beast, flames licking towards the sky, as sirens
> screamed and firemen shot gallons of water, taking away the life of the
> fire. But they were too late.

For the skillful writer, the subtle options of punctuation, fragments, and
run-ons are special effects, used to alter the shape of meaning. Such options
often violate conventions. However, the options for arranging and choosing sentence structures provide a similar hidden bag of tricks, but within
traditional rules.

Clauses and Phrases
With each choice of phrase and clause structure and each decision on its
placement, meaning changes. In turn, these choices are influenced by

what an author perceives in an image. Author Joan Didion explains it this way:

> The arrangement of words matters, and the arrangement you want can be found in the picture in your mind. The picture dictates the arrangement. The picture dictates whether this will be a sentence with or without clauses, a sentence that ends hard or a dying-fall sentence, long or short, active or passive. The picture tells you how you arrange the words and the arrangement of words tells you, or tells me, what's going on in the picture. (1984, 7)

Didion's point is easily illustrated. Compare the images in these two similar passages:

FIRST VERSION

Vast waves, each the size of a small house, were rolling in rapidly, close on each other's heels. Crossing the beach the wave would rise even higher, its crest curling in a question mark, then throw itself against the foot of the cliff in a rage.

SECOND VERSION

Rapidly, vast waves rolled in. Each was the size of a house. They were close, and as a wave crossed the beach, it would rise even higher. The wave's crest would curl. The curl looked like a question mark. Then, against the foot of the cliff, in a rage, the wave would throw itself.

Which did you perceive as more effective? The first was a carefully crafted passage from *Eye of the Needle* by Ken Follett (1978, 174); the second was a randomly scrambled rewrite. Although the information in both passages was essentially the same, the authors' selections and arrangements of structures created radically different feelings. Follett's passage captured the movement and fury of the waves. The second passage missed the mark.

Scott Rice, in his *Right Words Right Places* (1993), explains how the choice of clause and participle affects meaning:

> As a rule, clausal modification is heavier (but also more emphatic) because it contains a full verb. But a little emphasis goes a long way. Phrasal modification is more graceful and less obtrusive. If we think of a sentence as a drive, a dependent . . . clause is a sharp turn, and a participial phrase a gentle curve. (298)

Rice illustrates this idea by comparing a passage from an unidentified romance novel with his own rewrite. The original subordinates images with *as*, while Rice's revision links images with participles, creating a more powerful flow and a stronger emphasis:

THE ORIGINAL

She seemed to commune silently with spirits only she knew were there as she watched the tall grass rustle softly in the breeze, and felt the warmth of the sun shine down on her wheat-colored hair, as she began to sing softly. (299)

RICE'S REVISION

Watching the tall grass rustle softly in the breeze, and feeling the warmth of the sun shine down on her wheat-colored hair, she seemed to commune silently with spirits only she knew were there, then she began to sing softly. (299)

In addition to altering the meaning of images with choices of structure, writers can also change the flow and emphasis with choices of arrangement as with an inversion. A sentence such as "The runaway colt ran across the field into the woods" can be flipped to throw a spotlight on the colt with "Across the field into the woods ran the runaway colt." Inverting the sentence and placing the colt last focuses the camera on the last image in the sentence and gives it more importance. From these examples, we can understand why Francis Christensen, who spent much of his life examining sentence structures, noted that "solving the problem of how to say, helps deciding what to say" (1967, 5).

Creating Special Effects with a Greek Influence

For categorizing the special effects of structure, nothing matches the work of the ancient Greeks. Yet, rarely are Greek origins mentioned in the classroom. Most teachers introduce concepts like metaphor, simile, and personification, but not many have experimented with structures like the *antithesis, anastrophe, anaphora, antimetabole, polyptoton, zeugma, epanalepis,* or *chiasmus*. These structures, first catalogued by the Greeks, can enrich classroom writing and provide fascinating examples of structure and meaning for students.

Edward Corbett and Robert Connors (1999) have described more than seventy of these alternative structures in their book, *Style and Statement*, and demonstrate how these structural power tools add a rhetorical twist to a writer's ideas. Teaching students a few of the more common devices from this collection can improve awareness and appreciation for arrangement.

For example, if you are teaching S. E. Hinton's *Outsiders*, you might introduce a *zeugma*. A zeugma mixes unlikely images in a parallel structure. A writer might say, "She reached for Jerry's letter and her future." Two nouns are linked, but one is concrete and the other more abstract. Hinton opens *The Outsiders* with this zeugma: "When I stepped out into the bright sunlight from the darkness of the movie house, I had only two things on my mind: Paul Neuman and a ride home" (1967, 9).

Occasionally, intrigued with these contrasting images, students will experiment with them in their own writing. For example, eighth grader Kristen Parker opens her short story "The Eyes of Destiny" with this zeugma: "The wind catches my long auburn hair as I speed forward, away from the shackles of the castle, and toward my destiny—freedom, and perhaps a man with mysterious eyes."

Four Greek categories reoccur in much of the literature read by secondary students, offering frequent opportunities for discussion: the *antithesis*, the *epanalepis*, the *chiasmus*, and the *hyperbole*. The first three rely on the rhythm of the sentence to create emphasis; the last, on an exaggerated image.

The *antithesis* juxtaposes two contrasting ideas using identical sentence structures. In the sentence "If you *loved* the book, you'll *hate* the movie," the writer contrasts two views by contrasting the verbs in structurally similar sentences. This contrast can be done with other parts of speech as in the following example: "Leroy was *easy to like*, but *hard to live with*."

Epanalepis creates an hourglass feel. A sentence ends with the same word that started it, as in "*Kindness* comes to those who show *kindness*."

The *chiasmus* follows a reversible pattern of sentence structure, as in Kennedy's classic line "Ask not what *your country can do for you*, but what *you can do for your country*."

Hyperbole, another common structure, is a sentence that exaggerates an image to emphasis a point, as in these examples:

Sergeant Bolger's stare could crack granite.
A largemouth bass, the size of a Nautilus submarine, broke the water.

Hyperbole seems to be a favorite device of many sports writers. So, sports columns make great sources for classroom analysis. Bob Chieger and Pat Sullivan (1990), who have cataloged hundreds of snappy comments in their *Football's Greatest Quotes*, provide a rich source for hyperboles. Here are a few samples from their collection of comments by writers, players, and coaches:

Jim Murray on Mike Garrett: "He eats more dirt than a gopher. His throat has the fingerprints of every linebacker in the league on it." (215)

John Madden on Louie Kelcher: "If you can block a coke machine, you can block Kelcher." (78)

Lisa Gastineau on Mark Gastineau: "He's like Felix Unger, a total neat freak. He keeps his cereal boxes in alphabetical order." (77)

Mark Whicker on Joe Morris: "A flashbulb has about as much chance of catching him as a linebacker." (217)

Creating Special Effects with Mood Filtering

Special effects of meaning can also be achieved by working with mood. Using a technique he calls *mood filtering*, novelist Kevin Anderson reviews the emotional tone implied by words and phrases in his writing to see if they are appropriate. "You determine the way readers will view a setting or react to a sequence of events, simply by the way you choose to describe it," he explains. "Prose description is analogous to the soundtrack of a movie. How would the audience have reacted to the shower scene in *Psycho* if, instead of using terrifying music, the soundtrack played a frolicking tune lifted from a Walt Disney movie about otters?" (1995, 34).

To transform a dull description into one that moves the reader emotionally, Anderson reads a passage, decides on the dominant mood, and then filters out any words and phrases that are inconsistent. Once he filters, he then adds new images to further enhance the mood. Here are two short passages used by Anderson to illustrate this technique:

UNFILTERED FIRST DRAFT

I'm sitting at my desk in the living room of a suburban townhouse. The walls and doors are painted white; the carpet is tan. (34)

FILTERED SECOND DRAFT

The light bulb flickered, sending stark shadows up and down the walls. The carpet under my feet was brown, earthlike, the color of a freshly turned grave. (34)

The second passage communicates a foreboding tone, the mood that Anderson wanted to suggest. This approach to controlling mood, an idea that originated with Poe's analysis of the short story, can aid those students who paint descriptions indiscriminately.

Creating Special Effects with Tantalizing Titles

One last special effect that teachers can introduce to students is painting titles with appealing grammatical patterns. Short eye-catching title patterns can not only tease the interest of the reader, but also often provide a unifying idea or image for a work. Novelist Nancy Kress (1994) in an article for *Writer's Digest* suggests writers use twelve grammatical patterns to create this effect:

1. Possessive-Noun (*Finnegan's Wake* by James Joyce; *Sophie's Choice* by William Styron)
2. Article/Adjective-Noun (*A Clockwork Orange* by Anthony Burgess; *Jurassic Park* by Michael Crichton)
3. (Article)-Adjective-Adjective-Noun (*Another Marvelous Thing* by Laurie Colwin; "The Romantic Young Lady" by W. Somerset Maugham)
4. Noun-and-Noun (*Love and Work* by Gwyneth Cravens; *Pride and Prejudice* by Jane Austen)
5. (Article)-Noun-of-Noun (*Death of a Salesman* by Arthur Miller; "The Housebreaker of Shady Hill" by John Cheever)
6. Noun-for-Noun ("A Rose for Emily" by William Faulkner; *Requiem for a Heavyweight* by Rod Serling)
7. Prepositional Phrase (*Out of Africa* by Isak Dinesen; *After All These Years* by Susan Isaacs)
8. (Article)-Noun-Prepositional Phrase (*Appointment in Samarra* by John O'Hara; *Catcher in the Rye* by J. D. Salanger)
9. Infinitive Phrase (*To Kill a Mockingbird* by Harper Lee; *To Dance with the White Dog* by Terry Kay)
10. Adverbial Phrase (*Where the Wild Things Are* by Maurice Sendak; "When the Fathers Go" by Bruce McAllister)
11. The-Noun-Who (*The Man Who Melted* by Jack Dann; *The Cat Who Went into the Closet* by Lilian Jackson Braun)
12. A Command (*Remember Me* by Marry Higgins Clark; *Wait Until Dark* by Frederick Knott) (8–9)

Notice how eighth-graders played with these grammatical patterns in their titles:

His Loving Touch	by Shauna Reno
Scavenger Souls	by Tara Wongchaowart
When I'm Old	by Meredith Bucur
Remember This!	by Evan Frederick
Inescapable Time	by Molly Gallagher

A Family's Civil War	by Tina Grothe
Death Net	by Colin Culkin
Golden Betrayal	by Kristin Parker
Two Sides of Death	by Caitlin McNally
December Morning	by Julia Miller
Don't Forget Us	by Meredith MacMillan
Senses of a Storm	by Kate Cooke
An Evening to Remember	by Morgan McKinney
Being Stalked	by Megan McNiff
Arctic Sunrise	by Keir Marticke
Reflections of War	by Maria Verderico
Message from a Spectator	by Colin Culkin
The Winter with No Snow	by Lindsay Trump
Uptight and Scattered	by Phil Eskamani
The Eyes of Destiny	by Kristin Parker
The Pirate Who Stood on the Island	by Lindsay Davis

The grammatical patterns suggested by Kress reinforce conventional concepts of grammatical structures and cause little confusion for students. However, many special effects discussed in this chapter break the well-known rules of grammar. In these instances, author Gary Provost offers an excellent suggestion to help students discriminate:

> When you knowingly use poor grammar, you should ask yourself two questions. The first: Is my meaning clear? If the answer is no, rewrite. The second question: What am I getting in return for poor grammar? If you can't answer that, don't use the poor grammar. (1984, 21)

Provost's guidelines place the burden of correctness on students, urging them to analyze the way they use structures and encouraging them to distinguish between special effects that add to the artistry of writing and ineffective errors that simply violate conventions.

STRATEGIES

Strategy 1: Play with Fragments and Run-ons

Have students imagine a scene where events are almost out of control, such as a boy who is lost in a mall, an athlete making a critical play in a sporting event, a musical performer pushing his abilities beyond the limits, an individual caught in a natural disaster, or a cat being chased by a dog. Ask students to picture as many details as possible about the events—to listen to sounds, to look for details, to smell the aromas or odors, and to feel the texture of objects. Then have each student write a one-paragraph description using fragments and/or run-on sentences to capture the whirl of action.

Before students write, share this description of a stock car crash by Tom Wolfe, taken from *The Kandy-Kolored Tangerine Flake Streamline Baby*.

> The pack will be going into a curve when suddenly two cars, three cars, four cars tangle, spinning and splattering all over each other and the retaining walls, upside down, right side up, inside out and in pieces, with the seams bursting open and discs, rods, wires and gasoline spewing out and yards of sheet metal shearing off like Reynolds Wrap and crumbling into the most baroque shapes, after which an ash-blue smoke starts seeping up from the ruins and a thrill begins to spread over the stands like Newburg sauce. (1963, 30)

Strategy 2: Return to Erasmus

Here is a strategy that dates back to the fifteenth-century scholar Erasmus. Erasmus would give his students this sentence: "Your letter delighted me very much." Then he would ask each member of the class to play with the arrangement and the selection of words to create five new sentences that communicated a similar meaning in different ways. Corbett (Corbett and Connors 1999, 76) states that Eramus' students created a total of one hundred and fifty variations of the sentence and gives these as a few examples:

> Your epistle has cheered me greatly.
>
> Your note has been the occasion of unusual pleasure for me.
>
> When your letter came, I was seized with an extraordinary pleasure.
>
> What you wrote me was most delightful.
>
> On reading your letter, I was filled with joy.
>
> Your letter provided me with no little pleasure. (76)

Try a similar experiment. Divide the class into five teams. Give each team one of the sentences below and ask them to create five variations that communicate the same—or nearly the same—idea. The sentences below are taken from Ashleigh Brilliant's book *Appreciate Me Now and Avoid the Rush*:

> Group 1: Nothing is as good as it used to be—especially my memory. (1993, 132)

Group 2:   Slavery and torture were outlawed long ago, but for some reason, marriage is still legal. (1993, 145)

Group 3:   Tomorrow is another day, but I hope it's not another day like this one. (1993, 124)

Group 4:   The best thing about my lack of progress is that I can't fall back very far. (1993, 117)

Group 5:   Communication with the dead is only a little more difficult that communication with something living. (1993, 95)

Strategy 3: Listen to the Beat of Punctuation

An excellent strategy for teaching punctuation is to train students to hear the natural pauses in writing. As part of his language arts program first published in the 1970s, James Moffett (1968, 1992) developed a punctuation program based on listening. Students silently marked unpunctuated passages while hearing them being read either on tape or by the teacher.

Try this with your students. Distribute copies of Dawson's punctuation hierarchy (on page 95) and copies of the passages below. Emphasize that they are to place marks where they "hear" pauses and stops, using the hierarchy as a guide, as you read the passages A1 and B1 aloud.

PASSAGE A1

We read and studied out of doors preferring the sunlit woods to the house all my early lessons have in them the breath of the woods the fine, resinous odor of pine needles blended with the perfume of wild grapes seated in the gracious shade of a tulip tree I learned to think that everything has a lesson and a suggestion. The loveliness of things taught me all their use indeed, everything that could hum or buzz or sing or bloom had a part in my education noisy-throated frogs katydids and crickets held in my hand I felt the bursting cotton-bolls and fingered their soft fiber and fuzzy seeds I felt the low soughing of the wind through the cornstalks the silky rustling of the long leaves and the indignant snort of my pony as we caught him in the pasture and put the bit in his mouth ah me how well I remember the spicy clovery smell of his breath

PASSAGE A2 (PUNCTUATED)

We read and studied out of doors, preferring the sunlit woods to the house. All my early lessons have in them the breath of the woods—the fine, resinous odor of pine needles, blended with the perfume of wild grapes. Seated in the gracious shade of a tulip tree, I learned to think that everything has a lesson and a suggestion. The loveliness of things taught me all their use. Indeed, everything that could hum, or buzz, or sing, or bloom, had a part in my education—noisy-throated frogs, katydids and crickets held in my hand. ... I felt the bursting cotton-bolls and fingered their soft fiber and fuzzy seeds; I felt the low soughing of the wind through the cornstalks, the silky rustling of the long leaves, and the indignant snort of my pony, as we caught him in the pasture and put the bit in his mouth—ah me! How well I remember the spicy, clovery smell of his breath!

From *The Story of My Life* by Helen Keller (1996, 25)

PASSAGE B1

Of course the ordinary soldiers didn't have much fun for one thing there was the snow it came down in a great blizzard about a week after the troops had started to build their encampment their huts were not finished and they were forced to work in bitter cold and storm the cold was a problem the huts were really just tiny log cabins with big stone fireplaces making the whole rear wall in cold weather they had a lot of trouble getting the mortar to set because of this the chimneys leaked so badly that half the smoke blew back into the room the snow made hewing wood difficult, too Sam told us that they were having an awful time getting the huts finished even when they were done they weren't much to live in twelve soldiers jammed into a 14 by 16 room breathing more smoke than air and having to stumble over people whenever they wanted to move around and the snow never stopped falling by January it covered the countryside three feet deep so that the stone walls disappeared you could drive a sled over the snow anywhere you wanted without paying attention to where the roads were.

PASSAGE B2 (PUNCTUATED)

Of course the ordinary soldiers didn't have much fun. For one thing there was the snow. It came down in a great blizzard about a week after the troops had started to build their encampment. Their huts were not finished, and they were forced to work in bitter cold and storm. The cold was a problem. The huts were really just tiny log cabins with big stone fireplaces making the whole rear wall. In cold weather they had a lot of trouble getting the mortar to set. Because of this the chimneys leaked so badly that half the smoke blew back into the room. The snow made hewing wood difficult, too. Sam told us that they were having an awful time getting the huts finished. Even when they were done they weren't much to live in—twelve soldiers jammed into a 14 by 16 room, breathing more smoke than air and having to stumble over people whenever they wanted to move around. And the snow never stopped falling. By January it covered the countryside three feet deep, so that the stone walls disappeared. You could drive a sled over the snow anywhere you wanted without paying attention to where the roads were.

From *My Brother Sam is Dead* by James Lincoln Collier and Christopher Collier (1974, 177)

Strategy 4: Go Live on Channel Five

Explain to the class that they will be participating in a simulated television sports show. This show gives news on breaking events, but with comments and opinions by the sports commentators. The task of each commentator will be to research and create a commentary on some interesting sporting event in the news.

The only requirement of the commentaries will be to include a hyperbole. (Review the samples presented earlier in this chapter on page 101.) Ask students to search for information from any of these three sources: (1) magazines from the library or home, (2) sports articles in the evening newspaper, or (3) the Internet sources listed below.

ESPN
http://ESPN.SportsZone.com/

CNN / Sports Illustrated
http://www.cnnsi.com/

CBS Sportsline
http://www.sportsline.com/

ABC Sports
http://www.abcsports.com/

Once students have written their commentaries, conduct a "live" sports show in a mock news studio at the front of the classroom.

If you have a colorful local sports reporter who does commentary, videotape a few of his or her broadcasts to use as warm-up models.

Strategy 5: Search for Titles in the Amazon

Using the computer lab in your school or a computer in your classroom, have students go to <http://www.amazon.com> or <http://www.barnesand noble.com>, two of the largest online bookstores. Ask students to browse for works by their favorite authors or authors you have been reading in class. Explain that they will need to conduct a "search" by author.

Have each student locate five examples of titles that match the grammatical patterns described earlier by Kress, and then share these in class, discussing those that seemed effective and those that seemed ineffective.

6
Toward a Grammar of Passages
Linking Images Beyond the Sentence

CONCEPTS

Mina Shaughnessy in *Errors and Expectations* comments, "The mature writer is recognized not so much by the quality of his individual sentences as by his ability to relate sentences in such a way as to create a flow of sentences, a pattern of thought that is produced, one suspects, according to principles of yet another kind of grammar—the grammar, let us say, of passages" (1997, 226). Unlike the popular notion that limits grammar to words and sentences, Shaughnessy suggests that grammar extends well beyond these limits.

Exploring a Grammar of Passages

In a traditional context, a grammar of passages seems unnatural; however, when one views grammatical concepts as tools of the artist, extending the definition of grammar is necessary for understanding the wholeness of a writer's work of art. In the act of creation, the writer, like the artist, rarely makes decisions in isolation, but views words, sentences, paragraphs, and passages as a whole, each indispensably interconnected.

Several scholars have attempted to pioneer a grammar of passages—most notably, Richard Coe (1988), Chris Anderson (1992), Paul Rodgers (1966), and Francis Christensen (1966). However, their attempts have been complicated by one problem: the definition of the paragraph.

To understand their dilemma, try this experiment. Below is an excerpt from *Tiger Eyes* by Judy Blume. Read the passage and jot down on a separate piece of paper the words where you think each new paragraph begins:

I have learned plenty about the dynamics of this school in just two weeks. For one thing, everyone is classified by groups. There are Coneheads, Loadies, Jocks, and Stomps. Coneheads are into computers and wear calculators strapped to their belts. They are carbon copies of their fathers, grinding away for the best grades so that they can go to the best colleges. Loadies are into booze and drugs and there is plenty available. You can buy whatever you want out of the trunk of a car in the parking lot. Jocks are jocks. Every group makes fun of every other group. Coneheads laugh at Jocks. Jocks laugh at Loadies. Loadies laugh at Stomps. Stomps dress in ten-gallon hats and cowboy boots. They chew tobacco and spit and ride around in pickup trucks, looking for fights. I know that I will never fit here. Of course, there are other kids like me, other kids who don't fit in either. There is a girl, Ann, who screams in the hallways. I can't figure her out. Maybe she realizes the futility of trying to fit in, just as I do. There are guys who aren't really Coneheads, but who aren't anything else either. And it's tough on them. Because the kids here are very into putting down anybody and anything that is not exactly like they are. I sometimes think it would be terrific if all of us who don't fit in formed a group called Leftovers. Then we could get together and laugh our heads off at the Stomps, Loadies, Jocks and Coneheads. (1981, 94–95)

Do not continue until you have identified the paragraph breaks.

Blume divided her passage into three paragraphs. The first, of course, begins with "I have." The second begins with "I know that," and the last with "There are guys." If you had difficulty, you can take some solace in knowing that the problem of paragraphing has stumped scholars for decades. In the early seventies Columbia professor Arthur Stern enjoyed teasing his college students with a similar challenge. Dr. Stern would ask students to paragraph a 500-word passage from Brooks and Warren's *Fundamentals of Good Writing*.

What might seem like a simple task stumped his students. Out of the hundred who attempted the task only five managed to match the original. Ordinarily, the result of the experiment might not seem surprising—especially with a group of college freshmen. However, the students in Stern's experiment were all postgraduate English teachers (Stern 1976, 253).

From this experiment Stern concluded that the popular notion of the topic sentence paragraph was a myth, a fantasy that lacked validity when tested with professional writing samples and educated readers.

Other scholars have noticed the same inconsistency with paragraph structure. William Irmscher found that in paragraphs written by professionals, 50 to 80 percent did not contain a topic sentence (1979, 222).

Braddock found that a little less than half of the expository writing samples he examined contained a topic sentence and added that of these, only 13 percent of topic sentences came at the beginning of the paragraphs (1974, 301). Richard Meade and Geiger Ellis analyzed paragraphs from the *Saturday Review*, the *English Journal*, and the *Richmond Times-Dispatch* and discovered that 56 percent of the paragraphs were not developed by any of the traditional methods of development (1970).

Apparently, the notion of topic sentences originated in 1866 with Alexander Bain, a Scottish logician. Bain wrote a book entitled *English Composition and Rhetoric* in which he argued that paragraphs should always follow a strict logical pattern, one in which supporting examples followed a topic sentence. Of course, in the mid-nineteenth century statistical research was not a common tool for logicians, so Bain never tested his hypothesis against an extensive sample of paragraphs written by professionals. Instead, he developed this concept using logical relationships devised by Aristotle. Subsequent authors relied on Bain's analysis, and the topic sentence paragraph along with Aristotle's categories of development (proofs, examples, cause and effect, comparisons, process, and narration) soon became dogma.

So where does this leave Lena Holcheck, the twenty-year veteran English teacher who has been teaching traditional models throughout her career? How does she begin to teach a grammar of passages? Does she abandon a topic sentence program that seems intuitively beneficial, an approach that she and her colleagues have relied on for decades? Not entirely. Teachers know that in a well-written piece, while paragraphs often lack a topic sentence, they always make a point. This point supports either the main idea of a passage or the controlling idea of the entire piece.

For example, examine the following five paragraphs by writer Erma Bombeck from her essay on living cheap:

> By having coupons I got an extra carton of cat food, an extra bucket of swimming-pool chemicals, an extra carton of infant strained lamb, and a huge savings on calf's liver.
>
> The only problem was we didn't have a cat, a swimming pool, or a baby, and we all hated liver.
>
> Double stamp hours made a lot of sense. If I went to the store between 7:30 and 7:45 on a Wednesday morning following a holiday and was among the first ten shoppers to buy the manager's special and come within two minutes of guessing when the cash register tape would run out on the express-lane register, I'd receive double stamps, which when the book was filled would give me ten cents off a jar of iced tea that made my kidneys hurt.

I licked and pasted until the family said my mouthwash just wasn't cutting my glue breath.

I tried creative things with my leftovers, disguising everything with a blanket of cheese and a sprinkling of parsley to kill the taste. (1979, 130)

This mix of ideas doesn't fit the conventional topic-sentence paragraph mold. Only the second paragraph contains a topic sentence, and four of the paragraphs are only one sentence long. However, each passage describes attempts to save money by living inexpensively. All of the ideas support the main thesis of the essay, which makes fun of schemes to save money with bargains and shortcuts. This larger unity—beyond the points made by individual paragraphs—creates the essential structure.

A paragraph is not a closed entity but is related to paragraphs before and after it, part of an organic whole. Consequently, writers create paragraphs in context, and that context often doesn't require topic sentences. In this sense a single paragraph might be compared to a random bar of music in a musical score. Without seeing the entire composition, the selected notes have no context. Each passage derives meaning from the melody. Similar unifying elements are found in every art form.

Behind every painting, behind every sculpture, behind every musical score lies a controlling idea that unifies the art. Mortimer Adler explains:

> Everyone, I think, will admit that a book is a work of art. Furthermore, they will agree that in proportion as it is good, as a book and as a work of art, it has a more perfect and persuasive unity. They know this to be true of music and paintings, novels and plays. It is no less true of books which convey knowledge. (Adler and Van Doren 1940, 78)

If we agree with Adler that the writer's art has a persuasive unity, then we should be able to track the footprints of that unity through paragraphs, passages, and complete works. The structural elements of a genre should suggest a grammar for that art form.

Tracking a Grammar of Passages in Exposition

The footprints of unity in nonfiction can be found in the predictable patterns of expository text. Although the specific lists by scholars differ slightly, Vacca and Vacca (1996) state that five logical patterns are identified in most studies of exposition. These include description, sequence, comparison-contrast, cause and effect, and problem-solution. English scholars recognize these same patterns, but expand the list with slightly different terms, which are detailed in Chapter 8.

Both English and reading teachers have used these patterns for years as a partial grammar of passages to teach both reading and writing, and the research has supported this practice. Flood, Lapp, and Farnan (1986) demonstrated that teaching expository structure helped students not only write more clearly, but also helped them understand more difficult text structures when reading. Horowitz (1987) found that using text patterns helped students interpret information more accurately by providing a predictable format.

Text patterns help students visualize the canvas of the entire piece of writing. The logical shapes allow teachers and students to see the whole, the logic of passages weaving a controlling idea. Sometimes, teachers highlight these shapes with drawings that give form to text, called *graphic organizers*.

Graphic organizers "are visual illustrations of verbal statements" (Jones, Pierce, and Hunter 1988, 20). When a coach diagrams a play, he or she is using an image that represents smaller explanations. When a teacher charts the arguments of an essay on a chalkboard, he or she uses an image to show the logical relationship of numerous paragraphs. Both the coach and the teacher use a visual to explain blocks of text.

Look at Figure 6–1. These two graphic organizers represent two approaches to a comparison-contrast paper. The top graphic represents a paper in which the writer uses several paragraphs to compare and then follows with several paragraphs that contrast. The second graphic illustrates a paper in which the writer mixes one comparison with one contrast in each paragraph.

Jones, Pierce, and Hunter, who have illustrated a number of designs for graphic organizers, point out that, "A good graphic representation can show at a.glance the key parts of a whole and their relations, thereby allowing a holistic understanding that words alone cannot convey" (21).

Painting Passages Using Christensen's Approach

Another approach to a grammar of passages that can also be represented with graphic organizers is that of Francis Christensen. In his *Notes Toward a New Rhetoric*, Christensen charted sentences and paragraphs on levels of generality like steps on a stairway with the most general image at the top and the most specific images at the bottom.

Levels of generality in fiction and nonfiction, argues Christensen, come in six shapes. Of these six, three shapes—the coordinate sequence, the subordinate sequence, and the mixed sequence—provide starting points to

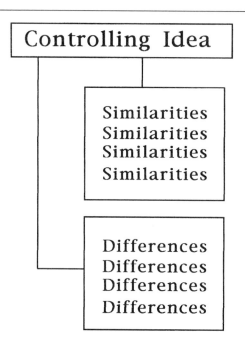

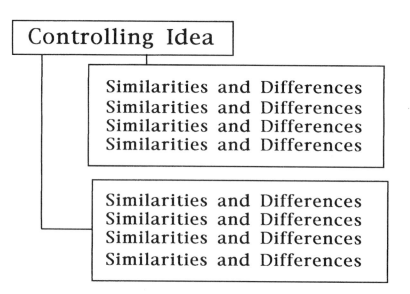

FIGURE 6–1. Two graphic organizers for comparison and contrast

help students make a transition from painting one-sentence brush strokes to painting passages. Viewed almost like a canvas as in Figures 6–2, 6–3, and 6–4, these graphic patterns illustrate a logic found in sentences, paragraphs, as well as entire works.

The Coordinate Sequence

As illustrated in Figure 6–2, the coordinate sequence is developed on two levels: a controlling idea (thesis in a long work, topic sentence in a paragraph) followed by several items of direct support. With paragraphs, the logic behind this design follows a topic sentence paragraph structure, which has caused some critics to question Christensen's entire approach. However, the last three of Christensen's sequences—a sequence without a controlling idea, a sequence with extraneous sentences (transitions, introductions, conclusions), and an incoherent structure—account for variations.

For students, the value of studying the coordinate sequence is not that it reinforces topic sentence development, but that it provides a miniature model of one type of logic found in larger works. A typical example of a coordinate sequence is this paragraph by eighth grader Brad Hannah:

> Underdogs were plentiful in 1997, but the greatest surprise of the tournament was the success of the Arizona Wildcats. Coming into the field as a number four seed, they won in the first round and then beat the 24-3 College of Charleston in the second round. Heading into the third round, the Wildcats faced top-ranked Kansas, the favorite of many to take the tournament. Pulling off that victory, they sailed into the finals to face the returning champions, Kentucky and Rick Petino. Triumphantly winning the championship, Arizona shocked the world as Miles Simon poured in 30 points and earned the right to cut the net down.

The Subordinate Sequence

Another model of a larger logical shape is Christensen's subordinate sequence (see Figure 6–3). The subordinate sequence is a pattern in which each succeeding step adds detail—not to the controlling idea—but to the previous step. A one-sentence passage from Ray Bradbury's "A Sound of Thunder" shows this logical progression on a simple level:

Level 1   Each lower leg was a piston,
      Level 2   a thousand pounds of white bone,
            Level 3   sunk in thick ropes of muscle
                  Level 4   sheathed over a gleam of pebbled skin like the mail of a terrible warrior. (1968, 210)

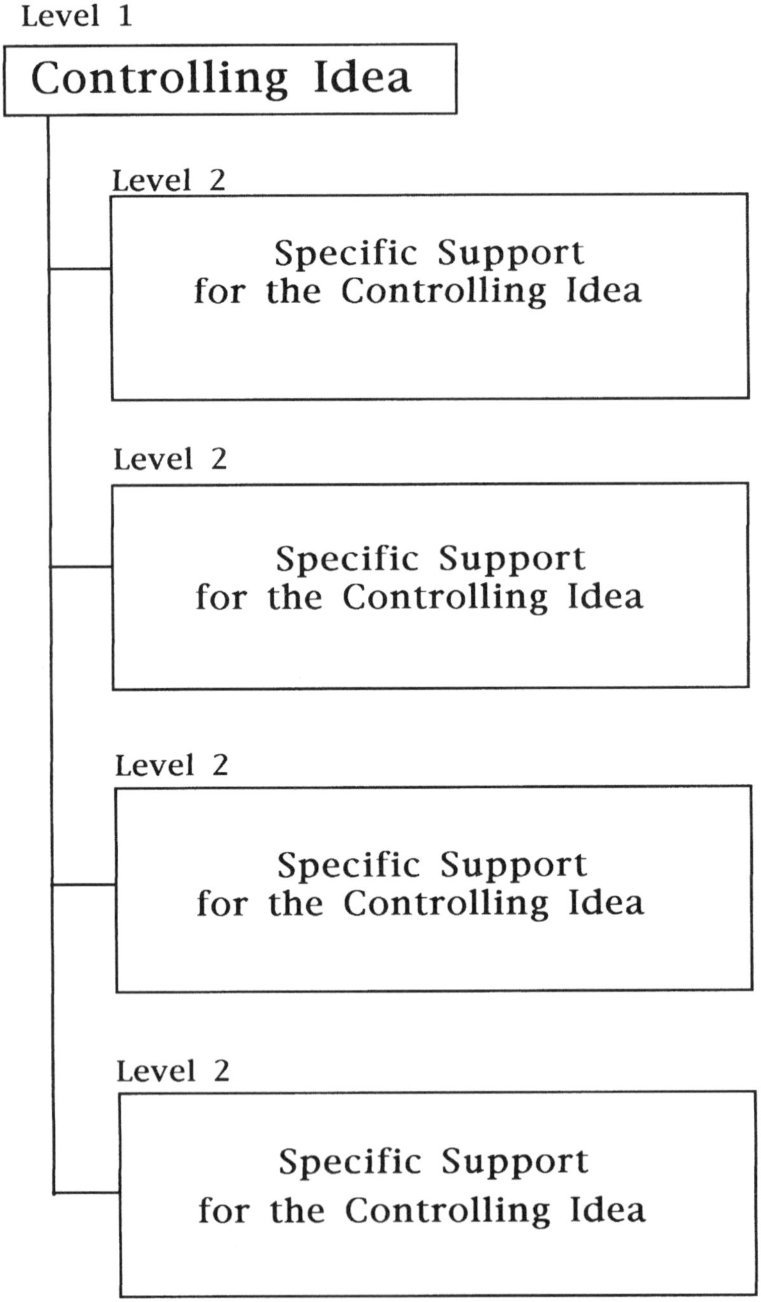

Level 1

| Controlling Idea |

Level 2

| Specific Support
for the Controlling Idea |

Level 2

| Specific Support
for the Controlling Idea |

Level 2

| Specific Support
for the Controlling Idea |

Level 2

| Specific Support
for the Controlling Idea |

FIGURE 6–2. A coordinate sequence

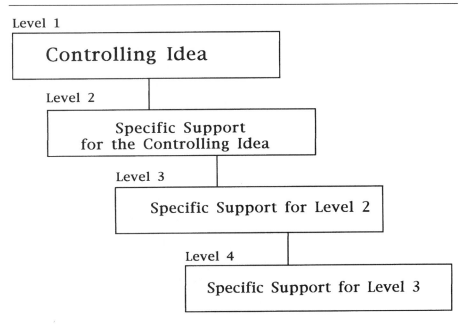

Level 1

Controlling Idea

Level 2

**Specific Support
for the Controlling Idea**

Level 3

Specific Support for Level 2

Level 4

Specific Support for Level 3

FIGURE 6–3. A subordinate sequence

The Mixed Sequence

Although a writer's imagination sometimes unfolds images and ideas in coordinate or subordinate patterns, more often, they create mixed sequences—another Christensen model (see Figure 6–4). This unfolds ideas in a zigzag pattern, mixing levels of support. For example, observe how John Steinbeck takes the reader on a zigzag image journey, moving from level 1 to level 2 to level 1, back to level 2 and on to level 3 in this passage from *The Red Pony*:

Level 1 Then Jody stood and watched the pony, and he saw things he had never noticed about any other horse,

   Level 2 the sleek, sliding flank muscles and the cords of the buttocks, which flexed like a closing fist, and the shine the sun put on the red coat.

Level 1 Having seen horses all his life, Jody had never looked at them very closely before.

   Level 2 But now he noticed the moving ears which gave expression and even inflection of expression to the face.

   Level 2 The pony talked with his ears.

Level 2   You could tell exactly how he felt about everything by
the way his ears pointed.
Level 3   Sometimes they were stiff and uptight and
sometimes lax and sagging.
Level 3   They went back when he was angry or fearful, and forward when he was anxious and
curious and pleased; and their exact position indicated which emotion he had.
(Steinbeck 1973, 25)

In the first sentence of this excerpt, Steinbeck sets up the main idea on
level one, explaining that Jody "saw things he had never noticed about any
other horse." Then, in the same sentence he adds specific examples at level
two. Next, with "Having seen horses . . ." Steinbeck returns to the first
level. The next three sentences return to the second level to illustrate the
expressiveness of the pony's ears. Finally, he concludes by zooming in to add
close-up shots of the ears with detailed images at level 3.

The coordinate, subordinate, and mixed sequence offer simple models
to help students see three logical patterns. Teachers can begin with activities using coordinate sequences, experiment with subordinate sequences,
and then move to mixed patterns. For example, after introducing samples of
tight coordinate sequences, a teacher could follow with a mixed sequence
containing just a slight digression to level three details. This paragraph from
Annie Dillard's *Pilgrim at Tinker Creek* follows this pattern:

Level 1   Other interesting things are going on wherever there is shelter.
Level 2   Slugs, of all creatures, hibernate, inside a waterproof
sac.
Level 2   All the bumblebees and paper wasps are dead except
the queens, who sleep a fat, numbered sleep, unless a
mouse finds one and eats her alive.
Level 2   Honeybees have their own honey for fuel, so they can
overwinter as adults, according to Edwin Way Teale,
by buzzing together in a tightly packed, living sphere.
Level 3   Their shimmying activity heats the hive;
Level 3   they switch positions from time to time so
that each bee gets its chance in the cozy
middle and its turn on the cold outside.
Level 2   Ants hibernate en masse;
Level 2   the woolly bear hibernates alone in a bristling ball.

Level 2   Ladybugs hibernate under shelter in huge orange clusters sometimes the size of basketballs. (1974, 48–49)

The value of these three logical sequences for students is that they offer explanations for essays like the Erma Bombeck example used earlier, in which individual passages of one or two sentences fill a logical slot and support the controlling idea.

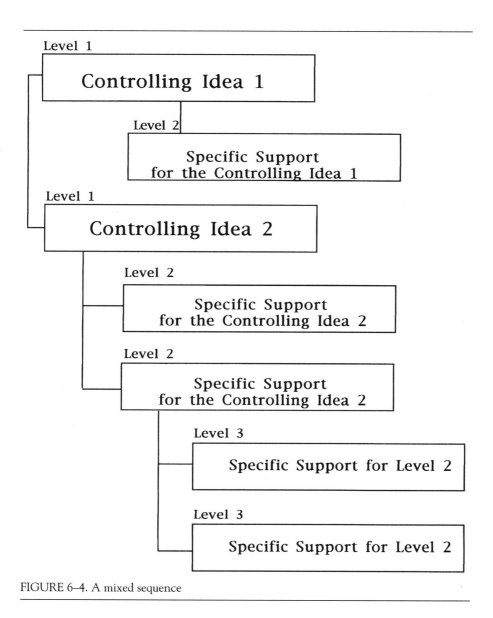

FIGURE 6–4. A mixed sequence

Introducing Logical Shapes with Periodic Passages

Working with students, teachers can introduce logical shapes with periodic paragraphs. A periodic technique, introduced with sentences in Chapter 3, delays the unifying punch line until the end. It is the reverse of Christensen's coordinate sequence. Instead of the controlling idea at the beginning, it comes last. Here is an example from a short essay by middle school student Maria Verderico. Notice how her surprise ending unifies the earlier images.

MY DOG OREO

My dog Oreo is not like any other dog you've seen. His eyes—big, warm, and friendly—almost seem to talk to you. When I'm upset, all I need to do is look into his eyes. They always seem to know what's going on, when in reality, the poor dog probably has no clue.

But, there's a comfort to him. His fur, a soft pillow, is black and white. I don't remember the last time Oreo kept his tongue fully enclosed in his mouth either. It constantly hangs over his bottom lip like a clothesline supporting a pair of pants. There's a certain look to his face that makes it seem like he's always smiling. His tail wags every time he sees me.

Whenever I need someone to listen, I turn to Oreo. Whenever I need a shoulder to cry on, I turn to Oreo. Whenever the whole world seems against me, I turn to Oreo. He always listens, soaks up the tears, and is never against me. There's something about him that always makes me feel better. You can never be lonely when he's around. It's almost like living with a small child.

So, there he is, my dog, Oreo—someone to turn to, someone to play with, someone who never lets you feel useless. There's just one thing I forgot to mention about him. He's not real.

This periodic form, of course, is not limited to single paragraphs or to nonfiction. Fiction abounds with short stories, novels, and plays structured with endings that generate a unifying surprise. Some short examples that work well as classroom models include Ambrose Bierce's "Occurrence at Owl Creek Bridge," Ray Bradbury's "Mars Is Heaven," Shirley Jackson's "The Lottery" and many of O'Henry's stories.

Introducing Logical Shapes with a Photo Shoot

Models such as these can help students understand how all parts of a work contribute to the whole. Teachers can also help students explore

Christensen's logical shapes by having them imagine that they are photographers on a photo shoot. After picking a location for the shoot (gym, athletic event, concert, lunchroom, televised event), the student visits the scene, observing as many images as possible. Next she or he decides what single impression the scene conveys, and then captures the images in a description that supports the single impression.

This exercise creates one or more paragraphs in which the impression serves as the controlling idea at level one and the still observed images create support at levels ranging from two to four. Visually, this is similar to a photographer collecting still photos (long shots and close-ups) for a thematic exhibit. Notice how this works with middle school student Emelia Hiltner's description of Tara Lipinski, based on images of Tara's gold metal Olympic performance:

> Tara Lipinski skated passionately. Her arms moved in perfect rhythm with the music. Her legs swung furiously, back and forth, gaining speed and momentum needed for her next jump. Determined to be the best, Tara leaped into the air, spinning and twirling. Timing exact, she landed with a swish, ice spraying out beneath her flashing skates.

In Emelia's description, the first sentence establishes the impression of Tara skating passionately, and then the sentences that follow support the impression with detailed images at different levels of generality.

The photo shoot strategy not only makes students aware of the importance of observed images, but also helps them add details with imagined images. In this paragraph, student Meredith Bucur paints an impression mixing the observed and imagined:

> An elderly man sits next to the creek. Heart aching, eyes watering, he thinks of his deceased wife, touching the water as if it were part of her. The water, calmer of people, helps comfort the man. It sheds tears for him as it streams along by his fingers. Slipping silently, the water leaves him to think.

Author and teacher Mina Shaughnessy used a variation of the photo shoot. Working with struggling college freshmen, she had success giving students collections of related photographs and asking them to form some conclusions about the images they were observing. Next, she asked students to develop short papers based on their generalizations, using details they had observed.

Shaughnessy explained that she motivated her students with photographs "so the shift from observation to generalization [would be] as sharply drawn as possible" (1977, 246). Here are descriptions of the slide collections she used, and sample generalizations reached by her students:

> *Slide group showing couples*
> Old couples sometimes look more like brother and sister than man and wife.
>
> *Slide group showing a variety of pregnant women*
> Not all expectant mothers react the same way to their pregnancy; some are joyful, some are sad, but others are afraid.
>
> *Slide group showing men at war*
> War changes men. Some for better, some for worse.
>
> *Slide group on children*
> Children playing alone can become very involved in an animal or object. (246–247)

Using Stadia to Explain Nontopic Sentence Sequences

Photo shoots usually create paragraphs and passages that follow logical patterns. However, teachers need to help students understand those paragraphs (better termed *passages*) that lack a clear topic sentence structure. These passages fall into two categories: they are either partial paragraphs that support a controlling idea or transitional passages that link sections of a piece.

In a symposium published in *College Composition and Communication*, both Christensen (1966) and Rodgers (1966) suggested redefining blocks of text as *stadia* (Christensen preferred the term *sequence*) to accommodate passages that didn't fit the definition of a paragraph. A *stadia* would represent any block of text—whether it included two paragraphs or one half of a traditional paragraph or a supporting passage that failed to meet the requirements of a paragraph.

With this conceptual framework, blocks of text would be viewed in the context of a work's controlling idea, instead of in the context of the internal structure of the paragraph. Those who write news already work from this perspective. Although motivated by mechanical considerations of appearance, by substituting one- to two-sentence passages for paragraphs, news writers have identified the critical element in prose as—not the paragraph—but the controlling idea.

Feature writers Clay Schoenfeld and Karen Diegmueller explain that "the number one principle in achieving readable exposition is simply this: Keep your objective uppermost in mind. . . . The question you must continually answer is 'What exactly am I trying to say?'" (1982, 160). The point is that news writers ask this question in relation to an entire work, not in relation to each isolated paragraph.

This concept helps students feel comfortable creating paragraphs that support a thesis but lack topic sentence development. For example, here are two paragraphs from an article written by middle school student Lauren Passell. Neither paragraph follows the traditional topic sentence/support design common to expository prose; but both paragraphs support the controlling idea, which describes the life of mystery novelist Terry White:

> Once, Terry was asked to write a short story involving a cat. Her story, along with others written by other authors, was going to be put in a collection. But when she sent it to the company, the story was lost along the way, and Terry was not paid. The company said that they were making a new collection about hit men, and she could just change her cat story to involve a hit man. "I made the change, but readers were probably thinking 'what's this cat doing in the story?'" Terry said.

> In the middle of our lunch conversation, Terry pulled out some of her books written in Japanese. Her novels are popular all over the world. Terry said, "I am pen pals with a girl from Japan. She writes to me after she reads one of my books. I love getting fan mail, but I don't very often. There are usually about three people who write to me more than once in one year. I respond to every fan letter I get."

Using Jon Franklin's Image Cluster Approach

Although he doesn't call it a grammar of passages, two-time Pulitzer Prize–winning journalist Jon Franklin suggests a similar approach to painting passages, but one based on unifying images. For Franklin, clusters of images not only create unity and coherence, but also provide a written work's basic building blocks. In *Writing for Story*, Franklin explains the relationship this way:

> Atoms are necessary to living things, insofar as they make up the molecules of life. Without them there's nothing. But it's the interaction of molecules, and not of individual atoms, that gives rise to the complexity of biology. Likewise, in literature it's "molecules" of words and not the individual words themselves, that impart life and vitality. We call this literary molecule the image. (1986, 94)

Franklin's molecule is a simple image—the smile on the face of a child building a castle of blocks, the twisted wrinkle in the eyes of an elderly woman being told she has breast cancer, a young guitarist lost in the rhythms of a blues tune.

From simple images like these, Franklin creates clusters, which he terms "focus images"—paragraphs and passages bound by actions and emotions. Focus images in turn join to form scenes—large blocks of prose, the planets in Franklin's universe. What began with a molecular image as simple as a vagrant standing in the snow next to the curling steam from a city laundromat, becomes an article on the homeless.

Franklin's universe of images might be combined with Christensen's sequences and represented in models like those in Figures 6–5, 6–6, and 6–7. Franklin's emphasis on images makes his model a natural fit with Christensen's sequences for sentences and paragraphs.

Franklin cautions beginning writers about missing the focus images in his model. Too many beginning writers, notes Franklin, will paint a summary instead of focusing first on one small image. For example, summarizing the reaction of a crowd of onlookers at an apartment fire isn't nearly as powerful as beginning with an image like the face of an elderly woman watching flames rip through the windows of her apartment. Without the molecular focus of small images, the galaxy of prose unravels into cosmic fog.

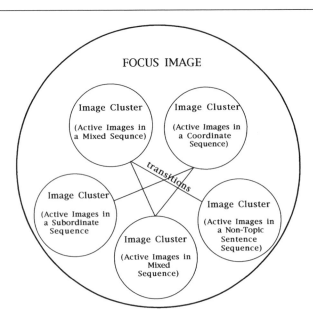

FIGURE 6–5. Franklin's focus image

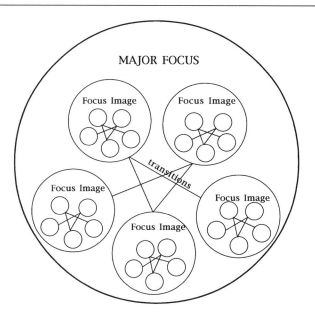

FIGURE 6–6. Franklin's major focus

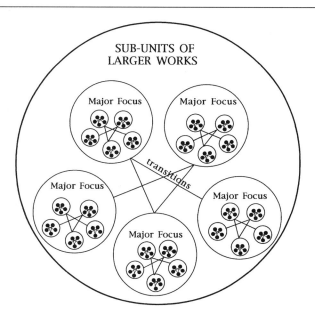

FIGURE 6–7. Franklin's sub-units of larger works

Connecting Images with Transitions

In his image approach to painting passages, Franklin emphasizes a component that many students treat casually: the use of transitions. For Franklin, connecting image clusters is as important as creating them (96). Transitions are the major expressways of Franklin's universe. They enable a quick flow of images from one central hub of activity to another. They bridge the flow of ideas from passage to passage.

Transitions between images and ideas can take two forms: (1) transitional words and short phrases that flash and clang like signals at a train crossing, and (2) subtle logical links that are almost imperceptible, often hidden in the middle of a sentence.

Transitional Signal Words and Phrases

Those words in the train-crossing category can be grouped as follows.

Addition: moreover, in addition, furthermore, also, and, too, again, and then, moreover, further, indeed, plus, likewise, besides, jointly, still, equally important, in the first place, next.

Contrast: however, on the other hand, on the contrary, in conclusion, still, nevertheless, regardless, instead, in spite of, but, yet, conversely, although, unlike, be that as it may, but at the same time, despite, even so, even thought, however, in contrast, notwithstanding.

Comparison: similarly, also, equally important, in the same way, also, comparably, equally, like, in the same way.

Emphasis: in fact, indeed, of course, after all, actually, certainly, perhaps, surely, naturally, really, to be sure, in truth, very likely, undoubtedly, assuredly without fail, truly, of course.

Examples: for example, for instance, specifically, mainly, that is, thus, an illustration of, even, in fact, to illustrate.

Place: above, at, below, around, near, nearby, beyond, in, opposite, adjacent to, under, next to, to the right, north of, east of, west of, south of, elsewhere, farther on, here, on the other side.

Pronoun Reference: this, that, those, these, he, she, it, you, they, we, such, some, many, none.

Restatement: in other words, in short, in summary, that is, again.

Result: therefore, consequently, as a result, accordingly, thus, for this reason, on this account, it follows that, hence, so, necessarily, otherwise, then.

Series: first, second, third, next, again, last, primarily, secondarily, in the first place, in the second place, finally, additionally, first and foremost, the former, the latter.

Summary: in conclusion, on the whole, all in all, in summary, finally, all in all, altogether, in brief, in other words, in short, therefore.

Time: first, second, third, next, the next morning, last, last night, finally, afterward, now, then, again, soon, formerly, eventually, subsequently, when, during, after, following, before, after a while, at last, at length, earlier, immediately, in the meantime, in the past, lately, later, an hour later, later that afternoon, presently, shortly, shortly before, at the same time, since, so far, thereafter, until.

Having students develop ideas from a list of transitions can improve student performance in timed exams such as proficiency tests. However, as students mature and experiment, teachers may want to encourage more subtle transitions, those that blend unnoticed in the writing. Author Gary Provost compares choosing an effective transition to selecting a getaway car for a robbery: "If you want to get from one place to another without being noticed, you drive a Ford, not a Maserati" (1990, 87).

The Fords of transitions are found at a level beyond one word or short phrase connectors. They occur in the logic of sentences, paragraphs, and passages, hidden in the natural flow of ideas. These subtle transitions can be classified into two categories: those signaled by ideas imbedded in sentences and those (primarily used in fiction) crafted as a sequel.

Transitions Imbedded in Sentences

Transitions from ideas are less obvious than signal word transitions because the words conveying the transition read like a natural part of the text. All of the examples have been taken from Carl Sagan's *Cosmos*.

Repeated Word. To create this transition, the writer repeats a word or a variation of the word. For example, a writer might mention that the ceiling is high and then follow with a comment on height. Or she or he might simply repeat the word high as a link to the next paragraph.

> The astronomers Derral Mulholland and Odile Calame have calculated that lunar *impact* would produce a dust cloud rising off the surface of the Moon with an appearance corresponding rather closely to the report of the Canterbury monks.
> If such an *impact* were made 800 years ago, the crater should still be visible. (Sagan 1980, 85)

Synonyms. Synonyms signal transitions by using a different word or phrase to refer to the same thing. An Olympic sportscaster might refer to "the gymnast" in one passage and create a transition by calling her "an athlete" in the next.

> He [Wallace] offered no *opinion* on microorganisms.
>
> Despite Wallace's *critique,* despite the fact that other astronomers with telescopes and observing sites as good as Lowell's could find no sign of the fabled canals, Lowell's vision of Mars gained popular acceptance. (109)

Whole-Part. With this transition a specific term creates a logical link to a more general term that preceded it.

> Through a break in the clouds of Titan, you might glimpse *Saturn and its rings,* their pale yellow color diffused by the intervening atmosphere. . . .
>
> To examine *the individual particles composing the rings* of Saturn, we must approach them closely, for the particles are small—snowballs and ice chips and tiny tumbling bonsai glaciers, a meter or so across. (162)

General Category-Specific Example. Using a transition similar to the whole-part, writers sometimes follow a categorical word with a specific member of the category.

> We approach *the planets* of our system, languish worlds, captives of the Sun, gravitationally constrained to follow nearly circular orbits, heated mainly by sunlight. . . .
>
> Finally, at the end of all our wanderings, we return to *our tiny, fragile, blue-white world,* lost in a cosmic ocean vast beyond our most courageous imaginings. It is a world among an immensity of others. It may be significant only for us. The *Earth* is our home. (11)

Comparison. Comparison transitions in sentences move the reader with sentences that suggest that two things have a similar significance. These are similar to one-word comparisons, but extended beyond a single word or phrase, resembling an analogy.

> Biology is more like history than it is like physics. You have to know the past to understand the present. (41)

Time. Transitions of time that are constructed with phrases resemble one-word transitions. However, unlike single words, phrases indicating time transitions are buried in the text.

> *Every evening* before Voyager 1's encounter with Jupiter, I could see that giant planet twinkling in the sky, a sight our ancestors have enjoyed and wondered at for a million years. And *on the evening of Encounter* . . . (160)

Question. Using a question can draw readers from one section to another.

> Why is there not a single satellite instead of a ring system around Saturn? (165)

Transitions Crafted as Sequels

Except for transitions of time and place, most mentioned so far occur primarily in nonfiction, linking the natural logic of exposition. Transitions in fiction, however, are more elusive. While writers of fiction use some single word and sentence transitions, more often they rely on a less-obvious technique that novelist Jack Bickham (1993) calls *sequels*.

Bickham believes that stories are composed of scenes—image sequences similar to scenes in a film and not unlike the image clusters described by Jon Franklin. Each scene is tied to another with a sequel, a passage containing four components of a character's response: emotion, thought, decision, and action. Not all sequels include all components, but Bickham claims that in the writing of fiction, most do. The pattern of Bickham's sequel looks like this:

> As she saw Brad slump back in the pilot's seat and the Cessna start to roll, Connie froze with terror. [Emotion] [Thought component skipped.] All she could do was try to take over. [Decision] She grasped the control yoke [Action] and . . . (1993, 58)

Unlike nonfiction transitions that hold ideas with the glue of logic, Bickham sees sequels as a blend of images centered on emotions, actions, explanations, and decisions. The combination creates a smooth flow from scene to sequel to scene. "Often you will see modern novels," he explains, "in which scene causes sequel, which leads into next scene, which causes next sequel, and so on. Indeed, most novelists plan their stories in just this scene-sequel, scene-sequel pattern" (51).

Whether in fiction or nonfiction, transitions create unity and coherence. They are an integral part of the whole and impose a connecting logic on what otherwise might seem like disconnected passages and paragraphs.

A true grammar of passages like a unified field theory may be years in coming. In the meantime, teachers can best help students by teaching them to view sequences of paragraphs, passages, and transitions as part of a controlling idea. Jack Hart, columnist for *Editor and Publisher* magazine, summarizes this well in his advice to writers of magazine articles:

> Any piece of writing that rigidly adhered to it [topic sentence development] would drive readers to the nearest TV Guide. . . . More impor-

tant, always remember to make a final check for paragraph unity and coherence. Does each paragraph deal with one main point or idea? (1998, 22)

STRATEGIES

Strategy 1: Paint Passages from Experiences of Touch

Inside four boxes (each about the size of a computer monitor) place several unusual objects: a fake Halloween nose, an oddly shaped piece of wood, a cloth puppet, some "silly putty," a hank of crepe hair, and other objects that would provide an unusual but interesting tactile experience.

After placing five or six of these objects into each box, seal the boxes with duct tape so that they are impossible to open. Then cut a small hole—just large enough to insert a hand into one end of the box. Over the hole of the box staple a small piece of cloth that's large enough to cover it.

Divide the class into four groups and have students in each group take turns exploring their respective boxes. Instruct students not to squeeze anything in the box too hard—especially if it moves. Follow these procedures:

1. Limit each student to one minute of exploration.
2. Explain that students are not to remove anything.
3. After their turn, have students return to their desks and write their descriptions.
4. Mention that similes and metaphors work well.
5. As students finish writing, give them the option of exploring a second box and writing a second paper for additional points.

As a follow-up, assign students a paragraph about memories of touch. As a model, share with them author Diane Ackerman's passage about smells:

> Nothing is more memorable than a smell. One scent can be unexpected, momentary, and fleeting, yet conjure up a childhood summer beside a lake in the Poconos, when wild blueberry bushes teemed with succulent fruit and the opposite sex was as mysterious as space travel; another, hours . . . on a moonlit beach in Florida, while the night-blooming cereus drenched the air with thick curds of perfume and huge sphinx moths visited the cereus in a loud purr of wings; a third, a family dinner of pot roast, noodle pudding, and sweet potatoes, during a myrtle-

mad August in a midwestern town, when both of one's parents were alive. (1990, 5)

Strategy 2: Construct Titles as Thesis Statements

Earlier we examined methods of generating titles from parts of speech. With nonfiction, titles sometimes imply the controlling idea of an article or essay. On these occasions, the title is often the only statement of a writer's thesis. To help students see how titles can contribute to a logical framework, schedule a period in the library and have them browse through popular magazines, each locating three titles that announce a thesis.

As a guideline, use Harry Crosby's categories of titles taken from *The Shape of Thought* (Bond and Crosby 1978). Crosby explains that titles often unify articles and essays, and he classifies them in four ways:

1. Titles Which Announce the General Subject
   Example: "The Age of Adolescence" by Archibald MacLeish
2. Titles Which Indicate a Specific Topic
   Example: "The Incredible Shrinking Attention Span" by W. B. Park
3. Titles Which Indicate the Controlling Question
   Example: "Can People Be Judged by Their Appearance?" by Eric Berne
4. Titles Which Announce the Thesis
   Example: "We Scientists Have the Right to Play God" by Edmund R. Leech (162–164)

After returning to the classroom, split into groups of four or five to compare titles and create a list of the two best examples in each category. After each group has shared its list, use the collected titles for a bulletin board.

A similar activity, one that could be done simultaneously with the title search, is to have students Xerox one article that develops its title clearly. Collect the articles, and on the following day read one of the best to the class without revealing its title. Ask students to guess the original title before announcing it.

Strategy 3: Draw Conclusions from an Ad Campaign

This strategy is designed to help students understand the logical structure found in most expository paragraphs and themes. Assign students the task of collecting all the print, audio, and video ads they can on a popular product. (So items can be shared, limit the class to a list of nine or ten frequently advertised products, such as Coca-Cola, Pepsi, Taco Bell, Microsoft, IBM, Wendy's, Ford, and Nike.) Assemble all the print ads on tables by product.

As a class, draw some conclusions about the advertising campaign. You might discuss the target audience, the product image, and the false conclusions used by advertisers to lure the audience into accepting as true. In addition, spend a day showing students videos of advertisements on the products.

Afterward, have students write an essay with a thesis relating to one of the ad campaigns. As an option, you might challenge students to imagine that they are from another planet and that the collected advertisements represent the only data they have about the inhabitants of Earth. What conclusions might an alien reach, and what examples from various ads would support those conclusions?

Strategy 4: Evaluate Henry's Paper on the Seasons

Divide the class into four or five small groups and distribute copies of "The Four Seasons." Mention to them that a middle school student wrote this after being given an assignment to describe the seasons. Without commenting on the piece, ask the groups to evaluate the essay for paragraph structure, unity, coherence, and supporting details. Ask students to assign the paper a grade.

THE FOUR SEASONS

There are four seasons in a year, Spring, Summer, Autumn, and Winter, I will begin with Spring. Now we see the ice beginning to thaw, and the trees to bud.

Now the Winter wears away, and ground begins to look green with the new born grass. The birds which have lately been to more southern countries return again to cheer us with their morning song.

Next comes Summer. Now we see a beautiful sight. The trees and flowers are in bloom.

Now is the pleasantest part of the year. Now the fruit begins to form on the trees, and all things look beutiful. In Autumn we see the trees loaded with fruit. Now the farmers begin to lay in their Winter's store, and the markets abound with fruit. The trees are partly stripped of their leaves. The birds which visited us in Spring are now retiring to warmer countries, as they know that Winter is coming.

Next comes Winter. Now we see the ground covered with snow, and the trees are bare. The cold is so intense that the rivers and brooks are frozen. There is nothing to be seen. We have no birds to cheer us with

their morning song. We hear only the sound of the sleigh bells.
(Sanborn 1917, 51–52)

After the class has discussed the merits of this work in small groups and
assigned it a grade, conduct a large class discussion with a spokesperson from
each small group sharing insights. After everyone has had an opportunity to
comment, average the grades given by all the groups. (Chances are that student evaluations will not be high.) Finally, reveal that the piece they graded was written by ten-year-old Henry David Thoreau. If the grade they
assigned was low, you might also add that the piece illustrates that even
great writers have humble beginnings.

Strategy 5: Solve the Gruesome Charles Benchley Murder

Divide the class into groups and explain that each group is a detective team
whose task is to solve the Benchley Murder. Charles Benchley, owner of the
multimillion-dollar Benchley Industries, was found shot to death in the
study of his Loch Side mansion. Tell students they will be competing in
teams to solve the mystery using the particular clues that each team member will receive (see Figure 6–8).

In analyzing the crime, these rules must be followed:

1. Students may not pass the individual clues they receive to other team
   members or line them up on a desk. They may read their clues aloud,
   discuss them in any way they wish, but the physical clues must remain
   in their hands.
2. Students may analyze the evidence any way they wish, organizing
   clues by character, each reading his or her clues, or by some other
   method.
3. When they solve the crime, they must elect a spokesperson to not
   only give the solution, but to also present the evidence that led the
   team to that solution.
4. The team with the correct solution and the most convincing evidence
   will win the game. If two teams should happen to reach the same solution, have the spokesperson write a list of the team's evidence before
   sharing it orally.

Before using this strategy, you will need to Xerox copies of the clue list
in Figure 6–8 so that each team has a complete set, and cut three or four
clues for each detective-participant. Emphasize that the winning team will

be the one with the best support for the correct solution and not the first team to arrive at a solution. Distribute the clues and let the teams begin.

Here is the solution:

> Mike Adams and Mimi Benchley, who had a romantic relationship, conspired to kill Charles for his money. Mike would become a major partner in Benchley Industries and Mimi would inherit a third of the Benchley estate. Mimi and Mike planted the scarf in Benchley's hand to incriminate Buddy.
>
> To further implicate Buddy, they also lied to the police. Mimi falsely said she saw Buddy arriving at the Benchley mansion, and Mike claimed Buddy had threatened Charles.
>
> Just by coincidence Buddy and Roco planned a robbery on the night of the murder. The bartender placed Buddy at the Hot Spot during the time of the crime. Roco passed a lie detector test that cleared him. Buddy refused to take the lie detector test because he didn't want to be implicated in the robbery.

After the spokesperson of each group gives a solution for choosing the guilty individual or individuals, discuss the logical relationship between their conclusion and the evidence given by the group. Point out that this logical relationship is a common pattern in writing.

Mysteries offer some of the best teaching tools for students to internalize the logical framework that holds passages and paragraphs together. Telling students the relationship between a thesis and support isn't nearly as effective as having them experience the process of logic by solving a mystery and then providing a logical explanation.

Charles Benchley, seventy-year-old owner of the multimillion dollar Benchley Industries, was found shot to death in the study of his Loch Side mansion.

Ballistics show that Charles was shot with a rare "Levinger Pistol," recovered at the scene. No fingerprints were found on the weapon. The coroner placed the time of death at 11:00 P.M. on Saturday evening, July tenth.

Mimi Benchley, the twenty-year-old wife of Charles, said she saw Buddy Benchley arrive at the mansion just as she was leaving around 5:00 on Saturday, the day of the murder.

Charles Benchley stipulated in his will that if he died, Mike Adams, his financial advisor, was to be named a major partner in Benchley Industries.

Buddy, the son of Charles Benchley, is in debt for $100,000 from gambling at Jungle Joe's, an illegal casino for high rollers. The casino is operated by several individuals believed to have Mafia connections.

FIGURE 6–8. Clues in the Charles Benchley Murder

Amy Benchley, the daughter of Charles, was at the Hot Spot nightclub Saturday evening with Buddy and another man. The owner of the Hot Spot said Amy was there from five until one in the morning.

Mimi told detectives that she was with Mike Adams, the Benchley investment advisor, reviewing legal documents at the time of the murder. She had stopped there on her way to her sister's, but did not return to the mansion after she left at five o'clock.

Annie Vorst, the cleaning lady, mentioned that two tough-looking characters had recently stopped by the house looking for Buddy. Annie said she never heard Buddy threaten Charles.

Buddy claims that he hasn't seen the murder weapon in years. He said he bought the gun as a gift for his father Charles, who collected weapons. He thought Charles had stored it in a cabinet with his gun collection.

Mike Adams confirmed to detectives that he and Mimi were working on legal and investment issues at the time of the murder. He said she appeared calm and composed. Nothing she said or did, in his estimation, suggested she had just committed murder.

The bartender at the Hot Spot said he is "almost sure" that Buddy was there from about seven until one on the night of the murder. Roco Fritz joined him around midnight.

Buddy told Detective Preston that he never visited his father the night of the murder and never threatened him at any time. He also claimed that didn't know anyone named Roco.

Amy Benchley, the daughter of Charles and brother of Buddy, has been in psychiatric care for years. Her father once had her committed for a year, and she has resented that ever since. Amy said that she often argued with her father, but Buddy rarely did.

Amy told detectives that she heard Rockin Rollins is in deep debt and may sell his house. Mimi Benchley will inherit one-third of the Benchley fortune when the estate is settled. Mimi says she doesn't trust Rockin Rollins and has often seen him wandering about the neighborhood late at night.

The owner of the mansion next door, rap star Rockin Rollins, says he saw two people—a man and a woman—leave the Benchley mansion around 11:15. He couldn't clearly identify either of them since they were some distance away, and the car they drove didn't look familiar.

Amy Benchley will inherit one-third of the Benchley estate now that her father is dead.

Buddy refused to take a lie detector test concerning the events on the night of the murder.

Rockin Rollins told detectives that Charles had a good relationship with Buddy and Amy, although Amy had mental problems. Benchley told him that Amy wasn't dangerous, but at times would lose touch with reality and sometimes not know where she was.

FIGURE 6–8. *continued*

Any family member implicated in the robbery will lose his or her inheritance because of legislation that prohibits criminals from profiting from their crimes.

Roco Fritz saw Mimi leave the house before he went in to burglarize it. This worried him because Buddy said only the old man would be there and that he would be sleeping.

Arny "The Fence" Jackson said Roco Fritz brought several items into his pawn shop—jewelry, three valuable paintings, and some computer accessories. Arny claims he didn't know these were stolen goods.

The bartender at the Hot Spot said two men "who looked like trouble" stopped by the bar a week before the murder looking for Buddy. He noticed that one of the men was carrying a gun.

Roco's prints and Arny's were found on the stolen merchandise. Rockin Robin's fingerprints were found in the study of Charles Benchley.

Annie says she doesn't trust Rockin Rollins. She has seen him outside walking late into the night.

A local art dealer called Detective Preston to tell him that a painting she had purchased from Arny's Pawn Shop might have been stolen from the Benchley mansion. After checking with relatives of Benchley, Detective Preston discovered that the painting was stolen from Benchley. Fingerprints were found on the painting that matched those of Roco Fritz.

The police lab found no fingerprints on the murder weapon.

Buddy will inherit one-third of the Benchley estate now that his father has died.

Annie Vorst, the Benchley cleaning lady, once saw Mimi kissing Mike Adams. Their embrace seemed more than just friendly.

Charles Benchley told Annie that Mimi would be visiting her sister Saturday evening and Sunday. So, she wouldn't need to clean her room Sunday morning.

Roco Fritz admitted robbing the Benchley mansion on the night of the murder, but claims he arrived after Benchley was killed. He didn't discover Benchley's body until he had collected several items.

Annie was once a nun, but left the church to marry.

Roco said that Buddy told him where to go and what to look for and the deal was that they would split the sale of the stolen goods. Roco passed a lie detector test that indicated he did not kill Benchley.

Mimi told Detective Preston that both Amy and Buddy were violent personalities who often lost their tempers quickly.

Buddy's scarf was found clutched in the hand of Mr. Benchley.

Rockin Rollins told police that he and Charles had developed a close friendship, although Charles was much older. Rollins said he often visited Charles just to talk as friends. He mentioned that Charles loved his children despite their problems. Rollins said that Buddy had recently told him he planned to stop gambling and become more involved in the company.

FIGURE 6–8. *continued*

Annie says that when she left the Benchley mansion at 5:00, the only two people left in the house were Mimi and Mr. Benchley.

Mike Adams said that Buddy had asked Charles for money to pay off gambling debts. When Charles refused, Buddy threatened him. Mike explained that Charles told him confidentially that he feared Buddy might harm him, and was considering removing Buddy from his will.

Rockin Rollins was once arrested (but not convicted) for attempted murder. The incident involved a knife fight at a concert when Rollins was 16.

Note: This mystery was designed by Harry Noden.

FIGURE 6–8. *continued*

Strategy 6: Perform a Magic Trick

Solicit three volunteers and ask them to stand in the hallway away from the door until you signal them to return. While the volunteers are in the hall, ask students to take out a sheet of paper and to write instructions on how to perform the magic trick you will demonstrate. Tell them that they need to watch closely but that you will demonstrate the trick several times. Ask students not to place their names on their instruction sheets and not to ask any questions until the entire experiment is over.

Before class you will need to tie the ends of a six-foot piece of rope to form a circle. To prevent students from copying the written instructions that follow, demonstrate the magic trick as you read these instructions silently to yourself.

1. Place the circle of rope around your neck like a necklace (see Figure 6–9).
2. Grab the right strand of the rope in your right hand and loop it once again around your neck, creating a double circle. Pull the rope tight so that a long loop remains on your chest (see Figure 6–10).
3. Next form an X by grasping the left stand of the rope with your right hand and crossing it to your right. This creates the appearance of a figure eight with the X in the center of the "8" at point D in the illustration (see Figure 6–11).
4. Grasp points A and B and fold the circle formed by the bottom of the eight so that point C rests under your chin. This forms one double-rope circle on your chest (see Figure 6–12).
5. Place your head through this circle by clasping both strands of rope at

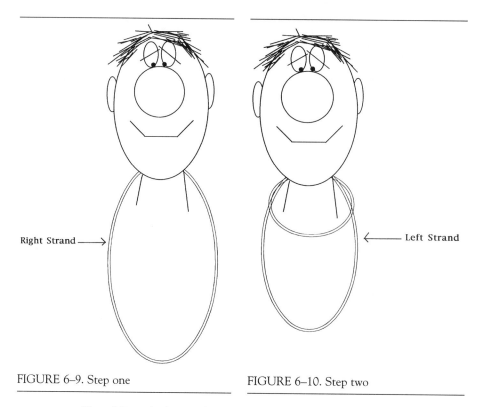

Right Strand ⟶

⟵ Left Strand

FIGURE 6–9. Step one

FIGURE 6–10. Step two

points E and F and placing both strands at H over your head (see Figure 6–13).

6. Announce to the class that you are either going to pull the rope directly through your neck or choke yourself. (It helps to practice!) Grasp any single strand of rope with both hands, grimace, and pull. The rope should pull free. If you slide your hands apart while holding the strand as you pull, you will create the illusion that the rope is penetrating your neck.

After students have written their anonymous instructions, collect them and lay them out on a large table. Have the volunteers return to the class and ask each to pick one set of instructions. Then, ask volunteers to take turns reading their instructions aloud while attempting to perform the trick.

Chances are that the volunteers will have difficulty. Explain to the class that they were tricked. Earlier, by having the class not ask questions, you reduced the chance that someone might pose the question "Can we draw pictures?" Such a question would have motivated everyone to think visually and improved their chances of creating clear instructions.

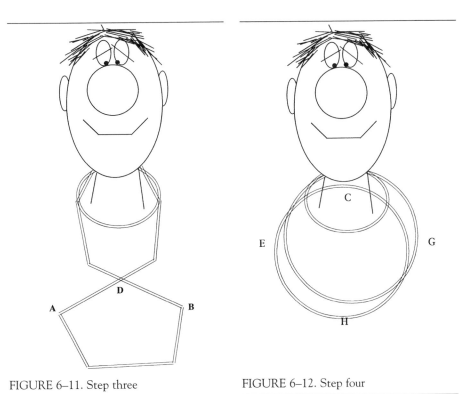

FIGURE 6–11. Step three

FIGURE 6–12. Step four

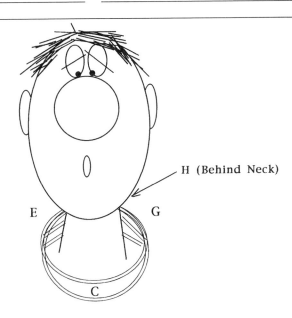

FIGURE 6–13. Step five

Why the deception? The point of the experiment is to show that without images in the instructions (both verbal and graphic), the chances for clear communication are almost impossible.

Strategy 7: Surf with Shaughnessy's Idea

Have students log onto the Yahoo Image Surfer at <http://isurf.yahoo. com/>. They will see six image categories:

1. Arts: Architecture, Landscapes, Painting
2. Entertainment: Comics and Animation, Rock and Pop
3. People: Actors and Actresses, Models
4. Recreation: Computer Games, Sports
5. Science: Animals, Space and Astronomy, Museums
6. Vehicles: Automobiles, Planes, Motorcycles

Using a variation of Shaughnessy's assignment, ask students to pick a category, travel to it, and examine at least ten images. After students formulate impressions from the images, have them write a short paper supporting one generalization about what they saw.

If you wish to use this as a bonus assignment, you might have students download their images and create multimedia presentations combining pictures and text.

7
Story Grammar and Scenes
Shapes for Fiction

"Today class," announced Ms. Elkins to her Advanced Placement English students, "in preparation for our short story unit, we are going to read three comic books."

In a high school or a middle school, most teachers would view such an assignment as inappropriate. Although many teachers are discovering the benefits of using children's books with secondary students, most still discourage students from reading comic books, assuming the cartoon format with limited words offers little to enhance student writing. Yet one of the country's foremost science fiction writers credits comic books for helping him understand the visual structure of stories. In his introduction to the comic-book collection *The Ray Bradbury Chronicles 2*, Bradbury explains how his fascination with visual images gave him an advantage over many Hollywood screenwriters:

> I discovered, later in life, when I began to work for the Hollywood studios, that no other screenwriter had "wasted his time" as a boy cutting out, and saving BUCK ROGERS or TARZAN or FLASH GORDON. No other writer, like myself had written a love letter to Harold Foster, creator of PRINCE VALIANT, telling him he was the greatest thing that charged down the road since the Crusades.
>
> No other writer had ever heard back from PRINCE VALIANT's papa, thanking him and sending on two gigantic PRINCE VALIANT original Sunday pages, four feet high and three feet wide, to be kept as treasures for a lifetime. No other writer had Walt Disney and MICKEY MOUSE for role models.
>
> So when I started out writing at UNIVERSAL STUDIOS, when I was thirty-two, I automatically wrote in metaphors. I could not help

but storyboard my screenplays in my mind as if they were Sunday comic panels. . . . There was no rubbish in my mind, only clear, clean, well-lit images of action and romance. (Gibbons 1992, 4–5)

Bradbury used the storyboards of his imagination as graphic organizers for developing fiction. He laid out plot sequences in blocks of comic book scenes, linking them together in visual story patterns. Bradbury's approach to building stories is not as unusual as it may first seem, for he constructed a visual layout using a fundamental writing and reading tool—a concept called *story grammar*.

With fiction, story grammar is an author's triple-A road map, charting a course from scene to scene. Like any map, it describes only the route, leaving the territory—the countryside, the cityscapes, and the sensory reality—for the traveler to experience. While a road map may be the same for many travelers, each journey is their own.

Understanding How Reading Teachers Define Story Grammar

For decades reading teachers have used story grammar to improve both students' reading and writing skills. Studies by Short and Ryan (1984), for example, suggest that reading comprehension and memory can be improved when students learn story grammar. Other scholars like Fitzgerald and Teasley (1986) conducted studies that indicated story grammar also enhanced student organization in writing. Summarizing the research on story grammar dating from 1975, Fran Lehr (1987) concluded: "One of the most effective ways to promote children's reading and writing skills is to help them develop a sense of story. Teachers can accomplish this through the use of story grammar" (550).

The potential benefits of story grammar makes it an essential teaching tool; however, defining it for students isn't easy. Reading and writing scholars define the term with similar but not identical components. Most reading scholars describe six common elements in story grammar:

1. **An initiating event:** Either an idea or an action that sets further events in motion.
2. **An internal response:** The protagonist's inner reaction to the initiating event, in which the protagonist sets a goal or attempts to solve a problem.
3. **An attempt:** The protagonist's efforts to achieve the goal or alleviate

the problem. Several attempts, some failed, may be in an episode.

4. **An outcome**: The success or failure of the protagonist's attempts.

5. **A resolution:** An action or state of affairs that evolves from the protagonist's success or failure to achieve the goal or alleviate the problem.

6. **A reaction:** An idea, an emotion, or a further event that expresses the protagonist's feelings about the success or failure of goal attainment/problem resolution or that relates the events in the story to some broader set of concerns. (Vacca and Vacca 1996, 257)

Understanding How English Teachers Define Story Grammar

Using very similar concepts, English teachers define story grammar with Freitag's Pyramid, which has been a standard analytical tool for writers since the nineteenth century when it was created by German critic Gustav Freitag.

Through the years scholars have refined Freitag's key terms to more closely represent the typical shape of contemporary fiction. So while there is no "definitive" model, Figure 7–1 shows one composite representation. In this variation, Freitag's symmetrical pyramid is redrawn as asymmetrical to

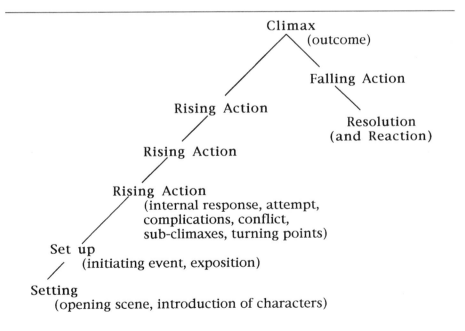

FIGURE 7–1. An adaptation of Freitag's Pyramid

illustrate the quick falling action common in most fiction. Also, synonyms for each label are included to account for variations of terms.

Just like the reading framework for story grammar, Freitag's Pyramid charts the struggle of the main character. First the character is introduced in a setting, and then caught in a situation (the set-up). Sometimes these two components are combined. Next the main character (he, she, or it) strives toward a goal and encounters conflict and complications (rising action). The conflict and complications continue through numerous episodes, depending on the length of the story. As the conflict builds, the main character reaches a crisis in the quest (the climax), and finally moves beyond the climax through falling action that resolves the story (resolution), often with a reaction.

Let's view this in the context of Richard Connell's classic short story "The Most Dangerous Game."

The Setting: The story begins with the introduction of the main character Rainsford, a big-game hunter, traveling on a ship in the middle of the ocean near a mysterious island.

Set-up: The first complication and subclimax occur when a reef rips apart the ship, causing it to sink. Only Rainsford survives, swimming to the shore of the nearby island. Here, Rainsford meets General Zaroff, a Russian soldier, and his servant Ivan, a mute giant.

Rising Action: The action accelerates when Rainsford discovers that Zaroff hunts humans for sport and invites Rainsford to join him. Rainsford refuses.

Turning Point: Zaroff announces that Rainsford will be his next prey and sets him loose on the island with only a knife to defend himself against Zaroff's rifle and hounds.

More Rising Action: Several additional complications and subclimaxes occur during the chase. Zaroff corners Rainsford, but lets him go to continue the hunt. Ivan and one of Zaroff's prize hounds are killed in traps set by Rainsford. The last subclimax comes as Rainsford appears trapped on a cliff and seemingly leaps to his death on the ocean rocks below, thinking he might survive. Zaroff sees no sign of him and assumes Rainsford is dead.

The Climax: When Zaroff returns to the castle, we learn that Rainsford survived his fall and has managed to enter the castle to confront Zaroff. The two men fight in a final climactic scene.

Resolution: Rainsford prevails by forcing Zaroff to plunge to his death off a balcony into a kennel of hungry hounds. This concludes the quick falling action. (No pun intended.)

Reaction: This story ends abruptly without a reaction scene.

The story grammar defined by the Freitag Pyramid is an important concept for fiction. Author Michael Druxman notes that Freitag's Pyramid is essential to any "story, be it a novel, screenplay, dramatic television show, one-act stage play, short story or whatever" and adds that the manuscripts of writers who ignored this primary structure have "wound up in trash cans, bonfires, and at the bottom of canary cages" (1997, 21). If a writer poorly designs the canvas of story grammar, she or he can destroy the effect of some of the most powerful detailed brush strokes.

Painting Plot Patterns

Some authors suggest that writers rely on their imaginations to spin plots. Other authors, like Druxman (1997) and Burroway (1987), encourage writers to build plots using just the basic structure of the Freitag Pyramid. Still others, like Kress (1997) and Tobias (1993), encourage writers to work from *plot patterns,* which are predictable sequences that tend to repeat in most fiction.

While all three approaches can help students, working with plot patterns gives students an added tool for understanding story grammar. Georges Polti (1917) in his classic work identifies thirty-six plot patterns. Robert Tobias (1993) claims that writers use twenty-five basic forms. Nancy Kress (1997) suggests there are thirteen archetypal plots. Although these models differ slightly, they provide students with predictable patterns that repeat in widely different tales. Just as two artists might paint the same cityscape with totally different results, two writers often follow the same plot pattern, yet develop radically different stories.

To help students understand this substructure, teachers can introduce them to a few of the more common patterns such as: (1) The Quest, (2) The Pursuit, (3) The Contest, (4) The Romance, (5) The Revenge, (6) The Mystery, and (7) The Surprise.

The Quest

In a quest plot the main character moves through the Freitag Pyramid in search of some object: a place, a thing, or an idea. *Don Quixote, Treasure Island, Grapes of Wrath*, and *Raiders of the Lost Ark* follow this sequence. The quest can involve a search for something as concrete as a lost will or something as abstract as freedom.

The Pursuit

Ahab pursues Moby Dick relentlessly. Quint pursues Jaws. The Americans and Russians compete to locate and secure the submarine *Red October*. The Alien hunts the astronauts. To chase or be chased is the motto of the pursuit plot. Unlike the quest plot, which deals with a search for an inanimate object or idea, the pursuit involves one character pursuing another.

The Contest

In a contest plot the main character struggles with a rival (person, animal, or nature). The crew members on board several ships struggle against an ocean hurricane in *The Perfect Storm*. Lenningen opposes thousands of army ants in "Lenningen Versus the Ants." The old man struggles to land the marlin in *The Old Man and the Sea*. Rainsford and Zaroff compete to see who will survive in "The Most Dangerous Game."

The Romance

Romance plots involve an obstacle between the lovers. In a *Writer's Digest* article on archetypes, Nancy Kress catalogues a number of the romance obstacles in several works: "Writers have used as obstacles parental disapproval (*Romeo and Juliet*), a preexisting engagement (*Sense and Sensibility*), a preexisting marriage (Edith Warton's *Ethan Frome*), class differences (Willa Cather's *My Antonia*), disagreements about having children (Avery Corman's *Fifty*), indifference on the part of one party (Maugham's *Of Human Bondage*), too-similar natures (Georgette Heyer's *Bath Tangle*), too-dissimilar natures (Philip Roth's *Goodbye Columbus*), strange personal scruples (Thomas Hardy's *Jude the Obscure*), war (Elswyth Thane's *Yankee Stranger*), revolution (Dickens' *A Tale of Two Cities*), murder (Daphne Du Maurier's *Jamaica Inn*), disease (Erich Segal's *Love Story*), abduction by pirates (Anya Seton's *Avalon*), abduction by Bolsheviks (Boris Pasternak's *Doctor Zhivago*), abduction by space aliens (Catherine Asaro's *Catch the Lightning*)—you name it" (1997, 7).

The Revenge

"I'll git you, ya varmit, if it's the last thing I do" is an old cliché found in stories of revenge. Poe's "The Cask of Amontillado," Shakespeare's *Hamlet*, and Stephen King's *Carrie* are a few examples of the revenge plot pattern.

The Mystery

A mystery plot invites the reader to solve a puzzle. Classic works by Arthur Conan Doyle, Agatha Christe, Sue Grafton, and even a few of the short stories of Edgar Allen Poe are built on this pattern. The basic idea is to pose a mystery for the reader, lining the story structure with clues, teasing the reader to match wits with the main character.

The Surprise

The surprise is a story where the ending startles or surprises the reader. Sometimes, as in O. Henry's "Ransom of Red Chief," the surprise is comical. More often it is shocking, as in Ambrose Bierce's "An Occurrence at Owl Creek Bridge." Many short stories developed into episodes for television's *Alfred Hitchcock*, and *The Twilight Zone* used the surprise plot pattern.

Teaching the Art of Scene Writing

Although these patterns represent variations of story grammar, they often establish a huge canvas, one more typical of a novel or a long short story. This poses no problem when students analyze works by professionals. However, without understanding the large scope of a plot pattern, students will often write two page stories with plots more appropriate for three-hundred-page novels. Here is one example of this common problem from an anonymous middle school student:

THE ESCAPE

Roger Zackery jumped into the cockpit of his X-3000 fighter jet, raced down the runway of the airfield in Bogata, and soared into the air. Roger was a member of the CIA on his way to a secret mission to find a smuggling ring in the jungles of South America. Two hours later, as he neared his target, he was hit by artillery fire. The damaged plane swerved toward the trees and Roger had to bail out.

Roger floated to the ground in his parachute. As he landed, he was struck on the head violently from behind. Three days later he awoke in a small wooden jail. His legs and hands were shackled together with a large chain. For two years Roger was a captive in this strange jungle prison where he was tortured and starved, living in horrible conditions. Finally, he saw a chance to escape.

One day, thinking Roger was sleeping, the guard turned his back to Roger's cell and lit a cigarette. Roger reached through the bars, grabbed the guard's neck and choked him unconscious. Using the key in the guard's pocket, Roger freed himself and scrambled into the woods, and three weeks later made his way back to civilization and freedom.

To help students who tend to construct mammoth plots, teachers can encourage them to paint "scenes" instead. The concept of painting scenes, mentioned briefly in Chapter 6, was first described by Walter Campbell

(1950) in his *Writing: Advice and Devices*, and then developed by Dwight Swain (1965) and more recently by Jack Bickham (1993). Bickham describes scene as "the single most important" concept in writing fiction (1996, 93).

A scene, according to Bickham, is "a segment of story action, written moment-by-moment without summary, presented on stage in the story 'now.' It is not something that goes on inside a character's head; it is physical. It could be put on a stage" (1996, 23). Long stories and novels are composed of many scenes. The concept of scene can be understood by recalling a time when a friend described the plot of a movie or book. The friend's summary lacked the power and detail found in the original: it failed to paint scenes, omitting the visual images that created a virtual reality.

Authors write in scenes, but most students tend to write summaries. To help these students learn the art of scene writing, teachers can limit the passage of time in an assigned story. For example, a teacher might require students to write a story that takes place in fifteen to thirty minutes. Or teachers might try the approach of junior high teacher Jay Richards. Richards has his students write 750 words describing a six-second event.

While this may be a difficult time restriction for many, Richards finds the assignment leads to papers that are "focused, detailed, and rich with character reflection and sensory imagery" (1998, 30). Other teacher/scholars have also found success with this approach and have given it a variety of labels. Gary Hoffman calls this approach "Splitting the Second" (1986, 77); Barry Lane refers to the technique as "Explode the Moment and Shrink a Century" (1993, 65).

Restricting time illustrates the influence of form on grammatical structure. A short scene compels writers to use brush strokes that zoom in on details. A long story, especially if written by students in a few pages, invites image blanks, that is, words and phrases that generalize. Observe how Robin Cook restricts the passage of time to create powerful images in the opening of *Outbreak*:

> A twenty-one-year-old Yale biology student by the name of John Nordyke woke up at dawn at the edge of a village north of Bumba, Zaire. Rolling over in his sweat-drenched sleeping bag, he stared out through the mesh flap of his nylon mountain tent, hearing the sounds of the tropical rain forest mixed with the noises of the awakening village. A slight breeze brought the warm, pungent odor of cow dung permeated with the acrid aroma of cooking fires. High above him he caught glimpses of monkeys skittering through the lush vegetation that shielded the sky from his view.

He had slept fitfully, and as he pulled himself upright, he was unsteady and weak. He felt distinctly worse than he had the night before, when he'd been hit by chills and fever an hour or so after dinner. He guessed he had malaria even though he'd been careful to take his chloroquine phospate as prophylaxis against it. The problem was that it had been impossible to avoid the clouds of mosquitoes that emanated each evening from the hidden pools in the swampy jungle. (Cook 1987, 1)

Compare this with the earlier student story entitled "The Escape." Both contain a similar number of words—Cook's has 183, "Escape" has 186. But in story time—the time the characters experience in the story—Cook's example takes only a few minutes, while "Escape" chronicles several years.

By describing a scene with a limited story time, Cook paints more vivid images, images captured with brush strokes that re-create the experience, images that *show* instead of *tell*. This is what mystery novelist P. D. James means when she describes her writing process:

I visualize the book as a series of scenes rather as if I were shooting a film. These can be written in any order depending on how I am feeling at the time. Some mornings I am attracted to dialogue, perhaps to scenes where my detective is interviewing suspects and there is the cut and thrust of verbal confrontation. On others, I draft descriptions of people, setting, scenery, weather, atmosphere, while sometimes I feel in the mood to tackle passages of violent action or horror. (James 1983, 24)

James writes her scenes with a limited story time, capturing images that are immediate. This in turn evokes grammatical structures that allow vivid details instead of vague images. Painting scenes with limited story time is a professional tool that students can use easily. Here is one example of how limiting story time helped middle school student Kristen Parker write an effective scene:

THE WAR

Tom took a step, and he felt the soft, torn grass at his feet. In the far off corner of his mind he heard a distant clanging, a horn or a bugle maybe. He dropped something in his hand as he swirled his head around and around, observing the madness. Next to him in the blood-stained grass lay a boy of no more than 17, shredded, torn by the mercilessness of a bullet. His face kept the broken, terrified glare of a rookie hardened by war. Bullets raged throughout the chaos, whizzing past his ear, a near miss. The smoldering gray sky acted like a blanket, hovering over the desperate men, puncturing their souls at the most vulnerable places. Across the dark field lay his opponents.

"These are not my opponents," he thought. "I hold no grudges against these men."

The stench of dry blood and disease filled his nostrils. His stomach began to turn as he watched young men to his left and right being cut down by the bite of small black devils. He glanced upward with a feeling of animosity and alienation as he peered at the American flag hanging limply from a makeshift pole. He pulled his damp, heavy head around just in time to see a bullet burrow into him, ripping his flesh as it went. He grabbed his thigh and crashed onto the ground, screaming in agony.

"Sir! Sir, are you all right?"

Tom opened his eyes and slowly looked around the small interior of an office building. He looked at the young man who was clutching his arm with a bewildered stare.

"You were just screaming then, Sir."

"Oh, ah, yes. Yes. So I was."

As Tom bent down and picked up his hat, he noticed a pen lying on the floor. He picked it up and stepped out of the building. Glancing up above him, he noticed a sign that read, "Army Testing Center for Psychological Warfare."

Scenes can be part of a larger story or stand alone as a short sketch. When part of a longer tale, they follow a pattern in which a character moves toward a goal and encounters conflict as obstacles thwart the character's efforts. This conflict causes readers to formulate story questions: Will Romeo marry Juliet? Will Ahab kill Moby Dick? Often, one question drives a story from scene to scene as a succession of minor disasters keep preventing the character from reaching the ultimate goal.

When students write scenes designed to stand alone, they often capture a slice of life that doesn't generate a story question. This should pose no problem for teachers. Such scenes help students learn to focus on a limited period of time—a significant incident that creates a mood or highlights a memorable life experience. For beginning writers, this type of scene writing should be a prerequisite to longer stories.

The following memoir by eighth grader Keir Marticke about time spent during summers with her grandmother is a good example of a scene without a story question. It is effective and complete in its own way, and serves a purpose much like a drawing in an artist's sketchbook, helping the artist to capture details of the moment.

WHISPERED WORDS BEFORE THE DAWN

Memories of her linger still in the folds of my mind, where the murmur of all pleasant things echoes, secluded from the scrutinizing harshness of reality. Closing my eyes, I see her as graceful footsteps carry her along the beach where we once walked, the iridescent light of evening dancing on her pale face. Hanging at her side, sandals dangle listlessly between her delicate forefinger and thumb, as sea spray splashes around her ankles and licks at the sandals' cork soles. She extends her hand and encloses mine. Turning, I grin at her, and she returns a soft smile.

We walk on the sands of time. The shallow imprints of my feet as a child deepen and grow wider, before the ocean tide erases each fallen step. No longer must I skip and stumble to match her smooth stride. Within hers, my grasp grows firmer. Gradually, I sprout taller, until I am not merely a small girl bobbing by her waist, but a young woman gazing equally into her eyes.

Simultaneously, she is aging. Wrinkles, the fragile tales of time, gather around her eyes from too many smiles. In her glance linger the memory of hardship and the pride of triumph. Her step, although it still emanates grace, slows and shortens. At her waist, she stoops slightly and braces herself with a hand. Once a deep and radiant brown, her hair is now silvery white, like the crystal perfection of fresh-fallen snow.

Swallowed by the joy of my own evolution, I fail to nurture her. Time creeps away on feline foot, and I realize my solecism too late. For velvety night has finally fallen, draping the beach and lapping ocean. Her grip over mine loosens and is lost. Frantic, I seek to redeem it, but cannot find her hand in the thickness of the night. Searching for the comfort of her smile, I find the dark betrays my probing eyes. A tear slips down my cheek.

"I love you," I whisper. But she is gone.

Providing Guidelines for Scene Writing

Teachers can encourage scenes like Keir's by giving students three guidelines. First, require students to work from a photograph, image, film, or a vivid memory. Second, ask them to limit the passage of time in the description. Finally, encourage students to use the brush strokes they've learned to zoom in on details.

Using these guidelines compels students to paint the "here and now." When students paint images with these guidelines, they emulate the way professionals focus on the present, creating more powerful passages. For example, notice how two middle school students, Alison Searle and Rick Miyajima, capture an immediate presence in the following two scenes. The first was written while viewing a photograph of destruction in the Middle East; the second, while viewing a slide of a grizzly bear near a river, feeding fish to his cubs.

A soft breeze blows through the naked forest, and a sharp silence fills the air with a feeling of death. Battle cries have been carried away into the blackness of night, and widows weep with agony. Tears fall slowly down a young girl's cheeks, as she stares through a shattered window pane trying to collect her thoughts.

Veiled bodies are strewn about the battlefield, and a dying man retrieves a tattered photograph of his wife and daughter, so as to remember them as he waits to greet them in God's kingdom. A small boy, victim of emotions, stands confused and afraid, wondering what happened to the father he never knew. When will mankind acquire sanity? (Alison Searle)

The grizzly bear, an excellent fisherman, grabs a leaping salmon. He wades through the water. The freezing temperature has no effect on him. Carrying the fish back to the bank, he gives it to his anxious cubs and they willingly accept.

Walking back to the river, he gives a low grunt and steps in. Catching a salmon for himself, he again returns to the bank, shakes his body to release the water from his fur and eats the wriggling fish hungrily. (Rick Miyajima)

Painting Characters in Scenes

Most scenes involve characters. Students can paint characters more effectively in both fiction and nonfiction with the help of a few painting techniques from professional writers. Maren Elwood (1966), Robert Newton Peck (1983), and Walter Campbell (1950) are just a few of the many authors who have formulated very similar methods for painting characters. Campbell, for example, outlines eight devices (see Figure 7–2).

Notice how Caleb Carr uses a combination of these techniques to paint the image of the narrator's grandmother in this excerpt from *The Alienest*:

> Back in the hallway I ran headlong into my grandmother, her silver hair perfectly coiffed, her gray and black dress unimpeachably neat, and her gray eyes, which I had inherited, glaring. "John!" she said in surprise, as if ten other men were staying in her house. "Who in the world was on the telephone?"
>
> "Dr. Kreizler, Grandmother," I said, bounding up the stairs.
>
> "Dr. Kreizler!" she called after me. "Well, dear! I've had about enough of that Dr. Kreizler for one day!" As I closed the door of my bedroom and began to dress, I could still hear her: "If you ask me, he's awfully peculiar! And I don't put much stock in his being a doctor, either. That Holmes man was a doctor, too!" She stayed in that vein while I washed, shaved, and scrubbed my teeth with Sozodont. (1994, 26)

1. By action of the character:
   Pete slunk out of the battle.

2. By speech of the character:
   "Hiya, pardner!"

3. By effect of the character upon other characters:
   Her loveliness was breath-taking.

4. By the character's own reactions to persons, things, and surrounding circumstances:
   John adored her, especially in blue.

5. By reporting what other characters say about the character:
   Said Tom, "Of course Sam is a heel!"

6. By explaining the traits and motives of the character:
   He loved good food.

7. By describing the character (in terms of the five senses):
   He had blue eyes, spoke with a Southern accent, smelled of the smokehouse, and his muscles were hard as nails.

8. By analyzing the psychological processes of the character:
   He was unable to overcome his shyness, which was the result of his being the son of a famous and terribly egotistical father.

Taken from Campbell, W. 1950. Writing: Advice and Devices. Garden City, New York: Doubleday and Company. (77)

FIGURE 7–2. Campbell's method for painting characters

In this passage, the author first paints a physical description with "her silver hair perfectly coifed, her gray hat and black dress unimpeachably neat, and her gray eyes, which I had inherited, glaring." Next, he characterizes with dialogue, and finally, he uses her actions to characterize by having her speak continuously while the narrator dresses, washes, shaves, and brushes his teeth. Our impression of Grandmother shows what she is like through Campbell's use of image devices.

Writers use these same techniques in nonfiction narratives. In the following excerpt, taken from a true story called "Life at Granny's," eighth-grade student Katie Price uses several of Campbell's techniques to paint a character sketch of her elderly, eccentric grandmother:

Granny lived alone until she was well in her 90s, and every day took the local bus down to Santa Cruz to attend the Santa Cruz Board of Supervisors meetings, which were public, and to criticize everything said. She slept on a carved wooden Chinese headrest. She didn't believe in baths or showers, and only took sponge and foot baths. (She had a sink installed on the floor of her bathroom for that special purpose.)

Once she went to an auction, and on the spur of a moment, purchased 35 marble sinks. Her crowning achievement, however, was Louella's Diary. Louella was the town lady who was, to put it politely, very popular with the men, and after she died suddenly, her estate went up for auction. It had hideous imitation French furniture, which Granny promptly bought, and hidden in one piece were Louella's collected diaries. The greatest delight of her life was to go up to businessmen in the Bubble Bakery downtown at lunch, shake her finger at them, and cackle, "I read about you in Louella's Diary!"

Students can play with any combination of these character-painting techniques and create image-rich portraits for both fiction and nonfiction.

Moving from Scenes to Stories

Once students acquire a sense of writing short scenes, they can begin to construct longer stories by connecting scenes. Using a variation of Freitag's Pyramid, teachers can illustrate how this works with Figure 7–3.

Viewing this graphic with an understanding of scene, students can see how scenes fit into larger works. As they write more complex stories, expanding time and adding images, they will be more likely to incorporate scenes. Eighth grader Jeff Jacobstein does this in his story, "Avenger." Here are his early scenes:

In the beginning, there was thunder, but it was not thunder. It was the roar of the gods, the roar of infinite power. It was the snarl of the heavens opening. When it was again silent, when the sound had circled the horizon twice, only then was the true dominance of the gods in full display. In the area where the sound had been, was a ship of the line. It had holes in a thousand different places. It was bubbling, as the water, denied entrance to the ship for so long, rushed into the ship with a vengeance.

In a small port, on the edge of the Atlantic Ocean, a frigate sailed in. It sailed slowly, barely moving fast enough to make a bow wave. Its sails shivered in the weak wind. They were more holes than cloth. It was a miracle that it was still afloat. On the stern, painted in chipped black paint, was the name "Avenger."

"Avenger, eh?" said the old man. The man's skin was a hunk of

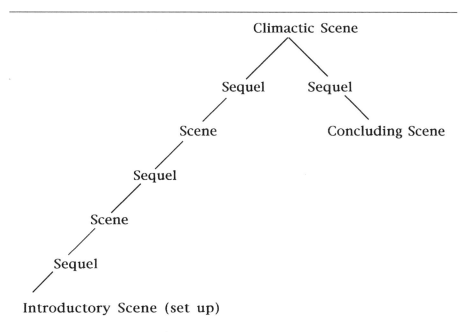

FIGURE 7–3. Scenes and sequels in Freitag's Pyramid

leathery meat caused by years of exposure as a sailor. "She always was a strong ship. Looks as if she had a run in with a big one, fifty gunner at least."

The man's voice rose with a bit of pride as he commented about the ship with the man next to him. "I used to sail on her before I lost me leg." The man gestured to where his leg should have been, but only a peg, a stump of rotten wood, remained.

Opening Stories with a Scene

A crucial element of any story is the *lead*, the opening designed to capture the interest of the reader. Authors create this lead with a scene that introduces a story question, a compelling question or questions the reader wants answered. Although the possibilities for teasing the reader's imagination are endless, teachers can introduce four general categories of opening scenes to help students get started: character scenes, setting scenes, action scenes, and dialogue scenes. Here is an example of each:

Character Opening: You don't know about me, without you have read a book by the name of "The Adventures of Tom Sawyer," but that ain't no matter. That book was made by Mr. Mark Twain, and he told the truth, mainly. There was things which he stretched, but mainly he told the truth. (From *Adventures of Huckleberry Finn* by Mark Twain)

Setting Opening: The tropical rain fell in drenching sheets, hammering the corrugated roof of the clinic building, roaring down the metal gutters, splashing on the ground in a torrent. Roberta Carter sighed, and stared out the window. From the clinic, she could hardly see the beach or the ocean beyond, cloaked in low fog. (From *Jurassic Park* by Michael Crichton)

Action Opening: The trawler plunged into the angry swells of the dark, furious sea like an awkward animal trying desperately to break out of an impenetrable swamp. The waves rose to goliathan heights, crashing into the hull with the power of raw tonnage; the white sprays caught in the night sky cascaded downward over the deck under the force of the night wind. Everywhere there were the sounds of inanimate pain, wood straining against wood, ropes twisting, stretched to the breaking point. The animal was dying. (From *The Bourne Identity* by Robert Ludlum)

Dialogue Opening: You know how it is there early in the morning in Havana with the bums still asleep against the walls of the buildings, before even the ice wagons come by with ice for the bars? Well, we came across the square from the dock to the Pearl of San Francisco Cafe to get coffee and there was only one beggar awake in the square and he was getting a drink out of the fountain. But when we got inside the cafe and sat down, there were three of them waiting for us.

We sat down and one of them came over.

"Well," he said.

"I can't do it," I told him. "I'd like to do it as a favor. But I told you last night. I couldn't."

"You can name your price."

"It isn't that. I can't do it. That's all." (From *To Have and Have Not* by Ernest Hemingway)

Each of these scenes has a mix of character, dialogue, action, or description, but in each the story question derives from one technique. For example, the question What will happen next? in the Hemingway cut emerges from the dialogue instead of the description of Havana that precedes it.

When writing fiction, two of the primary art forms are scenes and story grammar. As author Elizabeth R. Bills once commented, "Every work of art—a painting, a piece of music, a story—must have form. Without form it has no meaning, serves no purpose. Without some sort of disciplined structure, it won't even hang together. It is form—the rhythm of the lines, the color and tone, and economy of expression, the unity of the artist's conception—that gives a work of art beauty" (Bills 1964).

STRATEGIES

Strategy 1: Paint a Character from Eight Perspectives

Day One

To help students understand the options for building character scenes, divide the class into groups of four. With those students remaining, make one more group of between two to five.

Distribute copies of Campbell's Eight Devices for Characterization (Figure 7–2) so that each member in the group has a set. (This can also be found on the companion CD under Strategies in Chapter 7.)

Assign two of Campbell's techniques to each group member. With the odd-numbered, two-to-five group, use the same procedure, but assign Campbell's devices accordingly.

Explain to the class that they will be working as a team to create four group character sketches, and that their first task will be to pick four stereotype characters, one for each member of the group to begin writing about. Project the following list with an overhead and ask them to make selections.

School-Related Stereotypes: the class cut-up, the ladies' man, the impatient secretary, the deranged school cook, the hard-of-hearing custodian, the gullible girl, the computer nerd, the popularity seeker, a humorless teacher, the loner, the school's burn-out, a quick-tempered athlete, the constantly suspicious assistant principal, the complainer, the ultimate rule follower, the TV addict, the sports fanatic, the rock musician, the violinist, the star football lineman, the outstanding gymnast, the eccentric artist.

Society-Related Stereotypes: the rumor-spreading hairdresser, the pious reverend, the gum-chewing waitress, the talkative cab driver, the fanatical environmentalist, the exotic fortune-teller, the always-excited disc jockey, the smiling news anchor, the bigoted redneck, the hand-shaking politician, the introverted accountant, the professional wrestler, the cold-blooded hit man, the sleepy all-night security guard, the union-supporting truck driver.

Once students have chosen their characters, explain that they will need to use the two devices they've been assigned to write three to five sentences that characterize their stereotype. They will only have eight minutes to work. After that time, they should pass their passage to the person on their right, who will then continue the characterization using his or her two devices.

Continue the rotation every eight minutes until all four members of the group have contributed.

Day Two
Have students take turns in their small groups reading the team drafts. Ask each team to choose their best character sketch and then revise it as a team, adding and deleting whatever they feel will make the sketch more complete. After this, have an elected spokesperson from each group read the revised sketch.

Strategy 2: Build Visualized Scenes with Urban Myths

Help students transform plot into scenes by having them expand on urban myths, stories that circulate as part of American city folklore. Read the following urban myth to the class:

> Picture the following scene: On a warm summer night you are walking along the main street of your hometown past the Shalersville Funeral Home. As you pass the open door, you hear the somber music of a funeral service and notice several of your friends gathered near the entry. An icy tingle chills your spine, and you feel drawn into the service. As you enter the parlor, you find it odd that no one greets you. You gesture a hello to Ann Collins, one of your closest friends, but she ignores you, refusing to reply or even make eye contact. Other acquaintances turn their backs on you, continuing to talk as though you weren't there. Finally, you glance at the open coffin and discover your own smiling face staring up at you, blank eyes wide open.

Ask students to rewrite this myth by embellishing each scene with sensory images. They may change the characters, setting, and minor details, but they must follow the same plot.

For more variety, you may want to provide students with other tales. Two authors have anthologized summaries of these urban myths. J. Brunvand has written *The Choking Doberman and Other "New" Urban Legends* (1984) and *The Vanishing Hitchhiker: American Urban Legends and Their Meanings* (1981). Alvin Schwartz has written *Scary Stories to Tell in the*

Dark (1981) and *More Scary Stories to Tell in the Dark* (1984). All four collections contain excellent plot summaries for bridging scenes to stories.

Strategy 3: Discuss Comic Book Plot Paintings

Have students read a comic book—one appropriate for class discussion. While they read, they should search for a story line that best illustrates Freitag's Pyramid. Using an opaque projector, ask volunteers (possibly for bonus points) to share the story they found with the class and explain how it illustrates the plot development of Freitag's Pyramid.

Strategy 4: Write Scenes from Short Story Films

Many short stories have been made into films. For a list of about fifty titles, log online at <custsrv@filmicarchives.com>. Locate both a copy of the short story and its film version. Such combinations can often be found in your local library. After showing the film to students, have them select a five-minute scene and write it as a scene from the short story.

Be sure to explain to the class that while they are painting the same scene as the author, their images will be different. They will no doubt include details captured by the photographer and director, details never seen by the author when creating the text version. So student scenes will be unique to their own vision. Add that the purpose of this exercise is to learn about scene construction by comparing images captured by students with those in the author's original story.

After students have completed their descriptions, ask for student volunteers to share their scenes. Next share the written short story with the class and discuss the way the author handled his visual images.

You might mention that Arthur C. Clarke once used a variation of this technique. At the time the movie *2001: A Space Odyssey* was released, Clarke had not yet completed the final draft of the novel and used the film version as inspiration for his final written images (Negroponte 1995, 93).

Strategy 5: Use Music to Paint Scenes

Play an unusual piece of instrumental music. (Try works by Leo Kottke, Mia Jang, John Serrie, Harry Parch, or Robert Tree Cody.) As students listen, ask them to imagine this music playing in the background at some event. The event might be happening today; it might have happened centuries ago; or it might be unfolding in the far future. As the music plays, have students write a description of a short scene including the sights, sounds, and smells they picture.

Strategy 6: Build a Bulletin Board Photo Collection

Although convenient to use computer images with students, you may have limited access and want to seek out other photo sources. Here is another way to collect some colorful images. First try securing discarded magazines from the school or local library. Old issues of *Sports Illustrated* and *National Geographic* contain scores of powerful images, but many other magazines will do.

Second, ask students to locate three fascinating images (at least four-inches-by-six-inches) from old magazines at home and bring them to class. If each student brings three pictures, even if some fail to bring in any, you should end up with several hundred by the end of the day. These will provide you with enough images for both writing and posting.

As students write with magazine photos, you can display both their interpretations and the corresponding images on bulletin boards. Magazine images can also be laminated and used as a resource file. This will give you a collection to use at different times and in different ways when computer images aren't accessible.

Strategy 7: Write a Setting for an Exotic Scene

Take a virtual trip to an exotic location by logging on the Internet site <http://www.vtourist.com> and exploring a strange new world. Have students find a location that they feel would make a great setting for a short story. Ask them to write a scene with vivid images of that location for the beginning of a short story.

Have volunteers share their scenes in class and discuss the possibilities for stories written in these settings.

As an alternative, you may wish to have students explore these Internet options:

Web 66 at <http://web66.coled.umn.edu/schools.html>
This lists home pages for schools around the world. Visit another school and check their campus life for a story setting.

City Net at <http://www.city.net>
Visit one of the major cities around the world and consider an urban setting for a story.

Naomi's Photogallery and Travelogue at <http://www.bayarea.net/~emerald/photo.html>
Take a trip around the world in 80 photographs with one person's worldwide travelogue.

8
Nonfiction Form #5
A Close Examination of a Feature Article Form

> In the Brazilian Amazon, annual forest loss from all causes rose from less than 3 million acres in 1991 to an average of 4.8 million acres during each of the past three years—the equivalent of seven football fields a minute. In 1995 alone, more than 7 million acres were destroyed—an area roughly the size of Belgium. (Laurance 1998, 35)

This paragraph from feature writer William Laurance is a small piece of nonfiction art. With impressive statistics and a shocking comparison, Laurance grips the imagination of readers who come to understand the concept of five million acres of devastated rain forest by visualizing seven football fields vanishing every sixty seconds—a powerful personalized image, a type of image rarely found in fiction.

Just as the media of oil paint and clay provide different possibilities for expression, fiction and nonfiction generate different forms and different variations of content. Writers, like artists, select forms to express their content. Content stimulates form; form shapes content. Ben Shahn, a well-known painter, explains it this way in his book, *The Shape of Content:*

> Form is formulation—the turning of content into a material entity, rendering a content accessible to others, giving it permanence, willing it to the race. Form is as varied as are the accidental meetings of nature. Form in art is as varied as idea itself. . . . Form is the very shape of content. (Shahn 1985, 53)

With fiction Freitag's Pyramid lends shape; with nonfiction very different models control the form. To illustrate this difference, let us examine one

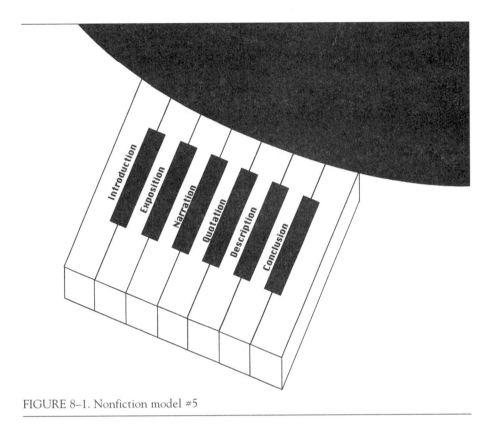

FIGURE 8–1. Nonfiction model #5

of the nonfiction models used for feature writing in many magazine articles. (This is not the *only* form, just one of the more popular choices.)

Nonfiction article form #5—the number five distinguishes this form from the others not described here—works well to illustrate the super structure of prose. It is analogous to a piano composition played on a limited keyboard (see Figure 8–1).

Articles constructed with this piano form begin with a lead on the first note, move to a conclusion for the last note, and in between, play combinations of four melody keys—exposition, narration, quotation, and description. The melody keys may be played in any sequence, using any repetitions that sound pleasing. While authors vary the notes they play to meet the demands of different types of feature articles and different styles of magazines, the keyboard for this form remains essentially the same for most feature articles. Leads provide choices for the first note in the nonfiction article.

Writing Introductory Leads

Writers sometimes refer to the lead as the *hook*. The opening of an article hooks the reader's curiosity and shouts subliminally, Read this! This is fascinating! Although writers such as Don McKinney, William Rivers, and Jerome Kelly have suggested varied categories of leads, eight seem to generate the most effective beginnings with students: the *narrative* lead, the *quotation* lead, the *statistical* lead, the *question* lead, the *mystery* lead, the *descriptive* lead, the *imagine* lead, and the *direct* lead.

The Narrative Lead

A narrative lead lures the reader with a compelling story in one to three paragraphs. Narrative leads wrap information in the humanity of a personal anecdote. Here is a narrative lead, taken from a chapter in Edward De Bono's *New Think*:

> Many years ago when a person who owed money could be thrown into jail, a merchant in London had the misfortune to owe a huge sum to a money-lender. The money-lender, who was old and ugly, fancied the merchant's beautiful teenage daughter. He proposed a bargain. He said he would cancel the merchant's debt if he could have the girl instead.
>
> Both the merchant and his daughter were horrified at the proposal. So the cunning money-lender proposed that they let Providence decide the matter. He told them that he would put a black pebble and a white pebble into an empty money bag, and then the girl would have to pick out one of the pebbles. If she chose the black pebble, she would become his wife and her father's debt would be cancelled. If she chose the white pebble, she would stay with her father, and the debt would still be cancelled. But if she refused to pick out a pebble, her father would be thrown into jail, and she would starve.
>
> Reluctantly the merchant agreed. They were standing on a pebble-strewn path in the merchant's garden as they talked, and the money-lender stooped down to pick up the two pebbles. As he picked up the pebbles, the girl, sharp-eyed with fright, noticed that he picked up two black pebbles and put them into the money bag. He then asked the girl to pick out the pebble that was to decide her fate and that of her father. . . . The girl . . . put her hand into the money-bag and drew out a pebble. Without looking at it she fumbled and let it fall to the path where it was immediately lost among the others.
>
> "Oh how clumsy of me," she said, "but never mind—if you look into the bag you will be able to tell which pebble I took by the color of the one that is left." (1967, 11–12)

DeBono's story entices readers to explore the nature of thinking. Like all effective introductions, it generates interest instead of providing information. Information comes later. In the sample that follows, eighth grader Zach Vesoulis accomplishes the same thing, using a narrative about a battle in computer cyberspace:

> All you can do is sit there and watch as your ship lurches, signaling the exit of hyperspace. Suddenly your ship is put into the middle of a fierce intergalactic battle. Energy beams float through space all around you and pretty soon a ship bursts into flames near you.
>
> Without thinking, your hand goes to the throttle control and instantly you are thrusting forward at half the speed of light. You glance quickly behind you before your targeting system picks up a stray enemy fighter. Now just a hundred yards in front of you is your quarry.
>
> With a sudden burst of adrenaline your heart begins to beat faster and faster as you wait for the targeting crosshairs to turn red. Now just moments away from turning your enemy into disarranged particles of carbon, a red light flashes on the visor of your battle helmet. You chance a glance down at the control panel of your fighter. You turn around just in time to see a missile of another enemy fighter slam into the right engine of you craft. You wait for next screen to appear, and you press "New Game."
>
> "Okay," you remark, "let's try this level again."

As these two examples illustrate, the narrative lead tends to be longer than other leads, often running several paragraphs. But its story appeal makes it one of the most popular introductions.

A shorter lead, one that gives the reader a feeling of a live news broadcast is the *quotation* lead.

The Quotation Lead

The quotation lead brings a conversational tone to an article with a comment that lures the reader. Notice how these tenth-grade students use unusual quotes to capture your interest:

> "Quack, quack!" Canada geese waddled across the road at a pace comparable to that of a tired turtle. Remembering her motto about the bothersome geese, Mom shouted, "Fly or die." (Nicole Passan)

> "When I'm a genetic engineer, I'm going to find a cure for cancer, and I'm going to make a chicken with six wings," she says. (Liz Botros)

> "I came to your house to die." (Daniel Simon)

The Question Lead

The question lead intrigues the reader by posing one or more direct questions. While this seems like a simple lead to construct, it is actually one of the more difficult, for the questions need to evoke curiosity, teasing the reader to continue. Here are a few student examples:

> John Grisham had always hated English. In college, he even earned Ds in freshman English. So, how did he become a writer with three suspense novels at the top of the charts? (Laura Faulkner)

> Would you like to see the only real pink elephants in the world? Or visit a barren lava bed whose name means "devil" in Swahili? Or watch hippos play in a bubbling spring? You can. Just visit Tsavo National Park in Kenya, Africa. (Meredith MacMillan)

> Have you ever had to glue your shoes to hold them together? Cut your own hair or make your own clothes? Watch as your older sister becomes pregnant at sixteen? Or, with sirens screaming and lights flashing, watch an ambulance take your mother to the hospital after she tries to commit suicide? And, after all this, would you have the strength to go on?
>
> These memories, dark and piercing, are from my mother's childhood. (Emily Coleman)

Just creating a question doesn't ensure a quality question lead. Suppose in this last example, Emily had opened with these questions instead:

> Have you ever wondered what it would be like to come from a poor family? Wonder what your clothes and food might be like? Ever wonder what problems a family like that might have? Well, my mother experienced a number of these things.

The effect of the hook would have been lost. This second lead lacks specific details and fails to "turn on" the reader's camera eye. Consequently, the question lead is the most difficult for students to create effectively. Unlike other introductions that have a natural appeal, questions must paint specific images that provoke curiosity. Simply asking questions isn't enough to create a psychological hook.

The Statistical Lead

Statistics impress readers. Numbers seem to generate some mystical spell, giving authority to the simplest information. Writers use this lure with lead paragraphs that present fascinating numbers. Eighth grader Molly Fitzpatrick experiments with this enticement by introducing an article with some surprising statistics on child abuse:

> Child abuse is becoming one of the fastest growing acts of violence in the United States. According to the American Humane Association, 1.4 million cases of child abuse were reported in the U.S. in 1982.

Nearly 1/5 of these victims were teenagers between the ages of 13 and 17. Last year, nearly 1,300 abused children died.

With a statistical lead, writers can personalize data by translating larger numbers to small applications. For example, if 25 percent of the nation's population seek out psychological help, a writer might say, "One out of every four of your friends may one day need psychological counseling." In the opening of this chapter, Laurance personalized the loss of 4.8 million acres of forest by comparing it to seven football fields vanishing every minute.

The Mystery Lead

The fourth lead, the mystery lead, parallels a fictional concept called *story question*. Both techniques keep the reader in suspense by posing unanswered questions. Watch how feature writer Margaret Bourke-White uses this device:

> The mysterious malady began so quietly I could hardly believe there was anything wrong. There was nothing strong enough to dignify with the word *pain*, nothing except a slight dull ache in my left leg when I walked upstairs. I did not dream it was the stealthy beginning of a seven-year siege during which I would face a word totally new to my vocabulary—incurable. (*Great Reading from Life* 1960, 471)

The author leaves unanswered questions: What type of medical problem would come with such little warning? Does the seven-year siege mean she recovered or that she is now hopelessly beyond help? Does the word *incurable* mean the author may soon die? To find the answers to these questions, the reader must read on.

The mystery lead teases by giving readers half of a story. Here are three student examples, the first from a middle-school student, the second and third from high school students:

> Embarrassed. That's the only emotion in the English language to describe a scenario that I shamefully remember as The Ballpark Incident. (David Haile)

> Heart thumping, palms sweating, my Dad watches as the enemy shows its face: nine men, all wielding weapons of war and destruction. Although the enemy does not outnumber my Dad's side, he realizes that their skill is far superior and that at any time one man could win the war. Still, he does not lose faith and holds his breath as he awaits the almost inevitable onslaught. (Patrick Mazanec)

> Grandma Mingo taught me to play poker when I was seven. (Liz Mesok)

The Descriptive Lead

Descriptive leads splash images like poetry, painting vivid characters, animals, objects, or unusual settings. Read this lead by William Newcott:

> The midsummer sun was high in a clear yellow-brown sky. The morning's filmy blue clouds had dissipated, and the temperature was 8 degrees Fahrenheit—way up from last night's low of minus 100 degrees. A breeze wafted from the west at about eight miles an hour.
>
> A perfect afternoon for a drive on Mars. (1998, 17)

Eighth grader Will Cleary relies on a descriptive introduction to puzzle the reader into speculating about his cat's unusual obsession:

> Leaping into the air and grasping the creature in her paws, the cat lands on all four legs victoriously. But, this is no ordinary cat. This is a cat named Sunny. Sunny is my one year old kitten that is full of enough energy to pull a semi across the country. Now, sure, she is like most other kittens in the world, except she doesn't use her energy the same way that most other cats do. Most cats use their energy to hunt rabbits or birds or even mice, but not Sunny. She uses hers to hunt for a different game. She uses her energy by catching insects.

The Imagine Lead

Closely related to the descriptive lead is the *imagine lead*, where the writer asks the reader to imagine something. Here are a couple of examples from middle school students—the first from an article on quarks, the second from a review of *Andromeda Strain:*

> Imagine dropping ten alarm clocks off the top of the Sears tower. Then, imagine if you had to rely on picture-taking sensors, like bubble chambers, to tell where the pieces fell. You would have tons of pictures of little trails of bubbles that represented part of the paths of the tiny fragments of the clocks. After collecting the data, you would have to do the impossible. Using only these pictures, you would have to figure out how one alarm clock works and what materials made it up. Even with the most powerful computers, it would take you a long time, working constantly, repeating the experiment, and guessing about what the trails represent, to come up with an educated guess.
>
> Brian Anderson, a pioneer detective of a world that would fit inside the tiniest speck of dust, works with such a problem. (Kati Moseley)

> Imagine this, you are sitting at home and the next thing you know you get this disease and your blood starts to clot. In other words, you freeze, right there. This is what happens in Michael Crichton's *The Andromeda Strain*. (Daniel Pipitone)

The Direct Lead

Finally, the weakest lead to use in this nonfiction model—but the best lead for a technical journal article, an essay test, or a business memo—is the direct lead. The direct lead defines the thesis of a long piece of writing in the same way a topic sentence generalizes the main idea in paragraphs. Although the direct lead lacks the imaginative appeal of other openings, its purpose differs. Other leads try to hook readers who lack a compelling interest in the topic. The direct technique assumes that the reader wants the information and doesn't need to be coaxed.

When appealing to the readers is unimportant, direct beginnings are efficient. This is why manuals, technical reports, scientific journal articles, memos, and business communications often begin with a direct technique. These forms of nonfiction, unlike the feature article, announce the topic as in this example taken from a book on chess openings:

> In this chapter we examine the Max Lange Attack, the Classical Variation of the Two Knights' Defense and a line in the Scotch Gambit that can arise if Black avoids the other two systems. (Levy and Keene 1976, 1)

The direct technique can also be used in the second paragraph when an article's title doesn't offer enough clarity to the thesis.

The Combination Lead

Often professional and student writers combine techniques. For example, student Linsay Davis combines a statistical and question lead in this introduction to a piece on the McCaughey sextuplets:

> What would cause you to go through 49 diapers each day? To go through 11 gallons of formula a week? To spend $1.25 million on medical expenses? To spend $1.45 million on 4 years of college education? Multiple births.

Writing the Body of an Article

Examine Figure 8–1 again. Returning to our piano analogy, after the writer plays the introductory note, he or she plays a melody using combinations of four piano keys: exposition, narration, quotation, and description. Each key, representing a passage of one or more paragraphs, can be played in any order, but like any musical composition, the tune will sound more pleasing if notes vary in duration, intensity, and in combination with each other.

Narration and Description

Narration and description, two introductory techniques, repeat as forms in the body of this nonfiction model. Narratives vary the melodic flow of nonfiction and also create psychological appeal. Moffett observed that "children use and depend upon narrative as their principal mode of thinking" (1968, 343). McNeil (1987) discovered that children acquire information more effectively when reading narratives. So the narrative plays a unique role in the reading and writing history of individuals.

Description, frequently woven in narration, adds the important sensory images such as color, detail, and sound. With description, authors can choose to inject phrases, sentences, or entire passages, as the writing demands.

Quotations

Quotation, another element of the body, adds authority and a conversational tone to the work. Reading a quotation, we feel like a television commentator has held up a microphone to an important personality. The cadence and phraseology of the quote create a change in the rhythm, adding variety and a feeling of presence.

The frequency of quotes varies with the style of a magazine. *People* magazine, attempting to capture a more "lively" feeling with a faster pace, uses quotes almost continuously, while *National Geographic*, more focused on places and ideas, injects quotes for emphasis and variety. Quotes appear less often in articles where the content is scholarly. Here, quotes often highlight clarifications by an authority.

Exposition

Exposition, the last of the four central elements, changes its shape like a chameleon to fit the content. Following the classic forms described in Chapter 6, exposition develops topics around the logical patterns of (1) details and examples, (2) proofs and reasons, (3) comparison and contrast, (4) process, (5) illustration, (6) cause and effect, (7) narration, and (8) enumeration.

By its nature, exposition reflects logical patterns, and as a result, teachers can illustrate these patterns in paragraphs, passages, and complete works. For example, the following paragraph might be used to illustrate "comparison and contrast" development. In this comparison-contrast paragraph, Nobel Prize–winner Konrad Lorenz argues that one of civilization's eight deadly sins is the "entropy of feeling." To support his thesis he uses a variety of expository passages including one that compares and contrasts joy and pleasure:

The psychologist Helmut Schulze has drawn attention to the remarkable fact that the word *Freude* ("joy") does not occur in Freud, who recognizes pleasure, but not joy. Schulze says, in substance, that when, sweating and exhausted, with sore fingers and aching limbs, we reach the summit of a difficult mountain, knowing that the even more difficult and dangerous descent lies ahead of us, this is not pleasure but one of the greatest joys on earth. Pleasure may be achieved without paying the price of strenuous effort, but joy cannot. Intolerance of unpleasurable experience converts the natural ups and downs of human life into an artificial plain, the great wave of mountain and valley becoming a scarcely noticeable ripple, and light and shade a monotonous gray. In short, intolerance of unpleasurable experience creates deadly boredom. (1973, 39)

Next students might be shown something like Bruce Catton's comparison and contrast of General Lee and General Grant, a passage that runs for several paragraphs in *Bruce Catton's Civil War*. In addition, students might be introduced to a book that compares two diverse views on a popular subject such as cloning, gun control, or euthanasia.

Using writing samples of different lengths illustrates the common logic of nonfiction and also demonstrates how other passages in the model—quotation, description, and narration—can support the logical framework of a longer work. This is useful since students are accustomed to viewing shorter models, which usually run one to five paragraphs in length.

Writing Conclusions

Endings are difficult for students. Many either stop abruptly with no sense of finality, ramble on well beyond the ideal stopping point, or use artificial expressions such as "in conclusion," "to summarize," and "finally." Teachers can help alleviate this common problem with a few guidelines that can shape a variety of conclusions. Author Leo Fletcher recommends three. A good conclusion, explains Fletcher, will "(1) emphasize the point of your article, (2) provide a climax, and (3) help readers remember your piece" (1997, 34).

If students keep these guiding principles in mind, they can more easily offer a variety of conclusions. For example, notice how the following three conclusions incorporate Fletcher's principles in different ways. The first meets Fletcher's guidelines by discussing the future; the next, ends with a summary, and the last, finishes with a quote.

Look to the Future
Concluding an article on the destructive power of tsunamis—tidal waves

created by earthquakes—feature writer Kathy Svitil suggests what might happen in the future in the United States:

> The fate of Arop, Warapu, Malol, and Sissano should be disquieting to residents of the West Coast of the United States. A Pacific earthquake could easily send a tsunami their way as well. If they were lucky and the quake was distant, they'd have a couple of hours' warning. But if the quake were closer to shore, they might not know what was happening until they saw the wave looming overhead. (Svitil 1999, 68)

End with a Summary

Just as Svitil's future ending on tsunamis emphasized the main idea, created a climax, and left something to reflect on, artist Lynn Newman accomplishes the same thing with a summary. In his first-person article on why and how he uses photographs as preliminary sketches for painting, Newman concludes:

> While I realize using snapshots as a sketchbook is no substitute for drawing or painting on location, it is a way to unravel at least one artistic quandary. Perhaps the wise use of snapshots can free some valuable time and rejuvenate your artistic sensibilities. (1999, 50)

Finish with a Quote

Similarly, a quote can bring resolution to an article as this example from an article on preserving wetlands:

> "As it's difficult to guarantee that we can re-create all that will be lost," Zedler says, "our primary responsibility must be to protect what's left." (Nadis 1999, 16)

In addition to these concluding techniques, students can shape endings with a question, a narrative, a surprise, or a host of other methods. As long as students follow Fletcher's basic guidelines, they can let their imaginations create any endings that fit the logic of their work.

Putting It All Together

Now that we have examined the parts of nonfiction model #5, let us return to our keyboard analogy and see how one student used this model to shape an entire piece. In the article that follows, tenth grader James Larson reminisces about how, at age eight, he first saw his mother lose her aura of strength. Each of the following passages is an excerpt from the longer original; this choppy flow is uncharacteristic of the original. However, notice how

James uses nonfiction forms—the piano-key techniques—to create variety. (Before each section, the nonfiction forms are identified in brackets.)

JOB HUNTING

[Lead: Mystery Technique]
Mom always prided herself on handling rough situations with great strength and determination. When grandma was in the hospital, strong enough for everyone was Mom. When Dad was laid off, money tight, she was as sturdy as an iron pillar supporting a skyscraper. But the day she walked through the front door an hour earlier than normal with a look of stunned fear on her face, I was nervous.

[Description Followed by a Quote]
When she walked through the door, she looked at me with brown eyes that could have torn me apart if I would have stared at them longer. They still advertised a deep love and respect for me, despite what she was about to tell me. Leaning against the dining room chair, face in hand, Mom heaved a great sigh. She looked at me once more with a determined look, determined to let it out, to get it over with. As a glistening tear rolled down the finely drawn lines of her cheek, she opened her mouth to speak. She said simply and understandably, "I'm out of a job sweetie." She then laid her face into her hands and wept.

[Exposition]
Cleaning in a quiet tedious sort of manner, Mom simply bumbled around the house, as if studying every inch of the house she had worked so hard for. . . . As any normal eight-year-old, I busied myself with school and such. I knew only that our future was uncertain, and uncertainty was frightening. I would hear my mother's sobs sometimes through the walls at night. I could feel her tears flowing. All I wished for was her to work once more and have everything back the way it was.

[Narration with Touches of Description]
Three months later, after plenty of waiting, the first glimmer of hope showed. This piece of hope came in a small white envelope with our address and my mother's name typed neatly on it. It was a letter for Mom to come to an interview. . . . My mother's face showed a new light, as if God had taken that glimmer of hope and attached it to her. The mother of old returned once more, laughed, and made jokes. The night the letter came, I caught her crying, and immediately assumed the worst. As it turned out, those were tears of happiness, not of sorrow. Those were the kinds of tears we had been lacking for a long time.

[Narration with Quote]
The day of the interview, I didn't pay attention in school whatsoever, too excited for Mom. Running from the bus stop, bursting through the

door, I rushed into the house after school. I looked into the eyes of my Mom. Without any words being spoken, with no looks exchanged to give the secret away, I knew she got the job. I could simply tell by the way her eyes shone bright and strong. She succeeded. I could tell we would be fine. I hugged her, and she started to cry once more from joy. I looked into her face and the first thing she said was, "I love you."

[Summary Conclusion]
My Mom always possessed a strength, which until it was missing, I never understood. That strength is what held us together through good times and bad.

The elements of this article play like a piano piece. From these excerpts, you can see how James mixes techniques for effect. He begins with a story question introduction, moves to a description with a quote, plays a little exposition, injects a quote, throws in a couple of narratives, adds another quote, and concludes with a thesis statement summary. The variety sustains interest.

Each technique adds to the meaning and psychological pace of the article in different ways. Quotes bring an authority to the work, giving the reader the feeling of an eyewitness newscast. Narratives enhance the central image of his mother and provide a story appeal, creating a release from the exposition that informs. Description, often mixed with narration, engages the senses. All these elements play notes that harmonize around the central theme of Mom's struggle.

Avoiding the Rigidity Trap

Using a form such as the nonfiction model #5 can help students avoid writing everything with patterns of pure exposition. However, forms function more like clay than marble. Teachers need to caution students that forms are created simultaneously with ideas. A writer shouldn't try to stuff ideas into predetermined boxes of form. This was the problem with the classic five-paragraph theme. Instead of teaching it as one of many forms, teachers taught it as *the* form, and students bent their thinking to match the structure. In time, critics began to ask, Where is the five-paragraph theme in professional writing? It didn't exist. Professionals allow their ideas to contribute to the form, and few published ideas matched the pattern of the five-paragraph theme.

Russell Baker discovered the importance of not imposing form early in his writing career. In *Growing Up*, Baker describes receiving an assignment from his eleventh-grade English teacher Mr. Fleagle to write an essay using the classic essay form. As he wrote about the comical images of his family eating spaghetti (a dish they rarely ate), Baker became caught up in the joy of sharing the experience and felt compelled to deviate from the form he had been taught:

> Suddenly, I wanted to write about the warmth and good feeling of it, but I wanted to put it down simply for my own joy, not for Mr. Fleagle. It was a moment I wanted to recapture and hold for myself. I wanted to relive the pleasure of an evening at New Street. To write it as I wanted, however, would violate all the rules of formal composition I'd learned in school, and Mr. Fleagle would surely give it a failing grade. Never mind. I would write something else for Mr. Fleagle after I had written this thing for myself.
>
> When I finished it, the night was half gone and there was no time left to compose a proper, respectable essay for Mr. Fleagle. There was no choice next morning but to turn in my private reminiscence of Belleville. Two days passed before Mr. Fleagle returned the graded papers, and he returned everyone's but mine. I was bracing myself for a command to report to Mr. Fleagle immediately after school for discipline when I saw him lift my paper from his desk and rap for the class' attention.
>
> "Now, boys," he said, "I want to read you an essay. This is titled 'The Art of Eating Spaghetti.'"
>
> And he started to read. My words! He was reading *my words* out loud to the entire class. What's more, the entire class was listening. Listening attentively. Then somebody laughed, then the entire class was laughing, and not in contempt and ridicule, but with openhearted enjoyment. Even Mr. Fleagle stopped two or three times to repress a small prim smile.
>
> I did my best to avoid showing pleasure, but what I was feeling was pure ecstasy at this startling demonstration that my words had the power to make people laugh. In the eleventh grade, at the eleventh hour as it were, I had discovered a calling. It was the happiest moment of my entire school career. When Mr. Fleagle finished, he put the final seal on my happiness by saying, "Now that boys, is an essay. Don't you see? Congratulations, Mr. Baker." (1982, 188-189)

Baker's willingness to allow form to emerge naturally taught him that content and form work as one. Just as the dancer cannot be separated from the dance, so the grammar of style cannot be pried from the grammar of form: both weave a harmony of purpose.

STRATEGIES

Strategy 1: Stuff a Sack of Shapely Ideas

Barry Lane in *After THE END* describes form this way: "Many writers talk about the power of visualizing the shape of the pieces they work on. A novel that loops back in time might be shaped like a coiling spiral, an essay centered on one central idea might look like a big duffel bag stuffed with examples" (1993, 93). Lane suggests asking students to draw the shape of something they have written, which is an excellent way to relate form to content.

Consider having your students do this with one of their writings, but first introduce the strategy with this exercise. Select two short pieces of professional writing—one fiction, the other nonfiction. Ask the class to draw two shapes, one representing each piece. To get them started, give them some shapes to consider sketching as models: a spider web, building blocks, Legos, beach balls, chains, sacks, bookshelves, planets, a wastebasket, a refrigerator, a basement, a desk drawer, a map, flashing Christmas lights, a pyramid, a stretch of river, boards, a garden plot, or a tree.

After students have listened to and drawn both pieces, share drawings and discuss how the content related to the form. You might also use this as a springboard for discussing Nonfiction Model #5 or Freitag's Pyramid.

Strategy 2: Run a Magazine Search Competition

Divide the class into four random teams. Explain that today they will be competing as a team for bonus points. The task of the team members will be to find as many examples of each element in Nonfiction Model #5 as possible in a one-period library search. Have each team pick a captain whose responsibility will be to check items found by other team members, verify them as valid examples, and turn in all of the team's examples.

Write on the board the following list of elements:

Introduction (narrative, quotation, question, statistical, mystery,
   descriptive, imagine, direct)
Body (narrative, quotation, description, exposition)
Conclusion (future, summary, quote, other)

Explain that they will earn one point for each example of any element they find. Examples must be correctly labeled for points to count. For introductions and conclusions, teams must identify the specific type: statistical, question, narrative, and so on. All examples must be copied in cursive or Xeroxed, labeled by the type of element, and turned in at the end of the period as a package with the names of team members listed on a cover sheet.

After the team packets have been turned in and scored, choose some of the best examples to use for review.

Strategy 3: Experiment with Forms

A common strategy among English teachers for years has been to have students rework a piece of writing in another genre. Teachers have asked students to create a poem based on a nonfiction article, to write a letter as one of the characters in a short story, or to develop a short story based on a news article. These crossover experiments not only help students understand how form shapes content, but also how the same thesis can be expressed in a variety of ways.

In recent years, crossing genres has led to the emergence of the "new journalism," a form of writing that blends nonfiction with fiction. Truman Capote's success with *In Cold Blood* inspired a succession of similar fiction/nonfiction works.

In the classroom students can have fun experimenting with this new form. Have students find a true narrative—either a nonfiction article or a filmed documentary—and write a short fictionalized story based on the events. Using a televised or video documentary provides one advantage: students can more easily experience and incorporate images. This makes their writing more detailed.

Seventh grader Stefanie Klaus transformed the events from an episode of the television program *Unsolved Mysteries* into a short story. Here is the beginning of her fictionalized nonfiction piece, which you can use as a classroom model. In this she adopted a first-person viewpoint, placing herself in the role of the main character.

WHEN NIGHTMARES COME TRUE

I swung open the refrigerator door, hoping to overcome the empty, nauseating feeling of hunger that lingered in my stomach with some edibles to nourish my feeble body. I had had a thoroughly exhausting day. Last night I lay in bed, assuming various restless positions with agitation. I felt racked with anxiety, just thinking the unbearable thought that after I fell asleep, I would have to wake up again the next day.

Something was going to happen. Something was wrong, very wrong.

A few things did occur the next day, things that I would have preferred to miss. From feeling so vexed the previous night, I hadn't fallen asleep until approximately 3:00 A.M. I slept in until 7:10—10 minutes before school began! Stricken with panic, I didn't eat or drink a thing for breakfast, and hustled frantically out the door, my hazel, watery eyes rimmed with tired circles. I was in such a hurry, I forgot my lunch.

In our seventh grade physical education class, we ran the mile. Ugh. Perhaps if I were more athletic, I wouldn't have found jogging nonstop up the track such a struggle. But I felt somewhat obligated to give it all my effort when I heard people comparing their times from last year.

"You got a 7:51?" I heard one tall and flexible girl boast, as she stretched in preparation.

"Well, I got a 6:50!"

My cheeks flushed absolutely scarlet with a sheepish embarrassment. Compared to those speedy times, my 10:03 must have been like molasses in slow motion!

If students have difficulty locating a written or a video source, suggest they search some of these news sources on the Internet:

The Nando Times: <http://www.nando.net>
The Newsroom: <http://www.auburn.edu/~vestmon/news.html>
The Washington Post: <http://www.washingtonpost.com/>
The Chicago Tribune: <http://www.chicago.tribune.com/>
The Los Angeles Times: <http://www.latimes.com/HOME/>
USA Today: <http://www.usatoday.com/>

Remind students that since they are writing fiction, they should feel free to add imaginary images, slightly alter actual events, and inject fabricated dialogue. However, mention that since their work is more fiction than fact, they need to change the names of any individuals mentioned in the original article.

You may also want to ask students to print copies of the original stories and turn them in along with their revised writing. This way, if you share stories in class, you can occasionally share the original piece the story was based on for comparison.

Strategy 4: Mix Forms with a Multigenre Research Paper

Each genre reflects content through different forms, creating insights unique to that genre. A poem expresses an idea in a radically different way than a news report. A short story and an essay on the same event open different doors of perception. To help students explore how different forms generate different types of information, Tom Romano in his book *Writing with Passion* suggests having students create a *multigenre research paper*. Using music, character sketches, comic book creations, art, short stories, poetry, monologue, news reports, and a host of other communicative genres, students piece together a research paper.

Try this variation of Romano's multigenre assignment. Divide the class into groups of five or six. As a team, have them select an individual, living or dead, who fascinates them. Explain that their task will be to create a multigenre paper examining this person. The individual can be an historical figure, an actor or actress, a musician, a scientist, an author, a politician, a general, a poet, a criminal, a comedian—any person the group finds engaging. The only requirement is that a mixture of magazine articles, books, and multimedia material be available for all members of the group to research this captivating individual. To avoid students selecting a person about whom little has been written, make sure each team creates a bibliography of available material to be submitted with their proposed topic.

After the group selects a person and checks on the available research material, explain that their task will be to create a multigenre research paper using some combination of the following genres and subgenres:

- *Art:* drawings, paintings, collages, photographs, VCR clips, ceramics, sculpture, jewelry, mixed media, cartoons, comic books, advertisements, T-shirts, logos, billboards, architectural designs, CD covers
- *Music:* original or found, instrumentals, songs with lyrics, tunes written with the flavor of blues, jazz, rock, rap, pop, country, or classical, electronic music, percussion music, Native American music, music from a specific time period
- *Drama:* one-act play, reader's theater, a film scene, a monologue, a formal speech, a dialogue
- *Fiction:* short story, character sketches, action dramas, fictional memoirs, fictional letters, fictional diaries, a legend, children's story, anecdote, short description, mystery, science-fi story, western, romance, humorous piece, horror story, a detective story
- *Nonfiction:* magazine articles, biographies, news reports, letters, diaries, sports features, personality feature, weather reports, opinions, movie reviews, film reviews, opinions, how-to pieces, scientific piece, historical piece, informational piece on music, art, entertainment, medicine, or technology

- *Poetry:* lyric poems, narrative poems, pop poems, shape poems, cinquains, syllable poems, haikus, and song lyrics
- *Photographs:* film, video, slides, photographs, Xeroxes

Each team member will be responsible for contributing two works from two different genres. While students may duplicate categories of genres, teams should strive for as much variety as possible. Each entry should contribute significant information on the chosen personality. Tell students that as a team they may share resources, interpreting different aspects of the same resource in different genres.

Each student on the team will receive two grades: one for individual effort, and one for the quality of the team project. Grades might be based on criteria such as:

FOR THE INDIVIDUAL GRADE

25%   Content: evidence of research, interesting insights, depth of details
20%   Form: powerful use of the elements of selected genre
20%   Style: quality of stylistic elements in sentence structures, paragraphs, passages and word choice
20%   Conventions: few conventional errors

FOR THE TEAM GRADE

15%   Unity of the Overall Project

As a model, Romano suggests using Michael Ondaatje's *The Collected Works of Billy the Kid*, a unique book that describes the life of Billy the Kid through multiple genres, such as songs, thumbnail sketches, poems, drawings, monologue, newspaper reports, and so on. You may want to make overheads of selected sections of the book for in-class illustrations.

Students should present their researched personalities to the class. If time permits, follow with a discussion on how different genres contribute different perspectives.

Strategy 5: Experiment with Images for Intros

Have students locate an interesting image at one of the following sites:

Discovery Gallery
<http://www.discover.com/gallery/index.html>
This site contains a wide collection of scientific images, including shots from the Hubble Telescope, computer-generated images, and illustrations by *Discovery*'s staff of artists.

Tom DiPace Sports Photography
<http://dipacephotography.com/dipace.html>
Tom DiPace's site offers an excellent collection of sports photographs, including images of football, baseball, basketball, tennis, hockey, golf, and NASCAR racing.

Using one of the introductory techniques explained in this chapter, have students write a brief introduction to a nonfiction article based on the image they choose. Ask students to label the specific introductory techniques they develop.

If any student has difficulty locating an appealing image, suggest he or she choose from the images on the CD that accompanies this book.

9
Systematic Revision
Form, Style, Content, and Conventions

"I seen it wit my mine own eyes," Thomas shouted.

"You mean I saw it with my own eyes," the teacher corrected.

"Oh, you seen it too?"

"Thomas, you must say I saw it."

"OK, I'll tell everyone you seen it too."

"No, you did not seen it!"

"But I did seen it," Thomas gasped!

The teacher interrupted, "No one seen it. Say, I saw it; you saw it. Somebody saw it."

"They did?" Thomas was surprised.

"Now, Thomas, why did you say, 'I seen it?'"

"Because I seen it."

"Let's try another way," the teacher suggested. "What did you see?"

"Thanks a lot. What I seen, you made me forgot." (Gendernalik 1984, 42)

This exchange, written by middle-school teacher Alfred Gendernalik, illustrates why asking many students to revise is a little like asking them to recite the first few lines of the *Odyssey* in the original Greek. For most students, revision is a mystery. The idea of Tolstoy rewriting *War and Peace* eight times or Doctorow revising *Ragtime* six times seems not just puzzling, but incomprehensible.

Part of their bewilderment comes from the tradition of teaching revision as editing conventions. Studies by Faigley and Witte (1981); Sommers (1982); and Joram, Woodruff, Byson, and Lindsay (1992) indicate that many teachers and their students equate revision with copyediting—correcting for spelling, punctuation, capitalization, and usage.

While this is important, editing for conventions is only one of four essential dimensions of revision. The other three, often overlooked, include revisions of form, content, and style. All four work in harmony to create effective writing.

Recognizing Revision Roadblocks

Several roadblocks can impede a teacher's effort to help students understand these four dimensions. First, a vague edict requiring students to revise for mechanics and usage can overwhelm them. When English teacher Ms. Latimeer says, "Be sure to proofread. I won't accept anything that isn't thoroughly edited," student Harvey Sloopwater glances at his three-hundred-plus-page grammar handbook in horror.

Judging from its sheer weight, Harvey guesses that the possible number of errors described within might total around two thousand. Since his knowledge of grammar is comparable to his knowledge of crop dusting in Upper Yalta, he fears disaster. "Proofread?" Harvey mutters to himself. "How do I proofread for errors? I don't know when I'm making an error. If I knew what a dangling participle was, I wouldn't have dangled it in the first place."

Since he needs a C average to continue playing right tackle for the Hincklebeck High Hellcats, Harvey sincerely wants to proofread. But where in that three-hundred-page handbook does he begin? In the past, when he has managed to correct his two most common errors—pronoun references and run-on sentences—Ms. Latimeer still lowered his grade because of shifting verb tense, weak supporting examples, or other problems he hadn't anticipated.

Another dilemma confronting Harvey is time. Why should he spend time revising if the time spent doesn't translate into better grades? From past experience, Harvey knows that he earns the same grade whether he spends five hours or five minutes revising. For Harvey, avoiding errors is like walking blindfolded through a swamp trying not to fall into unseen pits of grammar quicksand.

Using Short Checklists for Systematic Revision

How can a teacher help students like Harvey learn to revise? One approach is to emulate professionals who manage their revisions by using short checklists. Donald Murray, for example, uses a checklist of nine general concepts to revise (1995, 187). Richard Lanham works from a specific list of eight key

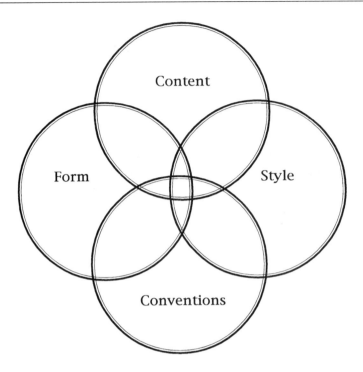

FIGURE 9–1. Scope of image grammar revisions

items (1992, 1). Novelist David Michael Kaplan revises with several frameworks, including an eighteen-point "Laundry List of Stylistic Glitches" (1997, 176–193).

These checklists share three qualities that provide possible solutions to Harvey's dilemma: (1) They narrow the focus of revision to a few significant items, (2) they outline a systematic approach, which makes revision manageable, and (3) they cover the complete scope of revision—form, content, style, and convention (see Figure 9–1).

By first introducing students to small checklists in each dimension (form, content, style, and conventions), and then later combining these to form more comprehensive lists, teachers can help students build a systematic approach to revision. Of the four dimensions, teachers may want to begin by having students revise for style. Alterations of style bring the greatest improvement with the fewest revisions.

Creating a Short Revision Checklist for Style

Teachers who have worked extensively with style find that the immediate improvement of stylistic revisions excites students. High school teacher Mark Jamison notes that his students were delighted and amazed by the effect of their revisions when they added brush strokes to sentences like these:

Original Sentence: He walked onto the game field.
Revised with Brush Strokes: He walked onto the game field, hands trembling from fear and adrenaline. (Jeff Branham)

Original Sentence: Shane Gordon appeared in the kitchen.
Revised with Brush Strokes: Shane Gordon appeared in the kitchen, his hair mussed like a startled porcupine. (Erin Nichole Jones)

Original Sentence: I walked up the stairs and down the dark hallway.
Revised with Brush Strokes: I walked up the stairs and down the dark hallway, shadows dancing on the walls. (Jonathan Triola)

Author and teacher Don Killgallon describes a similar response with Barry, one of his below-average tenth graders. Barry found writing frustrating and seemed unable to produce anything better than sentences like "The elephant is a slow person." Barry's success and attitude changed, however, when he began imitating stylistic structures and started producing sentences like this: "There is a flag, striped, colorful, and starry as a night sky" (Weaver 1996, 170–173).

To construct a checklist for style, one might begin with the five basic brush strokes described in Chapter 1 and later add additional stylistic devices as students expand their repertoire. Figure 9–2 is a handout that could be used to introduce revisions of style.

When teachers assign papers using a checklist as the basis for a grade, students like Harvey know exactly what they need to do to have success.

Creating a Revision Checklist for Conventions

The area of revision where teachers tend to have the most expertise is that of conventions—the rules for correct mechanics, usage, punctuation, and spelling. Because of this expertise, teachers need to be cautious not to overload their checklists with too many items. By limiting revisions of conventions to a small list of targeted problems, teachers can encourage greater student effort.

REVISION CHECKLIST FOR BASIC BRUSH STROKES

Name _____   Period _____

Revisions in this piece will be evaluated based on your use of five basic brush strokes. If you feel your piece contains examples of a specific brush stroke, circle "already used" and label the technique in the margin of your draft. If you haven't used a listed brush stroke, add one in the margin and label it. For each type of brush stroke correctly used in your writing (already used or added), you will receive 5 points. Points will not be given for a repeated technique, but add more strokes if they improve the effectiveness of your piece. In this exercise, you can earn a maximum of 25 points.

1. Absolute (already used / added)   _____

2. Appositive (already used / added)   _____

3. Participle (already used / added)   _____

4. Adjectives Out of Order (already used / added)   _____

5. Action Verbs (already used / added)   _____

Total Revision Points Earned = _____

FIGURE 9–2. Revision checklist for basic brushstrokes

Several scholars have created limited lists that teachers can use as models for short checklists. Cazort (1997) developed a short grammar textbook based on twenty-five of the most important grammar mistakes. Weaver (1996) identified five categories of grammar, each with a short list of key concepts in her *Teaching Grammar in Context*. Connors and Lundsford (1988) targeted twenty of the most common errors in their order of frequency, shown here:

1. No comma after introductory element
2. Vague pronoun reference
3. No comma in compound sentence
4. Wrong word
5. No comma in nonrestrictive element
6. Wrong/missing inflected endings
7. Wrong or missing prepositions
8. Comma splice
9. Possessive apostrophe error

10. Tense shift
11. Unnecessary shift in person
12. Sentence fragment
13. Wrong tense or verb form
14. Subject-verb agreement
15. Lack of comma in series
16. Pronoun agreement error
17. Unnecessary comma with restrictive element
18. Run-on or fused sentence
19. Dangling or misplaced modifier
20. Its versus It's error (58–59)

Similarly, using research on how people rank errors from serious to unimportant, Hairston (1982) developed a list of five categories in descending order of importance from "status marking" errors to items considered "minor or unimportant." And Noguchi (1991) cross-referenced Hariston's list with Connors and Lundsford's to create a combined list. So several well-researched lists are available to help teachers construct their own limited checklist appropriate for their students.

Many errors on these lists can be introduced to students as problems of image confusion. In sentences like "The malfunctioning gismo overheated the transformer. It needs repair," the pronoun creates a puzzling image. The reader can't clearly picture which item needs repair.

Two excellent sources for examples of image confusion are Richard Lederer's books *Anguished English* (1987) and *More Anguished English* (1993). Both catalog scores of comical images that arise from common errors with misplaced modifiers, pronoun reference, dangling participles, and logical slips. Here are a few examples taken from *Anguished English*:

> Yoko Ono will talk about her husband John Lennon, who was killed in an interview with Barbara Walters. (101)

> No one was injured in the blast, which was attributed to a buildup of gas by one town official. (104)

> When Lady Caruthers smashed the traditional bottle of champagne against the hull of the giant oil tanker, she slipped down the runway, gained speed, rocketed into the water with a gigantic spray, and continued unchecked toward Prince's Island. (105)

> Two cars were reported stolen by Groveton police yesterday. (102)

> Guilt, vengeance, and bitterness can be emotionally destructive to you and your children. You must get rid of them. (105)

Half the lies they tell me aren't true. (91)

Creating a Short Revision Checklist for Form

Every genre and subgenre follow a specified form. Novels, short stories, and plays, for example, share a common structure that identifies them as part of a particular genre. Even when two plays have nothing else in common, their structures are very similar. This is the case with screenplays, as scriptwriter and teacher Syd Field explains:

> If we were to take a screenplay and hang it on the wall like a painting and examine it, it would look like this diagram:

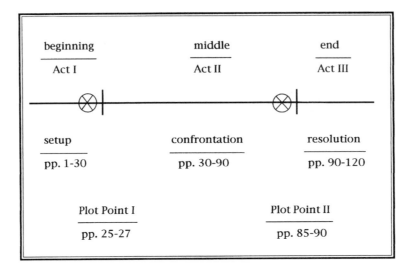

All screenplays contain this basic linear structure. This model of a screenplay is known as a paradigm. It is a model, a pattern, a conceptual scheme.

The paradigm of a table, for example, is a top with (usually) four legs. Within that paradigm, we can have a square table, long table, round table, high table, low table, rectangular table, or adjustable table. Within the paradigm, a table is anything we want it to be—a top with (usually) four legs.

The paradigm holds firm. (1984, 7–8).

Checklists for form outline the structural qualities of a work: the elements of fiction in relation to the Freitag Pyramid, the elements of nonfiction in nonfiction model #5, the structural design of a haiku, and so forth. For example, a teacher grading a paper based on nonfiction model #5 might use a short checklist like this:

ELEMENTS	POINTS:
1. Introduction	_____
2. Narrative	_____
3. Quotation	_____
4. Exposition	_____
5. Description	_____
6. Conclusion	_____
Total =	_____
Grade =	_____

In every genre, writers sift meaning with paradigm nets of form. The choice of form alters the writer's perception, influencing options for style, content, and convention. The structure governing a film script is just as different from the structure of a short story as the rules for playing baseball are from the rules for playing field hockey. Providing students with checklists of form gives them insights into these unique genre structures.

Creating a Short Revision Checklist for Content

Content from a writing perspective, ironically, ignores many aspects of the writer's ideas. For example, reading an essay in *Time* on the ethics of cloning, a historical scholar might focus on the religious-cultural-historic aspects of the article. To the historian, this is the essential focus. A scientist reading the same essay might see the piece as a testament to the advancement of science. However, a writer examining the piece would look for the essential content structures—a kind of grammar of content:

A CHECKLIST FOR CONTENT

Unity
1. Does the entire piece create one dominant controlling idea and is the idea sufficiently narrow?   _____
2. Does each paragraph or passage support the controlling idea?   _____

Development
3. Do the paragraphs and passages contain enough specific details to enhance clarity and contribute to unity?   _____

4. Are the logical relationships clear? Can the information be easily outlined with a classical outline or a Freitag Pyramid? _____

Coherence

5. Are ideas clearly connected from sentence to sentence and passage to passage? _____
6. Are transitions used to help ideas and images flow smoothly? _____

Clarity

7. Do words, sentences, and passages clearly express ideas? _____

Conciseness

8. Are excess words, sentences, and paragraphs eliminated? _____

Teachers for years used a grading system of two marks—one for content and one for mechanics. Students understood the basis of the mechanics grade, but they interpreted the content grade to mean the teacher either liked or disliked the information presented. Content checklists not only dispel this notion, but also provide a guide for revision.

Considering Some Special Concerns with Clarity

To help students improve clarity, teachers may want to discuss a concept of general semantics called the Ladder of Abstraction, an idea first described by Alfred Korzybski (1941). From a general semantics perspective, the relationship between words and the physical world follows a hierarchy. For example, describing Sniffer, a farmer's pig, a writer might choose to characterize Sniffer on one of many levels. The writer might refer to the pig simply as *Sniffer* or as a *pig* or as *livestock* or as an important *economic commodity*. Each label can be viewed on a scale ranging from the term that evokes the most powerful visual image to the one that loses all specific detail.

The phrase *ladder of abstraction* implies that some words cause us to mentally climb up a ladder, farther and farther away from the sensory reality at ground level. For example, at the bottom of the ladder, the word *Sniffer* generates images of a specific pig who likes to poke his wet snout through a wooden fence, who grunts and snorts at feeding time, and who even omits assorted odors on the morning breeze. But the higher one climbs the ladder, the less visual the images become. Compare the change in sensory referents as you move from *Sniffer* to economic commodity in Figure 9–3.

The words *economic commodity* include so many related images that the reader loses any specific focus. The trick in writing is not to eliminate abstract words, but to limit them, supporting those you use with many

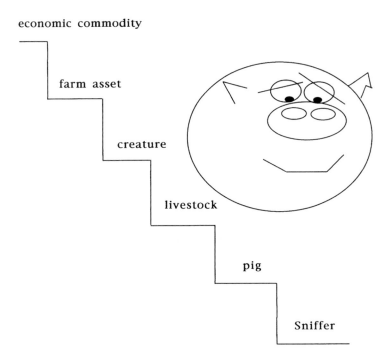

economic commodity

farm asset

creature

livestock

pig

Sniffer

FIGURE 9–3. Sniffer's ladder of abstraction

specific examples. Many well-written passages are constructed this way with an abstract controlling followed by specific supporting sentences. When writers use too many abstract terms or sentences, the words fog clarity.

This fogging quality motivated Philip Broughton (1968), a public service official, to create a Systematic Buzz Word Projector. Designed to illustrate how easy it is to create impressive statements that actually say nothing, the Buzz Word Projector provides writers three lists from which to construct one or more phrases.

COLUMN 1	COLUMN 2	COLUMN 3
0. integrated	0. management	0. options
1. total	1. organizational	1. flexibility
2. systematized	2. monitored	2. capacity
3. parallel	3. reciprocal	3. mobility
4. functional	4. digital	4. programming
5. responsive	5. logistical	5. concept

6. optional	6. transitional	6. time-phase
7. synchronized	7. incremental	7. projection
8. compatible	8. third-generation	8. hardware
9. balanced	9. policy	9. contingency

After building phrases by combining two or three words in each list, a writer can create the illusion of expertise by injecting these word combinations into their speech or writing. So, when someone asks what the superintendent in your school system actually does for a living, you can reply by choosing terms from each of the above columns and say, "The superintendent has been developing an *integrated reciprocal contingency* to make our school's *functional logistical time-phase* more effective." This sounds impressive, and may be as accurate a description as possible of what your superintendent does, but the mental images are blank.

Considering Some Special Concerns with Conciseness

Along with avoiding excessive abstractions, students need to be wary of what Richard Lanhan (1992) refers to as the "lard factor," the tendency to pack paragraphs with wasted words. In *Revising Prose*, Lanhan gives an example of squeezing out the lard in a passage written by a history professor:

> There is one last point in the evidence of Everard of Ypres, which deserves a comment before we leave it. This is the very surprising difference between the number of students at Gilbert's lectures in Chartres and in Paris. (20)

Lanhan squeezed these sentences, eliminating unnecessary words and leaving only this substance:

> One last question apropos Everard of Ypres: why did so few students attend his Chartres lectures and so many those in Paris? (21)

Lanham notes that the lard factor in this revision is 44 percent, meaning the final version contains 44 percent fewer words than the original.

Lard tends to develop when writing lacks a tight logical structure. Logic is the compass that leads the reader to a content destination. When students have no controlling idea influencing a paragraph or a passage, they wander like lost sailors in uncharted waters. When teachers ask students, "What is the point you're trying to make?" usually logic has been abandoned, and lard has emerged.

To avoid lard, corporate writers sometimes use a Fog Index to calculate clarity. To perform a fog index the writer must add the average number of words per sentence in a hundred-word sample to the percentage of polysyllables in the passage, and then multiply that total times .04. The result provides a number that correlates with the approximate grade level needed to read a passage. Requiring students to do this regularly would be time-consuming and more of an indication of mathematical ability than content clarity. However, most computer word processing programs now include a readability scale that can calculate text with one click of the mouse. For teachers with computer access, this is can be a useful teaching tool.

Combining Checklists

As the year progresses, teachers might combine checklists of form, style, convention, and content to give students a feel for the interrelationships of different dimensions of writing. Here is one example of a combined checklist for a nonfiction project:

A COMBINED REVISION CHECKLIST FOR NONFICTION MODEL #5

Name _____   Period _____

Be sure to review each of the following categories to see whether you have handled these elements well. Each listed item is worth from 0 to 5 points for a possible total of 140 points.

NONFICTION FORM	POINTS
1. Introduction	_____
2. Narrative	_____
3. Quotation	_____
4. Exposition	_____
5. Description	_____
STYLE	
6. Participles	_____
7. Absolutes	_____
8. Appositives	_____
9. Adjectives out of order	_____
10. Specific detail	_____
11. Use of parallel structure for effect	_____
12. Elimination of *being* verbs	_____
13. Use of figurative language	_____

CONVENTIONS

14. Elimination of run-on sentences   _____
15. Elimination of fragments   _____
16. Commas with introductory participles _____
17. Comma before a conjunction   _____
18. Commas with adjectives   _____
19. Quotation marks for dialogue   _____
20. Elimination of 10 common usage errors _____
21. Spelling corrected   _____

CONTENT

22. Topic is narrow.   _____
23. Passages support a central idea   _____
24. Ideas flow easily   _____
25. Details used are interesting   _____
26. Ideas and images are clear   _____
27. Controlling idea is supported with
    sufficient specific details   _____
28. Are excess words, sentences, and
    paragraphs eliminated?   _____

                         Total =   _____
                         Grade =   _____

This type of checklist makes grading easier. A teacher can determine quickly if a student has met the criteria listed and score points accordingly. While this practice should not replace marginal comments, conferencing, and self-evaluations, it is a useful way to reinforce wholeness in the revision process.

The systematic use of checklists can make grading easier and serve as a curriculum guide for portfolios; however, its primary benefit derives from helping students internalize their own personal framework for revision. Every writer revises from a checklist, but these are often subconscious lists, which have been composed over years of experimentation with form, content, style, and convention.

With students, the idea is to begin with four categories—form, content, style, and convention—and at first to teach just one or two concepts in each category. Then, as the year progresses, teachers can add additional items, building a kind of mental filing cabinet to store new insights, a first step toward a systematic approach to revision.

STRATEGIES

Strategy 1: Administer the Grammar Income Test

The Grammar Income Test is one of those ideas teachers wish scholars had invented. It is a test that measures a student's grammatical knowledge and then uses that measurement to predict the student's potential income. To motivate interest in conventions, give your students this test.

UNIVERSITY OF MOTTSBURGH OCCUPATIONAL INVENTORY OF GRAMMATICAL KNOWLEDGE

As demonstrated in the research of Dr. Edward McCormick, an individual's habits of grammar correlate with her or his income. Test results indicate that one can predict with 80 percent accuracy the income of an individual based on his answers to the questions below. Use this quiz to see what income level your grammatical patterns place you.

Instructions: Mark each sentence as C if it is grammatically correct, I if it is incorrect, or ? if you are uncertain. Wrong answers count as a minus two. A question mark, indicating you are uncertain, only counts as a minus one. Keep in mind that errors may be of any variety: spelling, punctuation, capitalization, or usage.

_____ 1.   Her choice will strongly effect the outcome.

_____ 2.   We have alot of work to do.

_____ 3.   Mottsburgh is a busy industrial city, thousands of cars and trucks move through it every day.

_____ 4.   "I suppose", she remarked "that success comes only with time."

_____ 5.   The company should receive the package tomorrow.

_____ 6.   Its impressive to hear what she has done.

_____ 7.   She was late, however, she did make the presentation.

_____ 8.   Give the book to whom?

_____ 9.   When the ship arrives we can begin the journey.

_____ 10. We rafted down the grand mountain river.

_____ 11. The name of the book was "Outbreak."

_____ 12. There were four in the group: Ann, Jim, Theo, and Amanda.

_____ 13. He sings good.

_____ 14. You shouldn't lie on the wet grass.

_____ 15. He paid all the interest on the principal.

_____ 16. I wish to go irregardless of his decision.

_____ 17. He doesn't know history very well. As you can see from his answers in class.

_____ 18. He imagined that Hawking would have all the answers but he just posed more questions.

_____ 19. Spiraling in the Andromeda Galaxy, Dr. Vilhelm insists that there is alien life on the Andromeda planet called Lanulos.

_____ 20. We packed all of our luggage, then we were on our way to the airport.

SCORING
Answer Key: 1. I, 2. I, 3. I, 4. I, 5. C, 6. I, 7. I, 8. C, 9. I, 10.I, 11. I, 12. C, 13. I, 14. C, 15. C, 16. I, 17. I, 18. I, 19. I, 20. I. (Corrected sentences are available on the companion CD.)

NUMBER WRONG	PROJECTED SALARY	OCCUPATIONAL LEVEL
0 to –4	$150,000 and above	top executive
–5 or –6	$90,000 to $150,000	upper management
–7 or –8	$60,000 to $ 90,000	key personnel
–9 or –12	$25,000 to $ 60,000	semi-skilled
–13 or –18	$10,000 to $ 25,000	unskilled
–20 or more	$0 to $10,000	unemployable

After students have taken and scored this test, explain that over the next few days you are going to increase their incomes by at least $30,000 each. Later, after you have worked with some of the grammatical concepts in this test, reveal that the test was fabricated. However, explain that the concept of the test is very real.

Every day individuals who make grammatical errors are victims of a pervasive but seldom discussed prejudice. People assume that those who make frequent grammatical errors are unintelligent, not very knowledgeable, and incompetent. None of this may be true. Language habits are more indicative of social background than education and ability. However, any business executive will support the notion that grammatical skill directly affects promotion. So, the idea behind the Grammar Income Test is valid, although the scored income level may not be.

Strategy 2: Punctuate That That Is Is That

To illustrate how punctuation shapes meaning, ask students to punctuate the following passage. Mention that this is an old puzzle once used in the film *Charly* to demonstrate the genius of the main character.

> That that is is that that is not is not that that is not is not that that is that that is is not that that is not is not that it it is

After students have tried punctuating this, use it as an illustration of how passages that sometimes sound logical to the writer, can be confusing to readers when pauses are not correctly punctuated. Then give the class the correct solution:

> That, that is, is. That, that is not, is not. That, that is not, is not that that is. That, that is, is not that, that is not. Is not that it? It is. (Ravenel 1959, 143)

Strategy 3: Editing the County Line Newsletter

Tell your class that the following paragraph was written as a brief overview of the Hollow Log Bluegrass Festival for the *County Line Newsletter*. Distribute a copy of the following to each member of the class, announce that they will be role-playing as an editor, and read the instructions to them.

As editor of the *County Line Newsletter*, you decide to conduct a short meeting to show reporters what you expect in revision. In preparation for this meeting, rewrite the paragraph below, showing how effective revisions might be made. Use your imagination to fill in needed details. Then follow your revision with a few written comments about why the original was ineffective.

HOLLOW LOG BLUEGRASS FESTIVAL

> The outdoor bluegrass jam was filled with music. Musicians played on all kinds of instruments. Dogs were wandering and sometimes barking. Kids were a bit disruptive, but the crowd was appreciative. Vendors sold a variety of souvenirs and great foods.

Strategy 4: Decoding Abstract Statements

This activity illustrates the problem of highly abstract words. Each of the following statements represents a well-known quote that has been paraphrased abstractly. Organize the class as teams to compete for bonus points by deciphering as many of these statements as possible in fifteen minutes.

ABSTRACTIONS

A. I'm unable to accurately perceive the possible directions that individuals might arbitrarily select, but given my predilection, I recognize only two viable alternatives: (1) restoring my emancipation from autocratic rule or (2) introducing me to the grim reaper.

B. The entire habitable and inhabitable regions of the third planet from the sun symbolically embody an elevated platform, and the two varieties of carbon-based bipedal life forms appear to be merely thespians.

C. Passageways for vehicles, humans and animals invited egress in two highly foliated directions, and I—I elected to traverse the access which appeared in better repair from less traffic.

D. The realm of the celestial expanse of the afterworld parallels a small, hard plat ovule of the genus Brassica.

E. A small move over a short distance to a specified place, accomplished by one individual; a forward bound of extraordinary proportions performed as a tribute to the human race.

ANSWERS

A. "I know not what course others may take, but as for me, give me liberty or give me death." (Patrick Henry)

B. "All the world's a stage, and all the men and women merely players." (William Shakespeare)

C. "Two roads diverged in a wood, and I—I took the one less traveled by." (Robert Frost)

D. "The kingdom of heaven is like a grain of mustard seed." (From Matthew, in the Bible)

E. "One small step for man; one giant leap for mankind." (Neil Armstrong) (Noden 1994, 63)

Strategy 5: Evaluate "Lost" by Ben Dover

This activity also illustrates the problem of highly abstract words. Divide the class into four or five groups. The task of each group will be to assign a letter grade and suggest revisions for the following short story, written by a high school sophomore. (Mention that the real name of the student has been deleted and replaced with Ben Dover.) The assignment given Ben was to create a short scene describing some incident, real or imagined.

After groups have discussed the story and recorded suggestions for revision, have a spokesperson from each group share the group's comments and evaluation. After all the groups have commented, ask the class this question: If the author of "Lost" later revised this piece, incorporating their suggestions, how much of a difference would it make in his grade? Also, ask them which types of revisions they found most important for improving this type of writing.

LOST

Tom was walking down the street. Suddenly he was dragged into an alley. He woke up three days later.

He didn't recognize the room he was in. A girl came through the door. She was dressed in a nurse's uniform.

"Must be a nurse," thought Tom.

"How are you?" she asked.

"Fine," said Tom. "But everything to me is a mystery. Where am I? Who am I?"

Yes, Tom was a mystery. He couldn't remember a thing. His mind was blank. He was suffering from what doctors said was amnesia. One doctor explained to Tom that he had been flown from Dunkirk, Maine to Denver, Colorado for brain surgery. It was a difficult operation, but Tom had survived. Since no one knew his name, they called him Danny. From then on he was known as Danny.

Danny felt confused. In three weeks he left the hospital, still confused. The doctors liked Danny, so they gave him a $4,000 loan and told him to return to Maine and try to find out who he really was.

"Good idea," thought Dan, and he left.

When Danny arrived in Dunkirk, he took a bus to the middle of town. Then, he walked up one street and down another. Again, he walked up one street and down another. All the streets looked the same. He was confused.

That night Danny got a hotel room and went to sleep. The next morning, he stepped out on the street and was excited when things looked familiar. His memory stirred. He was happy because things looked familiar. Then he realized that they looked familiar because he was there yesterday.

Days seemed to fly by. Danny was confused and sad. One evening it was getting late. Danny went for a walk in the darkness. The streets looked familiar, but he knew why. As he was walking back to the hotel room, all of a sudden, out of the darkness, a huge, black dog jumped from a bush. Danny thought the dog was up to no good.

Soon Danny saw that the dog just wanted to play. He examined the dog as it followed him to the hotel. Suddenly, Danny's memory stirred. Then it stirred again. He looked at the dog for a long time, very carefully, and it came to him that this was a Doberman Pincer.

Danny tried to get the dog to go home. "Go home boy," he said, but the dog just looked at him funny. "Go home I said," said Danny. But the dog wouldn't go. So Danny took the dog back to the hotel and they became good friends.

One night the dog was eating dinner. Danny opened the evening newspaper and his eye caught a large ad that read,

Wanted Lost Doberman Pincer
Answers to the name of Big Luke. $500 Reward
Boy's Pet

"Hmmm," thought Danny. "Could this be Big Luke? He doesn't seem that big."

Danny didn't want to take the dog back. He liked the dog.

"Finder's keepers," thought Danny. But Danny's honest up-bringing was fighting him all the way. So the next day Danny went to the address in the ad to return the dog.

He rang the doorbell and some old lady answered the door. She looked familiar.

"Oh, Oh" said the lady. "Herman," she yelled, "it's our son Tom. Oh Tom, I knew you would come back and I knew if anyone could find you it would be your dog "Big Luke.""

"I'm excited to be home," said Tom. "I've been in Denver."

"I'm so glad to have you back," said his mother.

"Me too," said his father.

Yes, this was Danny's mother and father. Dan's real name was Tom and his dog was really named "Big Luke." Tom's family would always be grateful to "Big Luke" for bringing Tom home.

The End!!!!!!!!!!!!!!!!!!!!!!!

If students have been working with image grammar, this paper should generate numerous comments on concepts discussed throughout this book—the need for brush strokes, the lack of parallel structures and special effects, the incorrect use of conventions, the failure to limit the passage of time in story—all elements that could easily be improved with revision.

After students have read and evaluated this piece, you may want to assign a rewrite—either as a group project or as an individual assignment—to illustrate the power of revising with image grammar techniques.

Strategy 6: Review Writings on the Web

On the World Wide Web there are hundreds of stories by middle and high school students. These offer an excellent resource for analysis. A writing taken from the Web can be analyzed freely in class without fear of hurting another student's feelings.

Below are several sites that publish student work. Preview the writing on these sites and download a few examples to use for a class discussion on revision.

Midlink Magazine for Kids
<http://longwood.cs.ucf.edu/~MidLink/>

KidPub
<http://www.kidpub.org/kidpub/>

Stone Soup (companion site for the magazine)
<http://www.stonesoup.com/>

The Ram's Horn, High School Newspaper
<http://www.chsn.org/ramshorn/index.htm>

Digital Storytelling Festival
<http://www.dstory.com/dsf5/home.html>
<http://www.dstory.com/dsf4/>

Salon Magazine
<http://www.salonmagazine.com/>

Mystery Net
<http://www.MysteryNet.com/>

A Concluding Note

Dominique Bouhours, the seventeenth-century grammarian, lay in bed, dying. A friend leaned over and asked how he felt. Bouhours looked up, smiled, and struggled to speak. "I am," he said, "about to—or I am going to—die." There was a brief pause. Then, Bouhours added, "Either expression is correct." Those were the last words he ever spoke (Conrad 1961, 48).

In my early years of teaching grammar, struggling with students who viewed grammar rules much like traffic violations and who saw me as the traffic cop, I often thought that students could very naturally perceive me on my deathbed making a statement like Bouhours. Fortunately, I don't think that is the case anymore—not because I have abandoned my concern for grammar, but because I have come to understand its hidden beauty.

Grammar is the soul of humankind. Its intricacies trigger our laughter, our tears, our dreams. Grammar is the secret muse of all expression, the portrait painter of life's emotions. It allows us to feel the touch of a lover's hand on a bridge in Madison County and hear the cracking voice of the oldest living confederate widow. It gives poets the syntax to paint brainteasers that will delight readers for centuries, and helps truck drivers with the "gift of blarney" to spin captivating tales for their buddies over a morning cup of coffee. Nothing in life is more essential, more sensitive, more intrinsic to the human soul. When students come to share this vision, grammar bridges the world of living to the world of writing, reading, and speaking. Image grammar attempts to build this bridge.

REFERENCES

Ackerman, D. 1990. *A Natural History of the Senses*. New York: Random House.

Adler, M., and C. Van Doren. 1940. *How to Read a Book*. New York: Simon & Schuster.

Allen, W. 1972. *Without Feathers*. New York: Random House.

Anderson, C. 1992. *Free Style*. Boston: Houghton Mifflin.

Anderson, K. 1995. "Getting Readers in the Mood." *Writer's Digest* (June): 34–35.

Auel, J. M. 1980. *The Clan of the Cave Bear*. New York: Crown.

Bachman, R. 1984. *Thinner*. New York: New American Library Books.

Baker, R. 1980. "Little Red Riding Hood." In *Effective Writing for Executives*, edited by S. M. Leblang, 46–47. New York: Time-Life Films.

———. 1982. *Growing Up*. New York: Congdon and Weed.

Barry, D. 1994. *The World According to Dave Barry*. New York: Wings Books.

Barthes, R. 1994. "Looking for My Mother." In *The Practice of Writing*, edited by R. Scholes, N. R. Comley, and J. Peritz, 44–45. New York: St. Martin's Press.

Beaumont, A. 1989. *Another Time, Another Love*. New York: Harlequin Books.

Benchley, P. 1974. *Jaws*. New York: Doubleday & Company.

The Best of Bad Hemingway. 1989. New York: Harcourt, Brace, Jovanovich.

Bickham, J. 1993. *Scene and Structure*. Cincinnati, OH: Writer's Digest.

———. 1996. *Writing and Selling Your Novel*. Cincinnati, OH: Writer's Digest.

Bills, E. 1964. "Writing the Magazine Article." Sound recording. New York: McGraw-Hill Sound Seminars.

Blau, S. 1995. *The Writer's Craft*. Evanston, IL: McDougal Littell.

Blume, J. 1981. *Tiger Eyes*. Scarsdale, NY: Bradbury Press.

Bombeck, E. 1979. *Aunt Erma's Cope Book*. New York: McGraw-Hill.

———. 1985. *Four of a Kind*. New York: McGraw-Hill.

Bond, G. R., and H. H. Crosby. 1978. *The Shape of Thought*. Lanham, MD: University Press of America.

Bova, B. 1995. *Orion Among the Stars*. New York: Tom Doherty Associates.

Bradbury, R. 1968. "The Sound of Thunder." In *R Is for Rocket*, 205–18. London: Hart-Davis.

Braddock, R., L. Lloyd-Jones, and L. Schoer. 1963. *Research in Written Composition*. Champaign, IL: NCTE.

Braddock, R. 1974. "The Frequency and Placement of Topic Sentences in Expository Prose." *Research in the Teaching of English* 8 (Winter): 287–302.

Brilliant, A. 1993. *Appreciate Me Now and Avoid the Rush*. Santa Barbara, CA: Woodbridge Press.

Broughton, Philip. 1968. *Newsweek* (6 May): 104.

Browne, G. A. 1976. *Slide*. New York: Arbor House.

Brunvand, J. H. 1981. *The Vanishing Hitchhiker: American Urban Legends and Their Meanings*. New York: W. W. Norton.

———. 1984. *The Choking Doberman and Other "New" Urban Legends*. New York: W. W. Norton.

Bunchman, J., and S. B. Briggs. 1994. *Activities for Creating Pictures and Poetry*. Worchester, MA: Davis Publications.

Burroway, J. 1987. *Writing Fiction*. 2d ed. Boston: Little, Brown.

Buscaglia, L. 1982. *Living, Loving, and Learning*. New York: Holt, Rhinehart and Winston.

Byars, B. 1986. *The Not-Just-Anybody Family*. New York: Delacorte Press.

CNN Interactive. 1997 (August 4). Showbiz Story Page. <http://www.cnn.com/SHOWBIZ/9707/30/romance.plagarism.ap/excerpts.html.>

Callahan, T. 1993. "Interview with Pete Hamill." *Writer's Digest* (Sept.): 45–46.

Campbell, B. 1981. *Raiders of the Lost Ark*. New York: Ballantine.

Campbell, W. 1950. *Writing: Advice and Devices*. Garden City, NY: Doubleday and Company.

Carli, W. 1994. We Are the Connectors. "Opening Day Welcome" speech given at Alliance High School, Alliance, OH, 25 August.

Carr, C. 1994. *The Alienist*. New York: Random House.

Carter, R., and W. Nash. 1990. *Seeing Through Language*. Cambridge, MA: Basil Blackwell Ltd.

Cassill, R. V. 1975. *Writing Fiction*. New York: Prentice Hall.

Catton, B. 1984. *Bruce Catton's Civil War*. New York: Fairfax Press.

Cazort, D. 1997. *Under the Grammar Hammer*. Los Angeles: Lowell House.

Chieger, B., and P. Sullivan. 1990. *Football's Greatest Quotes*. New York: Simon & Schuster.

Christensen, B. 1979. *The Christensen Method*. New York: Harper & Row.

Christensen, F. 1966. "A Symposium on the Paragraph." *College Composition and Communication* 17 (2): 60–64.

———. 1967. *Notes Toward a New Rhetoric*. New York: Harper & Row.

Christopher, J. 1967. *The White Mountains*. New York: Collier Books.

Clark, M. H. 1991. *Weep No More My Lady*. In *Three Complete Novels*. New York: Wings Books.

Clarke, A. C. 1986. *July 20, 2019*. New York: Macmillan.

Coe, R. M. 1981. *Form and Substance*. New York: John Wiley & Sons.

———. 1988. *Toward a Grammar of Passages*. Carbondale, IL: Southern Illinois University Press.

Collier, J. L., and C. Collier. 1974. *My Brother Sam Is Dead*. New York: Four Winds Press.

Connors, R., and C. Glenn. 1992. *The St. Martin's Guide to Teaching Writing*. 2d ed. New York: St. Martin's Press.

Connors, R. J., and A. A. Lunsford. 1988. "Frequency of Formal Errors in Current College Writing, or Ma and Pa Kettle Do Research." *College Composition and Communication* 39: 395–409.

Conrad, B. 1961. *Famous Last Words*. Garden City, NY: Doubleday and Co.

———. 1990. *The Complete Guide to Writing Fiction*. Cincinnati, OH: Writer's Digest Books.

Cook, R. 1987. *Outbreak*. New York: Putnam.

Cooney, C. B. 1990. *The Face on the Milk Carton*. New York: Bantam Books.

Corbett, E., and R. Connors. 1999. *Style and Statement*. New York: Oxford University Press.

Cormier, R. 1974. *The Chocolate War*. New York: Dell.

Crane, S. [1895] 1992. *The Red Badge of Courage*. New York: Barnes and Noble Books.

Crichton, M. 1990. *Jurassic Park*. New York: Alfred A. Knopf.

Dahl, R. 1984. "Beware of the Dog." In *Understanding Literature*, 86–94. New York: MacMillan.

Daiker, D. A., A. Kerek, and M. Morenberg. 1990. *The Writer's Options: Combining to Composing*. 4th ed. New York: Harper & Row.

D'Angelo, F. J. 1985. *Process and Thought in Composition*. Boston: Little, Brown.

Dawkins, J. 1992. "Rethinking Punctuation." ERIC ED 340 048.

———. 1995. "Teaching Punctuation as a Rhetorical Tool." *College Composition and Communication* 46: 533–48.

De Bono, E. 1967. *New Think.* New York: Basic Books.

Dickinson, P. 1992. *A Bone from a Dry Sea.* New York: Delacorte Press.

Didion, J. 1984. "Why I Write." In *Joan Didion: Essays and Conversations,* edited by Ellen G. Friedman. Princeton, ON: Ontario Review Press.

Dillard, A. 1974. *Pilgrim at Tinker Creek.* New York: Harper Perennial.

———. 1987. *An American Childhood.* New York: Harper & Row.

Doyle, Sir Arthur Conan. 1968. *The Hound of the Baskervilles.* New York: Dodd, Mead & Company.

Draper, S. 1997. *Forged by Fire.* New York: Atheneum Books for Young Readers.

Druxman, M. 1997. *The Art of Storytelling.* Westlake Village, CA: Center Press.

Eiseley, L. 1964. *The Unexpected Universe.* New York: Harcourt, Brace & World.

Elbow, P. 1985. "The Challenge for Sentence Combining." In *Sentence Combining: A Rhetorical Perspective,* edited by D. A. Daiker, A. Kerek, and M. Morenberg, 232–45. Carbondale, IL: Southern Illinois University Press.

Elledge, S. 1984. *E. B. White: A Biography.* New York: W. W. Norton.

Elwood, M. 1966. *Characters Make Your Story.* Cambridge, MA: Riverside Press.

Faigley, L., and S. Witte. 1981. "Analyzing Revision." *College Composition and Communication* 32: 400–10.

Field, S. 1984. *Screenplay: The Foundations of Screenwriting.* New York: Dell.

Fitzgerald, F. S. [1945] 1956. "The Crackup." In *The Crackup,* edited by E. Wilson, 69–84. New York: J. Laughlin.

Fitzgerald, J., and A. Teasley. 1986. "Effects of Instruction in Narrative Structure on Children's Writing." *Journal of Educational Psychology* 78 (Dec.): 424–32.

Fletcher, L. 1997. "Ten Ends for Any Article." *Writer's Digest* (Aug.): 34–35.

Flood, J., D. Lapp, and N. Farnan. 1986. "A Reading-Writing Procedure That Teaches Expository Paragraph Structure." *Reading Teacher* 37 (4): 556–62.

Follett, K. 1978. *Eye of the Needle.* New York: Arbor House.

Franklin, B. 1951. *The Autobiography of Ben Franklin.* New York: The Heritage Press.

Franklin, J. 1986. *Writing for Story*. New York: Penguin Books.

Gendernalik, A. 1984. "I Seen It." *English Journal* 73 (Dec.): 42.

Gibbons, D., ed. 1992. *The Ray Bradbury Chronicles, Volume 2*. New York: Bantam Books.

Goldberg, N. 1986. *Writing Down the Bones*. Boston: Shambhala.

Grafton, S. 1991. *H Is for Homicide*. New York: Henry Holt.

Great Reading from Life. 1960. New York: Bonanza Books.

Hairston, M. 1982. "Not All Errors Are Created Equal: Nonacademic Readers in the Professions Respond to Lapses in Usage." *College English* 43: 794–806.

Halberstam, D. 1991. *The Next Century*. New York: William Morrow.

Hall, E., C. Hall, and A. Leech. 1990. *Scripted Fantasy in the Classroom*. New York: Nichols Publishing.

Halprin, M. 1991. *A Soldier of the Great War*. New York: Harcourt Brace Jovanovich.

Hamilton, V. 1968. *The House of Dies Drear*. New York: Macmillan.

Hammett, D. 1930. *The Maltese Falcon*. New York: Alfred A. Knopf.

Hart, J. 1998. "Twenty-five Ways to Supercharge Your Manuscript." In *Writing for Magazines*. Cincinnati, OH: Writer's Digest Books.

Hayakawa, S. I. 1941. *Language in Action*. New York: Harcourt, Brace.

Hegi, U. 1994. *Stones from the River*. New York: Scribner Paperback Fiction.

Hemingway, E. 1952. *The Old Man and the Sea*. New York: Charles Scribner's Sons.

———. 1964. *A Moveable Feast*. New York: Charles Scribner's Sons.

Herriot, J. 1972. *All Creatures Great and Small*. New York: St. Martin's Press.

Hess, K. K. 1987. *Enhancing Writing Through Imagery*. Unionville, NY: Trillium Books.

Hesse, K. 1994. *Phoenix Rising*. New York: Penguin Books.

Hinton, S. E. 1967. *The Outsiders*. New York: Viking Press.

Hoffman, A. 1997. *Here on Earth*. New York: Berkley Books.

Hoffman, G. 1986. *Writeful*. Huntington Beach, CA: Verve Press.

Horowitz, R. 1987. "Rhetorical Structure in Discourse Processing." In *Comprehending Oral and Written Language*, edited by R. Horowitz and S. J. Samuels. San Diego: Academic Press.

Irmscher, W. 1979. *Teaching Expository Writing*. New York: Holt, Rhinehart and Winston.

Jacques, B. 1988. *Mossflower*. New York: Avon Books.

James, P. D. 1983. "A Series of Scenes." *Writer's Digest* (October): 23–24.

Jividen, S., and J. Jividen. 1997. *Goose Moon*. Ravenna, OH: SJ Productions.

Jones, B. F., J. Pierce, and B. Hunter. 1988. "Teaching Students to Construct Graphic Representations." *Educational Leadership* 26 (Dec.): 20–25.

Joram, E., E. Woodruff, M. Bryson, and P. Lindsay. 1992. "The Effects of Revising with a Word Processor on Written Composition." *Research in the Teaching of English* 26: 167–93.

Kafka, F. 1982. *The Castle*. New York: Alfred A. Knopf.

Kagafas, J. 1998. Interview at University of Akron. 1 December.

Kamins, M. 1986. "Images of Jim Murray." *Writer's Digest* (June): 26–28.

Kaplan, D. M. 1997. *Revision: A Creative Approach to Writing and Rewriting Fiction*. Cincinnati, OH: Story Press.

Kehl, D. G. 1979. "Composition in the Mimetic Mode: Imitatio and Exercitatio." In *Linguistics Stylistics and the Teaching of Composition*, edited by Donald McQuade. Akron, OH: University of Akron Press.

Keller, H. 1990. *The Story of My Life*. New York: Bantam Books.

Kelly, J. 1978. *Magazine Writing Today*. Cincinnati, OH: Writer's Digest Books.

Kennedy, J. F. 1961. Inaugural address given, Washington, DC, 20 January.

Kercheval, J. L. 1997. *Building Fiction*. Cincinnati, OH: Story Press.

Killgallon, D. 1997. *Sentence Composing for Middle School*. Portsmouth, NH: Boynton/Cook.

———. 1998a. *Sentence Composing for College*. Portsmouth, NH: Boynton/Cook.

———. 1998b. *Sentence Composing for High School*. Portsmouth, NH: Boynton/Cook.

King, M. L., Jr. 1986. "I Have a Dream." In *A Testament of Hope: The Essential Writings of Martin Luther King Jr.*, edited by J. M. Washington, 194–96. San Francisco: Harper & Row.

Korzybski, A. 1941. *Science and Sanity*. New York: International Non-Aristotelian Library Publishing Co.

Kress, N. 1994. "An Untitled Column." *Writer's Digest* (Dec.): 8–10.

———. 1997. "What's Your Archtype?" *Writer's Digest* (July): 6–9.

Kuralt, C. 1990. *A Life on the Road*. New York: G. P. Putnam's Sons.

L'Amour, L. 1990. *The Outlaws at Mesquite*. New York: Bantam Books.

Lane, B. 1993. *After THE END*. Portsmouth, NH: Heinemann.

Lanham, R. 1992. *Revising Prose*. New York: Macmillan.

Laurance, W. F. 1998. "Fragments of the Forest." *Natural History* 107 (6): 35–39.

Leavitt, H. D., and D. A. Sohn. 1964. *Stop, Look, and Write!* New York: Bantam Books.

Lederer, R. 1987. *Anguished English*. Charleston, SC: Wrick and Company.

———. 1993. *More Anguished English*. New York: Delacorte Press.

Lehr, F. 1987. "Story Grammar." *Reading Teacher* 40 (Feb.): 550–52.

L'Engle, M. 1962. *A Wrinkle in Time*. New York: Ariel Books.

———. 1994. *Troubling a Star*. New York: Farrar, Straus & Giroux.

Leno, J., with Bill Zehme. 1996. *Leading with My Chin*. New York: HarperCollins.

Levy, D., and R. Keene. 1976. *An Opening Repertoire for the Attacking Player*. New York: Mason/Charter Publishers.

Lincoln, A. "The Gettysburg Address." <http://www.loc.gov/exhibits/gadd.html>.

Lindemann, E. 1995. *A Rhetoric for Writing Teachers*. 3d ed. New York: Oxford University Press.

London, J. 1985. *Call of the Wild*. Pleasantville, NY: Reader's Digest Association.

Lorenz, K. 1973. *Civilized Man's Eight Deadly Sins*. New York: Harcourt, Brace, Jovanovich.

Lowry, L. 1993. *The Giver*. New York: Bantam Doubleday Dell Books for Young Readers.

Mailer, N. 1975. *The Fight*. Boston: Little, Brown.

———. 1983. *Ancient Evenings*. Boston: Little, Brown.

McKinney, D. 1994. *Magazine Writing That Sells*. Cincinnati, OH: Writer's Digest Books.

McNeil, J. D. 1987. *Reading Comprehension: New Directions for Classroom Practices*. 2d ed. Glenview, IL: Scott, Foresman.

Meade, R. A., and W. G. Ellis. 1970. "Paragraph Development in the Modern Age of Rhetoric." *English Journal* 59 (February): 219–26.

Mendelowitz, D. M., and D. A. Wakeham. 1993. *A Guide to Drawing*. New York: Harcourt Brace Jovanovich.

Meyer, C. 1987. *A Linguistic Study of American Punctuation*. New York: Peter Lang.

Michener, J. A. 1953. *The Bridges at Toko-Ri*. New York: Random House.

Miles, J. 1967. *Style and Proportion*. Boston: Little, Brown.

Moffett, J. W. 1968. *Teaching the Universe of Discourse*. Boston: Houghton Mifflin.

———. 1973. *A Student-Centered Language Arts Curriculum, Grades K–12*. Boston: Houghton Mifflin.

Morris, D. 1986. *Cat Watching*. New York: Crown Publishers.

Morrison, T. 1998. *Paradise*. New York: Alfred A. Knopf.

Murray, D. 1995. *The Craft of Revision*. 2d ed. New York: Harcourt Brace College Publishers.

Nadis, S. 1999. "When It Comes to Building New Wetlands, Scientists Still Can't Fool Mother Nature." *National Wildlife* (Dec./Jan): 14–16.

Negroponte, N. 1995. *Being Digital*. New York: Vintage Books.

Newcott, W. R. 1998. "Return to Mars." *National Geographic* 194 (2): 8–23.

Newman, L. 1999. "The Photographic Sketchbook." *American Artist* 63 (679): 46–51.

Nightingale, E. 1969. *This Is Earl Nightingale*. Garden City, NY: Doubleday.

Noden, H., and R. Vacca. 1994. *Whole Language in Middle and Secondary Classrooms*. New York: HarperCollins.

Noguchi, R. 1991. *Grammar and the Teaching of Writing*. Urbana, IL: NCTE.

Noonan, P. 1990. *What I Saw at the Revolution*. New York: Random House.

Nye, R. 1968. *Beowulf: A New Telling*. New York: Dell Publishing.

Obler, A. 1970. *Drop Dead!* Capitol Records ST1763.

O'Brien, T. 1990. *The Things They Carried*. Boston: Houghton Mifflin/Seymour Lawrence.

Olson, J. 1992. *Envisioning Writing*. Portsmouth, NH: Heinemann.

O'Neill, A. 1995. "A Good Yarn Teller." *Children's Book Review* (Summer/Fall): 36–37.

Parks, G. 1968. *A Poet and His Camera*. New York: Viking Press.

Paulsen, G. 1987. *Hatchet*. New York: Puffin Books.

———. 1988. *The Island*. New York: Orchard Books.

———. 1996. *Brian's Winter*. New York: Delacorte Press.

Payne, L. V. 1982. *The Lively Art of Writing: Effecting Style*. Chicago: Follett.

Peck, R. N. 1980. *The Secrets of Successful Fiction*. Cincinnati, OH: Writer's Digest Books.

———. 1983. *Fiction Is Folks*. Cincinnati, OH: Writer's Digest Books.

———. 1984. *A Day No Pigs Would Die*. New York: Alfred A. Knopf.

———. 1988. *The Horse Hunters*. New York: Random House.

Pedoto, C. 1993. *Painting Literature*. Lanham, MD: University Press of America.

Perret, G. 1982. *How to Write and Sell Your Sense of Humor*. Cincinnati, OH: Writer's Digest Books.

Poe, E. A. 1938. *The Complete Tales and Poems of Edgar Allan Poe*. New York: Random House.

Polti, G. 1917. *The Thirty-Six Dramatic Situations*. Translated by Lucille Ray. Ridgewood, NJ: Editor Company.

Probst, R. E. 1990. "Dialogue with a Text." In *To Compose*, edited by T. Newkirk. Portsmouth, NH: Heinemann.

Provost, G. 1984. "Ain't You a Little Too Concerned About Perfect English?" *Writer's Digest* (May): 20–22.

———. 1990. *Make Your Words Work*. Cincinnati, OH: Writer's Digest Books.

Rae, C. M. 1996. *Movies in the Mind*. Santa Fe: Sherman Asher Publishing.

Ravenel, W. B. 1959. *English Reference Book*. Alexandria, VA: Virginia Publishers.

Read. 1973. "Watch It, Hump Baby." 1973. *Read* (April): 22–23.

Reston, J. 1991. *Deadline*. New York: Random House.

Rice, A. 1989. *The Mummy or Ramses the Damned*. New York: Ballantine Books.

Rice, S. 1993. *Right Words Right Places*. Belmont, CA: Wadsworth Publishing.

Richards, J. 1998. "What Is the Most Effective Writing Assignment You've Ever Given?" *English Journal* 88 (2): 29–30.

Rivers, W. 1976. *Free-Lancer and Staff Writer: Newspaper Features and Magazine Articles*. Belmont, CA: Wadsworth Publishing.

Rodgers, P. C. 1966. "A Discourse-Centered Rhetoric of the Paragraph." *College Composition and Communication* 17 (1): 2–11.

Romano, T. 1995. *Writing with Passion*. Portsmouth, NH: Boynton/Cook.

Roosevelt, F. D. 1944. Tax Bill Veto Message. Speech given, Washington, DC, 22 February.

Ryan, C. 1959. *The Longest Day: June 6, 1944*. Kent, England: New English Library.

Sagan, C. 1980. *Cosmos*. New York: Random House.

Sanborn, F. B. 1917. *The Life of Henry David Thoreau*. New York: Houghton Mifflin.

Schoenfeld, C., and K. Diegmueller. 1982. *Effective Feature Writing*. New York: Holt, Rhinehart and Winston.

Scholes, R., N. R. Comley, and J. Peritz. 1994. *The Practice of Writing*. New York: St. Martin's Press.

Schwartz, A. 1981. *Scary Stories to Tell in the Dark*. New York: Harper & Row.

———. 1984. *More Scary Stories to Tell in the Dark*. New York: Lippincott-Raven Publishers.

Scofield, C. I., ed. [1945] 1967. *New Scofield Reference Bible*. New York: Oxford University Press.

Sebestyen, O. 1988. *The Girl in the Box*. Boston: Joy Street Books.

Seinfeld, J. 1993. *SeinLanguage*. New York: Bantam Books.

Seltzer, D. 1970. *The Hellstrom Chronicle*. Film transcript. David L. Wolper Productions.

Seutonius. *Lives of the Caesars, Julius*. section 37.

Shaara, M. 1974. *The Killer Angels*. New York: Ballantine Books.

Shahn, B. 1985. *The Shape of Content*. Cambridge, MA: Harvard University Press.

Shaughnessy, M. 1977. *Errors and Expectations*. New York: Oxford University Press.

Shepherd, J. 1966. *In God We Trust All Others Pay Cash*. New York: Doubleday & Company.

Short, E. J., and E. B. Ryan. 1984. "Metacognitive Differences Between Skilled and Less Skilled Readers: Remediating Deficits Through Story Grammar and Attribution Training." *Journal of Educational Psychology* 76: 225–35.

Slepian, J. 1985. *Getting on with It*. New York: Four Winds Press.

Smith, R. 1982. "Winning by Striking Out." In *The Red Smith Reader*, edited by D. Anderson, 154–56. New York: Random House.

Sommer, E., and M. Sommer. 1991. *As One Mad with Wine and Other Similes*. New York: Visible Ink Press.

Sommers, N. 1982. "Responding to Student Writing." *College Composition and Communication* 33: 148–56.

Speidel, J. D. 1977. "Using Art to Teach Writing." *Connecticut English Journal* 9 (1): 66–70.

Spiegel, A. 1976. *Fiction and the Camera Eye*. Charlottesville: University Press of Virginia.

Stein, S. 1995. *Stein on Writing*. New York: St. Martin's Press.

Steinbeck, J. 1953. *The Short Novels of John Steinbeck*. New York: Viking Press.

———. 1969. *Journal of a Novel*. New York: Viking Press.

———. 1973. *The Red Pony*. New York: Viking Press.

Stern, A. 1976. "When Is a Paragraph?" *College Composition and Communication* 27: 253–57.

Svitil, K. A. 1992. "A Deadly Wave." *Discover* 21 (Jan.): 66.

Swain, D. V. 1965. *Techniques of the Selling Writer*. Norman, OK: University of Oklahoma Press.

Thomas, C. 1977. *Firefox*. New York: Holt, Rinehart and Winston.

Tobias, R. B. 1993. *Twenty Master Plots*. Cincinnati, OH: Writer's Digest Books.

Tucker, S. 1992. *Writing Poetry*. Glenview, IL: Good Year Books.

Tuffte, V. 1971. *Grammar as Style*. New York: Holt, Rhinehart and Winston.

Twain, M. 1964. *The Adventures of Tom Sawyer.* In *The Complete Novels of Mark Twain,* ed. C. Neider, 385–559. Garden City, NY: Doubleday.

United Artists. 1996. Movieweb. March. <http://www.mgmua.com/lord /index.html>.

Universal Studios Online. 1995. <http://www.mca.com/universal_pictures /index.html>.

Vacca, R., and J. Vacca. 1996. *Content Area Reading.* New York: HarperCollins College.

Voight, C. 1986. *Izzy, Willy-Nilly.* New York: Atheneum.

Waddell, M., R. Esch, and R. Walker. 1972. *The Art of Styling Sentences.* Woodbury, NY: Barrons.

Warner, A. 1993. "If the Shoe No Longer Fits, Wear It Anyway?" *English Journal* 82 (Sept.): 76–80.

Weathers, W. 1980. *An Alternate Style.* Rochelle Park, NJ: Hayden.

Weaver, C. 1996. *Teaching Grammar in Context.* Portsmouth, NH: Boynton/Cook.

———. 1997. "Grammar Emerging in Writing." *Syntax in the Schools* 14 (2): 1–3.

Webb, F. 1983. *Watercolor Energies.* Fairfield, CT: North Light Publishers.

Weinberg, H. L. 1959. *Levels of Knowing and Existence.* New York: Harper.

West, J. [1945] 1971. *The Friendly Persuasion.* New York: Harcourt, Brace.

Whorf, B. L. 1964. *Language, Thought, and Reality.* Cambridge, MA: M.I.T. Press.

Williams, J. M. 1979a. "Defining Complexity." College English 40: 595–609.

———. 1979b. "Non-Linguistic Linguistics and the Teaching of Style." In *Linguistics Stylistics and the Teaching of Composition,* edited by Donald McQuade. Akron, OH: University of Akron Press.

Wolfe, T. 1963. *The Kandy-Kolored Tangerine-Flake Streamline Baby.* New York: Farrar, Straus & Giroux.

———. 1979. *The Right Stuff.* New York: Farrar, Straus & Giroux.

Yerka, J., and H. Ellison. 1994. *Mind Fields: The Art of Jacek Yerka, the Fiction of Harlan Ellison.* Beverly Hills, CA: Morpheus International.

Zicree, M. S. 1989. *The Twilight Zone Companion.* New York: Bantam Books.

Zinsser, W. 1976. *On Writing Well.* New York: Harper & Row.

About the *Image Grammar* CD-ROM

The *Image Grammar* CD is designed to help facilitate the "studio approach" to teaching grammar that is advocated in the pages of this book. It contains images to prompt student writing, strategies for teaching, and quoted examples from the book that can be printed out and used as handouts. The CD will work in both MacIntosh and Windows systems. To explore the CD, just place the CD in the CD-ROM drive of your computer. Next, using Netscape Navigator or Internet Explorer, open the file named "index.html," located in either the Student or Teacher section of the CD. Click on the links to explore the contents of the CD.

We would like to thank those who have given their permission to include material in this book and the accompanying CD:

Excerpts from COSMOS by Carl Sagan. Copyright © 1980 by Carl Sagan Productions, Inc. Reprinted by permission of the Estate of Carl Sagan.

Excerpt from *The Writer's Craft*. Copyright © 1994. Reprinted with permission of McDougal Littell Inc., a Houghton Mifflin Company.

Excerpt from "Teaching Punctuation as a Rhetorical Tool" by J. Dawkins in *College Composition and Communication* 46: 533–548. Copyright © 1995. Reprinted with permission of The National Council of Teachers of English.

"A Painting of a Script Paradigm" from *Screenplay* by Syd Field. Copyright © 1988 by Syd Field. Used by permission of Delacorte Press, a division of Random House, Inc.

Please note that there is an error on the CD in Strategy 1 of Chapter 9. Item 15 should read: "He paid all the interest on the principal."

214